"A treat for the mind, the heart, and the flesh. This moving meditation on God's 'divine desire placed in us by the Spirit' is a powerful theological commentary on how it is possible for us to break down our categories and barriers that separate us and journey, together, to the new, to our next. This is a book of hope and possibilities about a book of hope and possibilities . . . and this is good news."

—*Emilie M. Townes,* E. Rhodes and Leona B. Carpenter
Professor of Womanist Ethics and Society,
Vanderbilt University Divinity School

"Willie Jennings has long called us toward the truly Christian imagination needed for a post-Christendom and post-colonial (both contested notions and realities) world. Here he announces that such an imaginative revolution was long ago heralded by the divinely poured-out Spirit on the Day of Pentecost two thousand years ago that inspired cross-Mediterranean diasporic witness, a new form of Jew-Greek cosmopolitanism, and empire-resisting messianic citizenship. The book of Acts thus ignites faithful discipleship for a plurimorphic and polyglot people of God navigating the nationalisms, ethnocentrisms, and globalisms of the third millennium!"

—*Amos Yong,* Professor of Theology and Mission,
Fuller Theological Seminary, and author of
Who Is the Holy Spirit: A Walk with the Apostles

"Jennings writes as poet, preacher, and prophet. He takes the reader on a theological tour of Acts, and like a good tour guide, he describes the familiar places thoughtfully. Like the best of tour guides, he also takes the reader to places of importance that are often unnoticed. We are familiar with Paul's beatings and imprisonment, but Jennings invites us to think theologically about prisons and beatings. We are familiar with the Jewish-Christian struggles in Acts, but Jennings guides us to think more deeply about the Jewish diaspora and the trauma that empire imposes. These visits to neglected places engender new understanding and perspective on the events recounted in Acts. This commentary preaches as faithfully as it teaches."

—*Daniel Aleshire,* Executive Director,
The Association of Theological Schools

"The latest addition to the Belief series is a remarkable commentary. Through his fresh, stimulating interpretation of the book of Acts, Jennings offers profound and deep theological-ethical engagement with Luke's second volume. This beautifully written commentary will inspire readers who seek to listen with care to what Acts has to say to the theological and ethical challenges of contemporary life. Page after page, readers of Jennings's work, like the Saul of Acts 9, may find vision-obscuring scales falling away from their eyes. This is an important voice for our time."

—*John T. Carroll,* Harriet Robertson Fitts Memorial Professor
of New Testament, Union Presbyterian Seminary

"This commentary on Acts is unlike any I've read, for Willie Jennings is not afraid to read against the grain. His distinctive voice and prophetic reading is essential, especially in these days of social turmoil, days in which the church is seeking to make sense of its seeming loss of cultural power, days in which clarity about Scripture and its transformative power is needed more than ever."

—*Eric D. Barreto,* Weyerhaeuser Associate Professor of New
Testament, Princeton Theological Seminary

ACTS

BELIEF

*A Theological Commentary
on the Bible*

GENERAL EDITORS

*Amy Plantinga Pauw
William C. Placher†*

ACTS

WILLIE JAMES JENNINGS

WESTMINSTER
JOHN KNOX PRESS
LOUISVILLE • KENTUCKY

© 2017 Willie James Jennings

First edition
Published by Westminster John Knox Press
Louisville, Kentucky

17 18 19 20 21 22 23 24 25 26—10 9 8 7 6 5 4 3 2 1

Scripture quotations from the New Revised Standard Version of the Bible are copyright © 1989 by the Division of Christian Education of the National Council of the Churches of Christ in the U.S.A. and are used by permission.

Book design by Drew Stevens
Cover design by Lisa Buckley
Cover illustration: © David Chapman/Design Pics/Corbis

Library of Congress Cataloging-in-Publication Data
Names: Jennings, Willie James, 1961- author.
Title: Acts / Willie James Jennings.
Description: First edition. | Louisville, KY : Westminster John Knox Press,
  2017. | Series: Belief: a theological commentary on the Bible | Includes
  bibliographical references and index.
Identifiers: LCCN 2017005493 (print) | LCCN 2017007882 (ebook) | ISBN
  9780664234003 (printed case : alk. paper) | ISBN 9781611648058 (ebk.)
Subjects: LCSH: Bible. Acts--Commentaries.
Classification: LCC BS2625.53 .J46 2017 (print) | LCC BS2625.53 (ebook) | DDC
  226.6/07--dc23
LC record available at https://lccn.loc.gov/2017005493

Contents

Publisher's Note

William C. Placher worked with Amy Plantinga Pauw as a general editor for this series until his untimely death in November 2008. Bill brought great energy and vision to the series and was instrumental in defining and articulating its distinctive approach and in securing theologians to write for it. Bill's own commentary for the series was the last thing he wrote, and Westminster John Knox Press dedicates the entire series to his memory with affection and gratitude.

William C. Placher, LaFollette Distinguished Professor in Humanities at Wabash College, spent thirty-four years as one of Wabash College's most popular teachers. A summa cum laude graduate of Wabash in 1970, he earned his master's degree in philosophy in 1974 and his PhD in 1975, both from Yale University. In 2002 the American Academy of Religion honored him with the Excellence in Teaching Award. Placher was also the author of thirteen books, including *A History of Christian Theology*, *The Triune God*, *The Domestication of Transcendence*, *Jesus the Savior*, *Narratives of a Vulnerable God*, and *Unapologetic Theology*. He also edited the volume *Essentials of Christian Theology*, which was named as one of 2004's most outstanding books by both *The Christian Century* and *Christianity Today* magazines.

Series Introduction

Belief: A Theological Commentary on the Bible is a series from Westminster John Knox Press featuring biblical commentaries written by theologians. The writers of this series share Karl Barth's concern that, insofar as their usefulness to pastors goes, most modern commentaries are "no commentary at all, but merely the first step toward a commentary." Historical-critical approaches to Scripture rule out some readings and commend others, but such methods only begin to help theological reflection and the preaching of the Word. By themselves, they do not convey the powerful sense of God's merciful presence that calls Christians to repentance and praise; they do not bring the church fully forward in the life of discipleship. It is to such tasks that theologians are called.

For several generations, however, professional theologians in North America and Europe have not been writing commentaries on the Christian Scriptures. The specialization of professional disciplines and the expectations of theological academies about the kind of writing that theologians should do, as well as many of the directions in which contemporary theology itself has gone, have contributed to this dearth of theological commentaries. This is a relatively new phenomenon; until the last century or two, the church's great theologians also routinely saw themselves as biblical interpreters. The gap between the fields is a loss for both the church and the discipline of theology itself. By inviting forty contemporary theologians to wrestle deeply with particular texts of Scripture, the editors of this series hope not only to provide new theological resources for the church but also to encourage all theologians to pay more attention to Scripture and the life of the church in their writings.

We are grateful to the Louisville Institute, which provided funding for a consultation in June 2007. We invited theologians, pastors, and biblical scholars to join us in a conversation about what this series could contribute to the life of the church. The time was provocative, and the results were rich. Much of the series' shape owes to the insights of these skilled and faithful interpreters, who sought to describe a way to write a commentary that served the theological needs of the church and its pastors with relevance, historical accuracy, and theological depth. The passion of these participants guided us in creating this series and lives on in the volumes.

As theologians, the authors will be interested much less in the matters of form, authorship, historical setting, social context, and philology—the very issues that are often of primary concern to critical biblical scholars. Instead, this series' authors will seek to explain the theological importance of the texts for the church today, using biblical scholarship as needed for such explication but without any attempt to cover all of the topics of the usual modern biblical commentary. This thirty-six-volume series will provide passage-by-passage commentary on all the books of the Protestant biblical canon, with more extensive attention given to passages of particular theological significance.

The authors' chief dialogue will be with the church's creeds, practices, and hymns; with the history of faithful interpretation and use of the Scriptures; with the categories and concepts of theology; and with contemporary culture in both "high" and popular forms. Each volume will begin with a discussion of *why* the church needs this book and why we need it *now*, in order to ground all of the commentary in contemporary relevance. Throughout each volume, text boxes will highlight the voices of ancient and modern interpreters from the global communities of faith, and occasional essays will allow deeper reflection on the key theological concepts of these biblical books.

The authors of this commentary series are theologians of the church who embrace a variety of confessional and theological perspectives. The group of authors assembled for this series represents more diversity of race, ethnicity, and gender than most other commentary series. They approach the larger Christian tradition with a critical respect, seeking to reclaim its riches and at the same time to acknowledge its shortcomings. The authors also aim to make available to readers a wide range of contemporary theological voices from many parts of the world. While it does recover an older genre of writing, this series is not an attempt to retrieve some idealized past. These commentaries have learned from tradition, but they are most importantly commentaries for today. The authors share the conviction that their work will be more contemporary, more faithful, and more radical, to the extent that it is more biblical, honestly wrestling with the texts of the Scriptures.

William C. Placher
Amy Plantinga Pauw

Preface

I have enjoyed two sources of great help, instruction, and inspiration in the writing of this commentary. First, I am thankful for the scholarly work of many people that served as able and wise guides for me as I wrote this commentary. The commentary work and theological reflections of Clarice J. Martin, Luke Timothy Johnson, Beverly Roberts Gaventa, C. Kavin Rowe, Justo González, Ben Witherington III, Douglas Campbell, Chris Tilling, Jaroslav Pelikan, and John Calvin were immensely enlightening. As I was finishing this work, I received the incredible commentary of Craig Keener, all four volumes! It was fantastic, but it came too late for me to assimilate and incorporate as many of the powerful insights of this master work as I would have wanted. However, I am deeply grateful for this work as well. Every theologian should at some point in their life write a commentary. This was a beautiful labor of love that fed my soul and my mind as I meditated on Scripture. I understand better why ancient church writers did their most important theological work by commenting on Scripture. It has the profound effect of clarifying what you believe and what you hold dear and bringing those commitments into strong and loving confrontation with the Word of God. Confrontation is the right word, because the Bible parades the good, the bad, and the ugly without apology. Indeed, I, like so many others, feel a demand always placed on me when I read Scripture to make sense of my faith by striving for a real coherence between my life and the life of God depicted in the texts and between what I see there as the actions of God and the actions I should be taking in and with my life. This means that writing a commentary is always an occasion for confession. I am not the

Christian I ought to be. Daily I need the Spirit guiding me, and yet daily I must repent of my resistance to the Holy One. I am part of that great congregation that survives only by the grace of God.

The other source of instruction and inspiration has been the Moral Monday Movement that grew in North Carolina under the courageous leadership of the Reverend Dr. William Barber. I, like so many others, have marched, shouted, sung, prayed, been arrested, handcuffed, and jailed all while pressing for justice and advocating for those being hurt and killed by policies that advantage the rich and disadvantage everyone else. I (and on several occasions my wonderful wife, Joanne) have walked and stood in the North Carolina heat and sun, cold and rain, listening to speech and testimony, to cry and plea of women and men asking simply that their humanity and the humanity of others who could not be there be respected. I have seen astounding things, like women and men who have never marched, never protested, never voted, or never voted in any other way than straight party lines, lift their voices shouting together, "What do we want? Justice! When do we want it? Now!" I have seen Christians, Jews, Muslims, and peoples of many other faiths, people of no faith, people who hate faith, people from all sectors of the LGBTQ community, and people socially and political conservative singing and praying together that the state legislature would do right by the suffering people of North Carolina. I have seen young people, from junior high students to high schoolers, college students, graduate students, and even professors (!) marching, protesting, learning about public policy, legislative structures, and procedures, as well as learning how to organize. I watched the birth of a new generation of activists from all walks of life. I saw black folks advanced in age, tender of body but sturdy of spirit, raise their voices once again for justice and speak with a wisdom unrivaled in this world of how to protest and yet not hate, how to speak of evil and not be overcome by that same evil, how to call out unjust acts without name calling, and how to demand respect without showing disrespect. And in all this, I felt the Holy Spirit clearly, precisely, distinctly. I felt the Spirit at work in the common. A protest march is a fleeting moment even if it last for several hours, but it is exactly in such fleeting moments that we can sometime sense the permanent presence of the Spirit of God who never tires, never ceases to demand justice for love's sake, and never ceases to love a world mired in injustice. Acts is fundamentally about such fleeting moments that speak a more permanent reality, a new world. So this commentary is dedicated to Reverend Dr. William Barber and the Moral Monday Movement.

This commentary is also dedicated to others who have been inspirations to me in how they teach and live the Scriptures: To Amanda Diekman and Franklin Golden and the wonderful people they pastor together at Durham Church, a beautifully struggling, fledging church in Durham, North Carolina, formed in the hope and desire to be a community that embodies boundary-breaking love for one another. Amanda is no longer there as a pastor, but her powerful witness of reconciling life together remains. To Dr. James Earl Massey, Dean Emeritus of Anderson School of Theology in Anderson, Indiana, former Senior Pastor of the Metropolitan Church of God in Detroit, and former Dean of the Chapel of Tuskegee University; like the late Gardner C. Taylor and Peter Gomes, Dr. Massey has been a giant among us. I could not write this commentary without thinking of the brilliance and elegance of his preaching and exegesis. To Dr. W. C. Turner, my former colleague and pastor, whose ministry has been unparalleled in shaping generations of women and men in the art of listening carefully to the Scriptures while also listening to suffering and pain in this world and preaching in the small space between the two. I also dedicate this commentary to the Rev. Joanne L. Browne Jennings, my wife and colleague in life and ministry, who also happens to be one of the finest preachers I have ever heard. I am thankful beyond measure for her and for our wonderful daughters, Njeri and Safiya, and my mother-in-law, Elsie Browne. I also want to thank Dr. Justin Ashworth, a brilliant young theologian and ethicist who did an excellent job editing this book and offering perfect suggestions. Like so many others, I am deeply grateful for having known Bill Placher, who along with Amy Plantinga Pauw, established this commentary series. Bill was a theologian whose humanity matched his theology, both gracious, genuine, and inviting. I miss him terribly. Whatever is helpful I owe to this cloud of witnesses, but all the mistakes are mine alone. What I share with this cloud is the desire to answer in the affirmative the question, Is there a Word from the Lord?

Introduction
Why Acts? Why Now?

The Revolution of the Intimate

The book of Acts speaks of revolution. We must never forget this. It depicts life in the disrupting presence of the Spirit of God. Luke, its author, is a master storyteller. He is a master storyteller not because his skill in storytelling rises above all his contemporaries or because of his command of the historical archive of events, sayings, stories, and accounts of Jesus and his disciples' actions and decisions. His two volume work, Luke–Acts, exemplifies master storytelling because he follows God on the ground, working and moving in and through the quotidian realities of struggle, of blood and pain, suffering and longing. He never loses sight of God or of humanity, both locked in the drama of life together aiming toward life abundant. Although commentators remind us endlessly that these two volumes go together, the book of Acts has its own character, its own anointing.

Written probably in the 80s or 90s CE, the power of the story of Acts overwhelms, pulling the Gospel of Luke into its vortex and turning that book into a precursor of this radical beginning. The book of Acts is like the book of Genesis. It announces a beginning but without the language of beginning. Like Genesis it renders without pomp and flag-waving a God working, moving, creating the dawn that will break each day, putting into place a holy repetition that speaks of the willingness of God to invade our every day and our every moment. This God of Israel waits no more for the perfect time to be revealed. Now is the time, and here is the place. There is only one central character in this story of Acts. It is God, the Holy Spirit. This author's narration yields to the insurgency of the Spirit, but not as any kind of magical dictation. The Spirit is present in the storytelling. Although it is the story of the Spirit of God, Luke does not play off human agency against divine agency. God moves and we respond. We move and God responds. Nevertheless this is God's drama, God's complete exposure. Cards are on the table and the curtain is drawn back, and God acts plainly, clearly, and in ways that are irrevocable. There is no going back now. A history is being woven in front of our eyes that we cannot deny, or we deny only at our own peril.

History in Acts

The book of Acts creates a history that will show us how to think history. How to think history is not the same as thinking historically and certainly not the same as thinking like a historian. Too often the book of Acts is aligned with an historian's optic, a way of looking that asks honorable, even noble questions about what actually happened. The author of Luke–Acts is not against such nobility, but he is caught up in a different optic. He wants his readers to see a past unfolding in a future and making intelligible a present. In this regard, his history is now. The Spirit has come, and Luke will narrate how one discerns God's movement. This is his agenda. Luke is offering us instruction in historical consciousness. As such Luke is not offering a special kind of history. This is not a special revelation of history. Nor is this a gnostic return to a hidden history closed off to unspiritual eyes. This lesson in thinking history begins with a dogged refusal to imagine history as anything other than what it actually is, a creature, a creature embraced by God. History the creature needs its creator.

History, because it is a creature, must always be treated in its truth. It is created. It is storytelling that comes to life from the minds and mouths of other creatures. It shares in the beauty and majesty of the creature and through the incarnation has been embraced by the Creator. God has entered the life of the creature and joined the storytelling that is history. Now the divine life may ride on the multiple narrations of creatures. God has joined in the storytelling as well, but with God a different procedure explodes on the scene. God plays in the telling, moving back and forth from past to present to future. There in the storytelling of the past, now in present storytelling and ready, anticipating future telling. History understood as creature means that storytelling never aims to fully capture anything, especially not God. Yet it is ever useful to the Creator. History understood in this way aims at one thing: witness. Why witness? Witness lives. Witness is about the living and the ways we chose to live. History that becomes witness is history that shapes the paths of the living, bound up with their heartbeats and their breathing. Witness reveals the telling of history without the false pretense of history for history's sake. Witness is history being honest about its wishes. Witness exposes the storytellers and their desires to shape worlds, large or small.

The book of Acts then is honest history revealing the creature that is history. Just as there are many creatures, so too are there many histories; and just as some creatures will yield to the Spirit of God, so too Acts is a history yielding to the Spirit. In this regard, Acts has an interesting relation to what will later emerge as the rule of faith and the idea of tradition. In truth Acts helped to establish the rule of faith and the tradition in the ways it narrates the "and then" and the "what follows." Such establishment does not aim at immutability but irrevocability. Now that the life of Jesus and the way of discipleship has been marked in space and time, it cannot be denied. Now that God has shown the divine life to be this way and not another way and now that women and men have been extravagantly embraced by the Spirit of God, there is no going back.

This irrevocability in Acts sometimes gets confused with immutability so that Acts gets interpreted as the historical foundation of the church's life, as if Acts reveals the marble, stone, brick and mortar of ecclesial existence. Acts as architecture, in this sense, creates monument thinking about this narrative. Monument thinking turns the book of Acts into an ecclesial museum, the purpose of which is to show us the earlier forms of church life, religious ritual, or theology. That way of reading Acts has given into a colonialist procedure that places Acts inside the processes of knowledge acquisition and accumulation. The Book of Acts becomes an artifact. In this frame of reflection we turn to Acts in investigative analysis. The conversation about this book pivots on archival speculations. How does the book of Acts match up against other artifacts? What traces of ancient life and ancient ways of thinking and writing can we tease out of its accounts? These are not illegitimate questions, and they do not reflect inappropriate concerns. They do, however, miss an opportunity provided by this history to enter a life-giving historical consciousness found in the divine life made flesh.

The book of Acts beckons us to a life-giving historical consciousness that senses being in the midst of time that is both past and present and that pulls us toward a future with God in the new creation. That future with God, however, does not discount the now, the present moment. This is the work of the Spirit, who relishes each moment with us, never discounting our time and never treating the time of creation and each creature as inconsequential time. The book of Acts reveals the Spirit, who joins us in time, sharing our spaces and partaking in the places we inhabit as places fit for divine activity. Such historical consciousness, growing out of meditating on the book of Acts, does not romanticize the past. Indeed it is attuned to histories that claim what Walter Benjamin calls ". . . the crude and material things without which no refined and spiritual things could exist."[1] It is keenly aware of suffering and those who cause it, and it also sees God working toward the good in the midst of pain. Life-giving historical consciousness builds from the truth that history is a creature, and we are invited through the creature that is Luke–Acts to allow our seeing and sensing to align with the presence of the Spirit here and now. This history then requires that we grapple with three things: (1) a spatial history we enter, (2) a history we tell, and (3) a history we realize.

A Spatial History We Enter:
Faith between Diaspora and Empire

How can faith be found inside of empire? The book of Acts takes place in empire—the Roman Empire—and this is not a fact that we should ever let escape our attention. The goal of the Roman Empire

1. Walter Benjamin, *Illuminations* (New York: Schocken Books, 1968), 254.

was to shape the world in its own image. This is always the desire of empire. Rome understood its task as the reconstruction of land, space, and life under its rule. This was a civilizing mission at its deepest level where construction of place would mean reconstruction of life. As Justo González notes, ". . . Romans understood their civilizing task was precisely the 'cityfication' of the world. For them, the greatest human creation was precisely the city, and their purpose in history was to promote city life throughout their empire."[2] That city life came with a cost as peoples were displaced by the expansion of large agricultural estates that serviced the growing markets of the city. Small farmers had the choice that is no choice: either come under the Roman aristocracy and farm for your new masters or join the displaced masses in the cities. City life under Rome was city life permeated by the logic of slavery. In slaveholding society, one's humanity was not a given. The body of a slave was a commodity and not a human being. Only by birth into the right family or by purchasing one's freedom or by manumission could one claim a humanity, which was an elusive dream for many.

An aesthetic regime came with the Roman Empire that was woven into its building projects and that gloried in the visual. Beautifully colorful public buildings, temples, and homes covered the Mediterranean world. Beautiful buildings were not merely a signature of aesthetic design but also social desire as Rome sought to inculcate its vision of domesticity and community life. Such a vision, built on a slave economy, accommodated cultural difference and promoted a controlled cosmopolitanism that allowed for a diversity of beliefs as long as those beliefs were not a threat to the divinity of the emperor or the empire. Yet controlled cosmopolitanism is always cosmopolitanism in decline and diversity in retreat as the sensibilities of Roman life made their way ever more deeply into the quotidian realities of peoples. Thus life under empire is always life under threat of assimilation and transformation through the weakening and even loss of cultural identities and religious sensibilities. For Israel, such threat was woven into its history, and in the book of Acts we see the agonizing pain of such threat. Israel in Acts is diaspora Israel.

---

2. Justo L. González, *Acts, The Gospel of the Spirit* (Maryknoll, NY: Orbis Books, 2001), 10.

Acts =
Diaspora
Israel

Diaspora means scattering and fragmentation, exile and loss. It means being displaced and in search of a place that could be made home. For Israel it means life among the Gentiles. Danger and threat surround diaspora life. Diaspora life is life crowded with self-questioning and questions for God concerning the anger, hatred, and violence visited upon a people. We must never confuse voluntary migration with diaspora, because diaspora is a geographic and social world not chosen and a psychic state inescapable. The peoples who inhabit diaspora live with animus and violence filling the air they breathe. They live always on the verge of being classified enemy, always in evaluation of their productivity to the empire, always having an acceptance on loan, ready to be taken away at the first sign of sedition. They live with fear as an ever present partner in their lives, the fear of being turned into a *them, a dangerous other, those people* among *us*. They also remember loss—of land and place, of life and hope, and even for some of faith. Yet diaspora is also power, the power of a conviction to survive and the power of a confession to never yield to the forces that would destroy them. Diaspora is life by any means necessary. The condition of diaspora is often bound up with life under empire.

In Acts we find faith caught between diaspora and empire. Faith is always caught between diaspora and empire. It is always caught between those on the one side focused on survival and fixated on securing a future for their people and on the other side those intoxicated with the power and possibilities of empire and of building a world ordered by its financial, social, and political logics that claim to be the best possible way to bring stability and lasting peace. The book of Acts is read poorly when we forget this double bind or forget the pain of Israel in its pages. There is palpable fear flowing through the narrative and not just the fear of the Israel who resists Messiah Jesus and his followers but also the fear of the Israel who embraces King Jesus but is unclear about the Spirit's leading. The Spirit always confronts our fear in order to free faith to live in its true home in God. But this is not easy. Indeed the context of Acts is struggle. The content of Acts is also struggle. It is struggle in two senses. It is the struggle against the powers and principalities that exploit the emotional currents of diaspora and empire, seeking to drive people to kill, steal, or destroy for the sake of securing diaspora or empire's futures. The second sense of struggle is the struggle to yield to the Spirit, following God into the new that God imagines and is bringing about for the world.

The Spirit of God intervenes between diaspora and empire, offering a new world to both. Both diaspora and empire have just cause for their visions of life. Israel in diaspora remembered correctly those whose aim was their elimination. Diaspora Israel was rightly on guard against those who would threaten its common life and its way of faith. It was clear eyed about oppressors and liberators; friends and enemies; and plans, ideas, and belief systems that would help them or hurt them. The Roman Empire was clear too about its supporters and loyal subjects or those who harbored sedition in their communities or their bodies. The Roman Empire was about building a world that made order a material reality that everyone could experience and inhabit. Every people hold the dream of an ordered society, safe, secure, and productive, and Rome understood itself as the world's best hope for realizing that dream. Who would possibly imagine life, good life apart from diaspora or empire? To imagine whole life, good life apart from diaspora or empire comes only by the Spirit of God. We must hear in the Acts story the pathos of life caught in the grip of diaspora and empire—of people angry, confused, and frustrated as the resurrected Jesus calls them to envision the new creature in the Spirit, which is a mind-altering new life together. Fundamental to that new reality is the joining of Jew and Gentile.

A History We Tell—Jew and Gentile Joined

Acts presents the interruption. The established storytellers have been halted in their tracks and their stories have been disrupted. These disciples of Jesus are now telling the story of Israel differently, and they are emerging as new storytellers. Indeed the writer of Luke–Acts is performing a great feat of storytelling, presenting himself as a new narrator of Israel's story. The stories that had been told are now being told differently, and the established storytellers are being challenged. The storytellers are the most powerful people in the book of Acts and in every time and every place. They conjure identity through their stories, weaving together a vision of the past of a people with implicit instruction about how they should see themselves in the present. Yet the power of storytellers is most potent when they draw that self-definition, that sense of self woven through narration toward destiny. Storytellers seek to turn self-definition and identity toward determining how life ought to be lived and how a people ought to imagine building a life.

The interruption in Acts was not the destruction of Jewish identity, but many of those in the story perceived it as such. That destruction in their view would ride in on the Gentiles who, like water leaking into a boat at sea, threaten to drown Jewish faith and life. From the perspective of diaspora, the followers of Jesus, especially Paul, have become tools for Jewish assimilation that would mean nothing less than social death. This interruption is for them terrifying and absurd. Gentiles outnumbered the people of Israel and must not be allowed to enter and trample over sacred space. Yet the interruption is less entry and more expansion. The space of Israel is expanding by the Spirit and the number of people who worship the God of Israel is growing. Acts renders the Gentiles as a profound question to the Jews of diaspora: What will you do if I join you at the body of Jesus and fall in love with your God and with you? The Gentiles of Acts are on their way to communion with Jews while remaining Gentiles. This is the most terrifying aspect of interruption: love.

The Gentiles have not arrived at love of Israel in Acts, but they are surely on their way. That journey toward love is already a journey in love through the Spirit who has revealed a God creating an intimate space of joining between Jew and Gentile. There at the body of Jesus the futures of Israel and the Gentiles are being drawn toward a new destiny in God. This does not mean the loss of identity but its expansion. But there is loss involved, especially for the Gentiles. The radical nature of the story being told by the Spirit through these disciples is most acute at the site of Gentiles. Gentiles gain a new story of their existence told by the storytellers of Israel. They hear that they, too, like Israel, have been claimed by God through God's outstretched arm and mighty hand. They, too, have been freed from the powers and principalities and released from captivity to the demonic forces at work in this world. Indeed the Spirit of the living God finds them a suitable home for the divine life.

New life with the God of Israel beckons and yet it requires that the Gentiles turn away from other gods. This is no simple matter because that turning away touches the ground in every way and throws everyday life into crisis, touching friendships and relationships, habit and custom that form the fabric of life. These multiple peoples touched by the Spirit find their worlds undone. First they find out that they are indeed Gentiles, those outside the covenant of promise and at the margins of concern of a people born of Abraham and Sarah. But then they learn that they are indeed included by grace, by the sheer overwhelming love of Israel's God, who has the power over life and death. This God is their God too; Israel's creator is their creator too and now their friend. For those Gentiles touched by the Spirit, this story has become their story, a life-defining, life-directing story, but for those unconvinced, the story is sheer folly, and the Gentile followers of a Jewish God have descended into madness and cultural and ethnic betrayal.

The book of Acts reminds us that to follow Jesus is to already be a betrayer of one's people. That betrayal is at the point of diaspora concern and imperial desire. The disciples of Jesus do not betray an identity but a destiny, not a history but how the story of my people will be used to dictate to me a future and plan my life projects. The imperial project of the Roman Empire also dies in the body of the disciple who has joined her or his body to the risen savior, Jesus. The Spirit is crumbling imperial design from within by destroying the divide between those enslaved and their masters. The hierarchies nurtured so carefully by the Roman Empire are being undone by the Spirit, who will not release slave or free, Jew or Gentile, to their own self-interpretations but who will relentlessly prod them to open themselves toward one another in a life that builds the common. Now in the Spirit the common is not the bottom, not the despised humble beginning, and not the launching pad into social and economic hierarchies. It is the goal of life together in God.

The common is the condition of joined life where the haves and have-nots are bound together in clear sight of one another and in shared support. The common is the redistribution of life where the Spirit invites us to a sharing of space and place, resources and dreams. The common takes from empire its designs for building a world and from diaspora its plans for surviving in it. Instead the common joins, weaving together purpose and hope in the life of discipleship to Jesus. Neither Roman Empire nor diaspora Israel could tolerate the common, because it represented a massive disruption to political, religious, economic, and social designs. And anyone caught promoting the common was deemed a criminal, a heretic of the faith, and an enemy of the state. Incarceration, prison, and torture often go hand in hand with being of the common, and the disciples of Jesus were of the common. The story of Acts brings us into contact with the carnal weapons of this world: violence and the threat of violence. These weapons represent the seductive power of death that tempts us to envision a world made right through its uses. Death invites us to imagine creation through its power. We are often seduced into believing that killing and destroying can create and sustain peace and order. This has always been a fool's gold. The enemies of the Way repeatedly believed that violence would thwart the Spirit of God and end discipleship to Jesus. They misunderstood not the power of religious conviction but the nature of divine desire.

A History We Learn—The Desire of God

At heart, the book of Acts exposes divine desire inside a writer's desire. God's desire is for the living. We are the pearl of great price sought after by the Spirit. Yet the new thing Luke narrates is intensification of divine desire in flesh. The heart of Israel's God is laid bare and presented to all flesh through the Spirit. Now is revealed the divine fantasy of a creation turned in love and embraced by its creator. This divine fantasy for people is what God brings to the disciples who follow the Son who has made concrete God's intentions. God intends to join. God has offered God's body to be taken in, eaten, chewed, and swallowed. Divine desire is of the earth, of flesh and blood, body and dirt, of hunger and passion and *eros*. The Spirit announces God's seeking of pleasure in the joining. This is what the Spirit seeks to impart to the disciples, a new fantasy desperately needed by the world. The prevailing fantasy of people is to have power over others, to claim the power of self-determination, and to make a world bow to its will. This is the fantasy of nations and clans, peoples and corporations. But the Spirit offers us God's own fantasy of desire for people, of joining and life together and of shared stories bound to a new destiny in God. This desire for people is not the desire for their utility but for their glory, to draw them into the divine pleasure and joy at the sight of the creature in communion and formed in hope. The disciples are to make evident divine desire, reveal it to be the central gift of the Spirit.

Where the Spirit of God is, there is divine desire not simply for God but for one another and not simply for one another but for those to whom we are sent by the Spirit, to those already being drawn into communion with God and sensing the desire of God for the expansion of their lives into the lives of others. The deepest reality of life in the Spirit depicted in the book of Acts is that the disciples of Jesus rarely, if ever, go where they want to go or to whom they would want to go. Indeed the Spirit seems to always be pressing the disciples to go to those to whom they would in fact strongly prefer never to share space, or a meal, and definitely not life together. Yet it is precisely this prodding to be boundary-crossing and border-transgressing that marks the presence of the Spirit of God. Clearly, one disciple in particular emerges as a crucial figure in the narrative: Paul. Yet it might be better to read Paul less as foreground and more as background to the agency of the Spirit. This is not to discount Paul's important role in the story, but by focusing too strenuously on Paul, Acts too often gets read with a masculinist optic as a heroic tale, and as the exploits of a virtuoso apologist who wields an incredible intellect.

We must notice who Paul joins, who accompanies Paul, and whose company Paul keeps. We must attend to the places he goes and the people who inhabit those places, as well as the responses not only to his message but to his companions. Paul yields to the Spirit. This is the sum total of his story in the book of Acts, but inside that story is the story of a God who desires us and all of creation and will not release us to isolations, social, economic, cultural, religious, gendered, and geographic. This is why the book of Acts will always be contemporary, always of this present age and this current moment. We are constantly trying to catch up with the Spirit and keep pace with a God who is calling forth the new creature in the Spirit. That new creature in the Spirit collapses diaspora and empire into each other and seeks to weave together a breathtaking joining. Yet the Spirit is being resisted by flesh and the desire of God is being denied by women and men both inside and outside the church. We have yet to hear the message of Acts of an erotic God who seeks to place in each of us desire for those outside of us, outside our worlds of culture, clan, nation, tribe, faith, politics, class, and species.

The Acts of the Apostles is about aesthetics before it is about ethics. It is about a God whose weapon of choice is the divine desire placed in us by the Spirit. That desire has the power to press through centuries of animosity and hatred and beckon people to want one another and envision lives woven together. Such a life never asks people to forget their past or deny their present, but to step together into a future that will not yield to the given order of isolations, but yields to the Spirit that is poured out on all flesh. Segregation is an ancient strategy for creating a world, and it continues to work because it teaches us to see the world in slices, fragmented pieces of geographic space that we may own and control. Segregationist ways of thinking and living permeate this world including the church, dimming our sight of ourselves as creatures and our connection to other creatures, and weakening our ability to discern where and to whom the Spirit wants to lead us. We need people of faith who will yield to the Spirit in this present moment. God fills the world with God's own life. God fills the disciples of Jesus, and they speak the languages of others. God fills Gentiles as well, as they too speak words of peoples not their own. God drives some into the lives of others for the sake of Jesus and the hope born of love. This is the book of Acts for us. Welcome to the real.

1:1–4:37

The Revolution Is Here!

1:1–12

The Death of Nationalist Fantasy

The Book of Acts . . . [is] . . . a call to Christians to be open to the action of the Spirit, not only leading them to confront values and practices in society that may need to be subverted, but perhaps even leading them to subvert or question practices and values within the Church itself.[1]

1:1–4

The revolution has begun. The disciples of Jesus have seen its beginning. It is a beginning without an end in sight. Part two of Luke's Gospel, known to us as the Acts of the Apostles, narrates stunning newness. The newness begins with Jesus. Not an idea, not a principle, not even a memory, but an impossible reality, flesh and blood on the other side of death standing in front of the disciples, alive and well. No one survives death. Their words spoken in life, eloquent or clumsy, powerful or weak, meet their end in death, silenced by its power and remembered only by fragile memory and tentative technologies, ancient or modern. Flesh and word are separated by death, until now, until Jesus. His word spoken before his suffering, spoken during his suffering and betrayal, is now the same word he speaks. He watches over his word to perform it. This performance is of the Holy Spirit. Divine instruction comes only

---

1. Justo González, *Acts: The Gospel of the Spirit* (Maryknoll, NY: Orbis Books, 2001), 8.

by the Holy Spirit, and Jesus will continue his lessons for life for his disciples through the Spirit.

This is a different reality of instruction, one born of the Spirit and the resurrected Word. This form of instruction flows over and through the disciples flooding their senses with the divine urging. This new reality of instruction intensifies God's guidance of Israel, pressing them to follow where the Son of God leads. God speaks, and Israel must follow; this has been the order from the beginning. Luke gestures in the old order but clearly intends the new. As of old, the prophetic word is being spoken, but this is a new reality of the prophetic. Luke invokes the very reality that he renders historiographically. He writes history, but he is inside the history he writes, and he offers us a picture of Jesus who is alive, reading what Luke wrote, watching over its reading, and ready to speak through its words, his words. There is always danger in reading Luke's narrative. It sounds like the old way, history done correctly. But his is history that threatens history: that is, it threatens a vision of the past that is reachable only through the imaginations of the storytellers. Luke gives us history that stands in what Michel de Certeau calls history's "rupture between a past that is its object, and a present that is the place of its practice."[2] This is not history writing trapped in that rupture and caught in what the philosopher Gotthold Lessing called history's ugly ditch. This is history writing that will not be drawn into the illusion that it is speaking for the dead and in so doing bringing someone back to life. This is history that shatters both hagiography and historiography and then lays their shards across the bodies of witnesses and the body of a living witness.[3]

Luke cannot do otherwise, because he is witness to the One who rose from the dead, Jesus, Mary's Son. Jesus speaks of the reign of God, a reign that has begun in his body. The faith that is being born at this moment is a faith of the body, of this life, of this time and this place. Jesus is present, here, now. Jesus inaugurates a new way of speaking about God and about life. This is truly the God of the

2. Michel de Certeau, *The Writing of History*, trans. Tom Conley (New York: Columbia University Press, 1988), 36.
3. De Certeau, *The Writing of History*, 36, 270–72.

living, the God who overcomes death. Theological speech that does not carry this tenor, this rich flavor, is not theological speech birthed in newness but is religious discourse yet bound to death. God, who overcomes suffering and death, presents Godself. Jesus gives himself (*paristemi*) to be viewed, touched, and even handled over many days. This giving of himself continues what began with the Mary's touch of her child; through the crowds that pressed in to grasp hold of his healing body; to the brutal hands of a Roman military committed to practices of torture; to this moment when disciples, confused, fearful, unclear of the future, needed to hear the words of Jesus: here and now touch me (Luke 24:38–40). Jesus always presents himself  to be touched. *accessible human.*

The disciples are being introduced to the revolutionary way. Faith will not be rooted in a phantasm. Whether they believe or not, Jesus is alive. Present to be touched, in league with all the senses. Surely the resurrection of Jesus is closer to the erotic than the evidentiary. He is not a slab of living meat stretched out across a medical examiners table or a judge's bench, waiting eagerly to be held up as proof in front of a skeptical world. Luke does speak of convincing proof (*tekmēriois*), but this moment of summation should not be used to turn us away from the sheer thankfulness of the surprise. The friends who held him before his anguish and their anguish, before his abandonment and their guilt, who wished to see him one more time, hold him once more, maybe even now to say I am sorry, maybe now to hold him again, see him again, hear him again. This moment is more than proof; it is forgiveness, reconciliation, and peace. The body of Jesus is not simply evidence, it is much more. Love bound in bodies can now continue through death: touch can be eternal. Jesus presents to his disciples a way through the fear of death by simply touching him. It will be the way of his disciples. Disciples must touch and be touched. Could it be that the church weakens its grasp of the resurrection precisely in its timidity to present itself to be touched by the world? Even at this moment, the church is yet plagued by a fear of touch, shaped in worship services where people sit or stand side by side, hermetically sealed in their private piety. Some ecclesial quarters harbor a profound disdain for touching as nothing more than modern sentimentality and a sign of weakness of mind and will.

Touch, of course, is clothed in discourse and performed through the logics of cultures, adding complication to its execution. Touch means different things to different people. And touch for many has been the occasion of violence and suffering, exploitation and pain. For others touch has been lost to a distorted sexual imagination and made only a precursor to intercourse. But now God invites touch, announcing a new order of things, a new possibility of knowledge and even truth discovered through hands touching a sanctified body. Handling Jesus, as the disciples will soon come to understand, will happen as they put their hands on those whom he chooses to embrace. Jesus took bread and wine into his hands just as he took the disciples into his life. Now both will re-present his life and invite grasping. These are not replacements for Jesus. He yet gives himself to be held, and he asks of his disciples to do the same.

1:5–12

He will seal this new order, this revolution over death and the power of violence through the Holy Spirit. The Spirit is the promise of the Father to the Son and those joined to him. Indeed Acts narrates the journey of the Spirit even more deeply into the way of Jesus and the journey of Jesus more deeply into the way of the Spirit. The Spirit, companion with Jesus and his disciples, will soon spread the body of Jesus over space and time opening his life as a new home for the faith of Israel. So this new Israel, an Israel staring at Jesus, staring at life after death, is commanded by Jesus to wait in Jerusalem.

Geography matters. Place matters to God. From a specific place the disciples will move forward into the world. To go from place to place is to go from people to people and to go from an old identity to a new one. Jesus prepares them for the journey of their lives by holding them in a place where the Spirit will be given to them in *that place*, and from *that place* they will be changed. But first Luke shows us signs of the old, the old identity of the disciples: After the command of Jesus, the disciples ask the crucial question: "Lord, is this the time when you will restore the kingdom to Israel?" (1:6a). This is an understandable question, yet it is still an astonishing and tragic question. It is understandable because Jesus is now, without doubt, the One with power over death; the One who has overcome violence; and the One with all power in his hands. The greatest weapon that any people might use is violence. No people have ever resisted the tempter's snare to make use of violence in order to have their way in the world and to secure their future.

The disciples ask the nationalist question: When will we rule our land, and become self-determining, and if need be impose our will on others? All this would, of course, be for the good of the world, they suppose. A resurrected Jesus cannot stop such a request from being made, nor could he thwart nationalist desire. Nationalist desire has tempted Israel from the beginning and in fact tempts all peoples. The nationalism suggested here is not a historical nationalism bound to the anatomy of Israel, but the deeply human desire of every people to control their destiny and shape the world into their hoped-for eternal image. Nationalist desire easily creates a fantasy of resurrection and the fantasy of resurrection appeals to peoples, calling forth a triumphal vision of a nation that rises from death and is filled with conquerors and the powerful. Jesus, however, is not a sign of resurrection. He is its Lord. Resurrection will not define him. He will define resurrection's meaning and resurrection's purpose. It will not be used by these disciples as an ideological tool for statecraft. Nor will it constitute them the winner's circle. Such ways of thinking resurrection turn Jesus into the greatest victor in an eternal competition and produces disciples who follow Jesus only because they worship power.

Nationalist fantasy has seeped into faith both Jewish and Christian and finds its ways into other faiths as well. Such fantasy dreams are completely understandable and quite compelling because they help us cope with the vulnerability that is creaturely life, and they reflect the power of accumulated wounds. The greater the number of wounds inflicted on a people, the greater the fantasy dreams of being self-determined and wielding power over others, and power to control our own destiny. It drives the creation of walled communities, border patrols, and checkpoints and turns violence and segregation into the proper exercise of the state's right to life.

Jesus does have power and the reign of Israel will be restored, but not as the disciples anticipated it. The power of God will be released

on them through the Holy Spirit, and the life of Jesus will be insepa-
rably bound to their lives. They will become, in ways more complex
than they could ever have imagined, his witnesses. Witness here carries two fundamental connotations for these disciples. They carry
the real history of life with Jesus. They are now in the position of
the master storytellers. Like elders of the village who remember well
the old ones and the old ways, so too the disciples will soon speak
of when they walked with Jesus, drawing from fragile memories the
fragments of sights, sounds, and the words of the man from Galilee. They will be an irrefutable presence. They will also be witnesses
of divine presence. They will give room to *the witness*, making their
lives a stage on which the resurrected Jesus will appear and claim
each creature as his own, as a site of love and desire. This second
sense of witness reaches into the first sense. Although there will only
be a few who knew him according to the flesh (*kata sarka*, 2 Cor.
5:16), countless more will follow these disciples in rightly claiming
to be an irrefutable presence of an experience with Jesus even as they
give space through their lives for Jesus himself to speak to others.

Witness in this twofold sense is already in conflict with nationalist desire, and against the fantasy of any people for global influence
or world domination. The disciples will be formed by the Spirit as
witnesses. They will be turned out to the world not as representatives of empires but those who will announce a revolution, *the
revolution of the intimate*, God calling to the world. They will enter
new places to become new people by joining themselves to those in
Judea, Samaria, and the ends of the earth. As Jesus announces this
divine desire, he ascends. The ascension of Jesus continues to play
so small a role in ecclesial imagination precisely because we struggle
to think spatially. As Vine Deloria Jr. suggested, one of Christianity's
historical weaknesses is that it knows how to read the world tempo-
rally but not spatially.[4]

We more easily imagine the time of Jesus Christ, the time in which
he wishes to announce his reign, and the time between his ascension
and his return, than we do the space of Jesus Christ, the spaces he
wishes to inhabit and to enter in. If the ascended Lord embraces our

---

4. Vine Deloria Jr., *God Is Red: A Native View of Religion* (Golden, CO: Fulcrum, 2003), 121–31.
Also see his *For This Land: Writings on Religion in America* (New York: Routledge, 1993), 145.

time as his time to be made known, then he also seeks to walk in the places of this world to announce his life as the life given for the world. It is true that the ascension of Jesus certainly marks the new time of his reign and the time of the Spirit. In this time what will be constituted is the moment of gathering that will become the church. Yet as Jan Milič Lochman noted, Jesus' "journey to heaven" becomes the disciples' "journey to the ends of the earth."[5] Jesus ascends not only to establish presence through absence, but he also draws his body into the real journeys of his disciples into the world. He goes to heaven for us, ahead of us. He goes with and ahead of his disciples into the real places of this world. He is Lord of time (past, present, and future) yet walking in our time, and he is Lord of space (here and there) yet taking our spaces and places with utmost seriousness.

His ascension marks less his power and more his scope. He will reign over the whole cosmos and yet he rises to raise us into heaven, as John Calvin said, and to overcome the distances between us and God and between one another.[6] Jesus' ascension is in fact God claiming our space as the sites for visitation, announcing God's desire to come to us. God's desire will be seen in the pouring out of the Spirit in a specific place in order to enter specific places and specific lives. He ascends for our sake, not to turn away from us but to more intensely focus in on us.

As he ascends, the disciples watch, and here the danger of watching becomes clear. Jesus is no action figure, no superhero to be consumed in spectacle. Watching Jesus and watching for Jesus was and is a significant temptation for his disciples. Such watching can easily undermine movement and easily undermine the priority of the journey. Luke presents to us two men in white robes standing by the disciples, just as they did at the tomb of Jesus (Luke 24:4–5). These men echo a similar question to the one asked in the Luke passage, a question that basically means, Why are you performing actions that contradict the actions of Jesus? The women (in Luke) sought the living among the dead; these other disciples at this moment look into the heavens concerned by absence rather than looking forward to

5. Jan Milič Lochman *The Faith We Confess: An Ecumenical Dogmatics* (Philadelphia: Fortress Press, 1984), 167.

6. John Calvin, *The Institutes of the Christian Religion*, 4.17.31.

see presence. These disciples consumed in spectacle may easily turn toward monument thinking and building. They could easily have begun to consider how they might mark the spot of his departure and forget his instruction given through the Spirit. This is a moment of loss, even as they know that they must go forward in faith. We must never discount the next step that must be taken at the sight of Jesus' leaving. Such a step is understandably a labored step, unsure and unclear. Nevertheless it must be taken because faith always leans forward to Jerusalem, toward the place where God waits to meet us. We are always drawn on by God to our future. For some of us that drawing will not take us away from what we have lost or what we feel or what we see. But for others that drawing will mean leaving behind such loss, if it would be an obstacle to our moving toward what God wants to do in and through us. The Holy Spirit always waits for us to enter the journey of newness.

> The old definitions have not served us, nor the earth that supports us. The old patterns, no matter how cleverly rearranged to imitate progress, still condemn us to cosmetically altered repetitions of the same old exchanges, the same old guilt, hatred, recrimination, lamentation, and suspicion. For we have, built into all of us, old blueprints of expectation and response, old structures of oppression, and these must be altered at the same time as we alter the living conditions which are the result of those structures. For the master's tools will never dismantle the master's house.[7]

FURTHER REFLECTIONS
Christians, Jews, and Nationalism

Nationalism is a seductive way of understanding collective existence. It has become almost impossible to not see the world as a collection of nations, nation-states, and peoples who are not nations but are on their way to becoming nations. Nationalist vision

---

7. Audre Lorde, "Age, Race, Class, and Sex: Women Defining Difference," in *Words of Fire: An Anthology of African-American Feminist Thought*, ed. Beverly Guy-Sheftall (New York: The New Press, 1995), 291.

even infects the way we read the Bible and understand biblical Israel's existence, gauging their actions according to the protocols of nation-states. However, it would be better to read Scripture against nationalist vision and nationalist form that interprets peoples on a plain of group sameness, each seeking self-determination, control of their land and resources, and desiring full membership and participation in the global economy. Such a way of understanding peoples necessitates borders, cultural and racial segregation, and military forces to maintain independence. Nationalism always engenders zero-sum calculations, where we win by controlling our borders and/or controlling our identities, or we lose by being overrun with aliens who confuse our identities and resist assimilation. Nationalist vision is weakness and fear masquerading as strength and courage, because it beckons the world's peoples to postures of protectionism and leans toward xenophobia. In our global contexts, nationalism always sets the stage for commerce and capitalism. Only money and those with money may flow freely between nations. This however is a false freedom that depends on a history of conquest, uneven exchange, debt deployment and manipulation, violence, and war. To think toward national existence is already to be thinking toward captivity and death.

We struggle to imagine collective life beyond nationalist form. The pre-Pentecost events of chapter 1 remind us of the dynamic of collective life that the triune God is drawing Israel toward—a people who receives peoples, welcoming the stranger, and thereby expanding their identity without loss or violent assimilation. The multiple stories of Israel in Scripture show us a people pressed by God not to be like other peoples who desired a king and a world inscribed by the visible trappings of power and influence and forms of interaction controlled by such realities (1 Sam. 8). Israel got precisely what they longed for: a king and a royal lineage. God, however, overturns what we might anachronistically call Israel's nationalist desire through nationalist form—the son of King David, King Jesus, will not form nationalists even as he forms a new people, but disciples. Should disciples of Jesus love their nation, the one they claim and are claimed by? This is the wrong question. The question we are compelled to ask and answer by our lives is, How might we show the love of God for all peoples, a love that cannot be contained by any nation, a love that slices through borders and boundaries and reaches into every people group, every clan, every tribe, and every family?

The love of God exposes our modern nations for what they are—simple fabricated containers for the rich multiplicity of peoples who each and every one are beloved creatures of the Creator God. The disciples of Jesus are called to reach into this rich multiplicity (Luke 24:47) and like quilters joining beautiful fragments of cloth, invite a weaving together of peoples within nations and beyond them as well. Nationalisms resist such weaving, preferring instead the logics and technologies of assimilation so that they might cover peoples over with forms of patriotism and nationalist self-determination that reduce options for life together. The question for Christians and Jews is whether we can imagine life beyond nationalist consciousness; its seductions remain strong, and we easily fall freely into its collecting gaze. Biblical Israel's hopes and dreams for self-determination and freedom from Roman oppression as witnessed in the desires of the disciples of Jesus prior to Pentecost were understandable, but Jesus collapses all such hopes and dreams into his own life and turns us toward the coming of the Spirit and a new cultural politic of joining.

Nationalism remains a powerful way of imagining life together because it is a theological vision that mimics the desire of God for our full communion with each other. It is communion without God or God simply used as a slogan. This is why nationalism for us moderns is the first idolatry, because it places another god before God. It places a god-bound-to-our-nation over the God of all nations. The god-bound-to-us nationalism, whether we articulate it through a theocracy, a monarchy, a democracy, an oligarchy, a socialism, the plight of an exiled people, or even a global corporation, always seeks to turn our imaginations toward a form of desire that is border controlled and boundaried by distinct objects of affection, for example, a flag, or founding documents and founding historic figures, or songs or stories of heroic sacrifice for the sake of the business or the nation.

The horror of the god-bound-to-us nationalism is not that it wants our respect; it wants our desire. It constantly presses respect toward desire because secretly it wants our worship. Karl Barth, in his commentary on the book of Romans, noted that both the supporters of nation-state and those who wish to limit or topple governments want to inscribe our lives in their fabricated pathos and drama. They long for us to join our passions to their constructed nationalist passion and earnestness within a narrative that would define our hopes and dreams. Barth's answer to such efforts to seize our desire is starvation.[8] We must starve all who would offer us a god-bound-to-us nationalism of their pathos and drama, turning our attention away from their stories of heroic sacrifice, ingenious founders, eternal nationalistic or business principles, or schemas for prosperity. To do so is not an act of disrespect or a denial of their significance for a nation. It means that we acknowledge that our desire for life together flows from another source, and any other claim to be that source can only gain from us an ironic smile that hides serious laughter that anyone could believe that their nation could actually be a comprehensive and enduring reality for a life together that gives life.

Desire for a people and desire for a place belong to God having been born out of the divine life expressed in the gracious act of creation. What belongs to God, God seeks to direct. God seeks to direct such desire in us toward holy ends and not the ends of statecraft or global or local markets. This is why the book of Acts is a direct, unequivocal assault on nationalism in all its forms. God from the very beginning of the Acts drama will not share holy desire with any nationalistic longing that draws borders and boundaries. The Holy Spirit will break open what we want closed and shatter our strategies of protectionism for the sake of a saving God who will give back to us precisely what we cannot hold onto with our own efforts and power, the continuities of our stories, our legacies, our hopes and dreams for a good future and a thriving life. God who will be all in all desires to bring all into all, the many into the many, just as the One is now in and with the many. Nationalism give energy to the false belief that only by its own single efforts can a people sustain

---

8. Karl Barth, *Commentary on Romans* (London: Oxford University Press, 1968), 483.

its story, its hope, and its life. Such belief is unbelief for a Christian, because we know that God offers a new way found in a new life, a joining that brings stories, hopes, and life in a shared work of knowing, remembering, and testifying.

1:13–26

Grasping for the New

It will soon happen again. Obedience to God will make way for the Holy Spirit to touch human flesh and create the new. At the beginning of Luke's Gospel, Mary is the place of obedience that begins the new; and now in part two of Luke's narrative, Mary is again present at the edge of destiny, but this time with the other disciples of Jesus. There is no map for this moment, just as there were no models for Mary. Like Mary, Jesus remains fully within the story of Israel, fully within the trajectories of Jewish faith, hope, and life, yet Jesus has already normalized the unconventional with his motley band of followers—former tax collectors, people who farm the sea, even political revolutionaries, and his mother—all positioned in emergence, ready for transformation. Into what, they do not know. Here is where God likes to sit disciples of the Son, waiting, hoping in prayer.

God gathers not according to our wishes, but through holy desire for those who desire the holy. Thus we have here an interesting group, Mary and her other children, the disciples who walked with Jesus, and certain women: 120 people that could not be confused with a clan, a class, or family, extended or nuclear. This group is not necessarily predisposed to the old practices of patriarchy, but the apostles may be. They prepare for an unknown future, aware of a troubled past. The past contains betrayal that now requires consideration of a replacement. Judas must be replaced. But first Judas will be placed, inscribed in the narrative as the one who was the tool of the empire in the imprisonment, torture, and death of Jesus.

Peter does this important work. He functions in the power of the storyteller. He will tell the story of Judas in a way that moralizes his life and, as Ray Anderson suggests, places on Judas the whole history of their betrayal.[9] Peter and the other disciples are free, but Judas will carry the burden of collective guilt, the one and only betrayer of Jesus, the one and only failure in ministry. There is in this passage the necessary and magisterial ambiguity of divine opinion on this matter. The text could be read as saying that Peter is telling the story in exactly the way God tells the story, or it could be read as saying that Peter is telling the story in the way we tell the story about the dead and their mistakes, and their suicide, and their silence. Yet Peter does expose the logic of this kind of storytelling. The logic moves from the end back to the beginning, the end of a body destroyed to its beginnings in a demonized heart. Judas died a horrible death. Nothing good is coming of his legacy; he betrayed Jesus, and therefore he was and is the betrayer. This logic is crystal clear.

This is the logic, however, of the waiting, the logic of the before. Pentecost is yet coming. It is true that the Holy Spirit is already speaking, according to Peter, in their reading of prophecy: a betrayer was foretold and Judas is that man. But the last word on Judas will not come from Peter. It will come from Jesus. Divine opinion is separate from Peter's opinion. Peter narrates Judas's life for a purpose. Judas is the setup for what he really wants to see happen: replacement. This is the awesome power of storytellers. They can invoke lives and play with them, juggling them like balls in the air. The dead cannot answer back. They have no control over how their lives are used or how they are remembered. There is what Judas did, but now we are in the additional realm of what Peter is doing. Both realms of past and present merge in storytelling and only an ethic born of the resurrected life of Jesus can guide us in how to flow in both realms. At this moment, Peter has no flow.

However, Peter is not the problem here. The problem is a group of Jesus followers who are only at the beginning of coming to grips with his resurrection from the dead and what it means for how we speak of those who have died in shame, died in pain, died in guilt. Last words no longer belong to us. They have been seized by a savior. Jesus' power now reaches into the grave, into Judas's grave. Peter's deepest concern at this moment is for the trajectory of

9. Ray S. Anderson, *The Gospel according to Judas* (Colorado Springs: Helmers & Howard, 1991).

representation. Without falling into anachronistic thinking, it would be appropriate to see the politics of representation at play in Peter's speech. Like the question to Jesus about the restoration of Israel' reign in the world, their concern now was who would fill out the number. The disciples understood that they represented the twelve tribes of Israel. Each one of them was positioned to rule alongside of the Messiah.

Luke is not presenting to us in Peter a man moved only by political motivations. This is also a matter of faithfulness to the ministry and apostleship bestowed on the twelve. Faithfulness requires continuity. So the need was for someone who had been with them from the beginning, from baptism to the ascension of Jesus. Replacement indeed. This is a unique moment in an unrepeatable event and to find someone whose life stands between the unique and the unrepeatable is no small accomplishment. Yet here are two possible witnesses, and make no mistake, they are looking for someone worthy to give witness to Jesus. Such a weighty mantle could only fall on someone elect in the same way that the disciples themselves had been elected by Jesus, and such election demands prayer for its discernment. John Calvin was right to see the implications of this text for the awesome task of congregations choosing ministers.[10] Matthias is chosen, and it would be easy to read this selection as the completion of divine election or to read it in the oppose direction, seeing this as only a signature of the old world, the old way, rooted in the casting of lots.[11] But neither reading reaches into the risk of this moment.

Someone has been chosen for an uncertain future with the memory of betrayal still very fresh. How might anyone enlist with the way forward so utterly unclear? Matthias is called. That is now clear, but he is called to the same upper room with the other one hundred and twenty, with men and women he probably knows very well, and he is called to one work, pray and wait, wait and pray. Like the others

---

10. John Calvin, *Commentary on the Acts of the Apostle* (Grand Rapids: Christian Classics Ethereal Library, https://www.ccel.org/ccel/calvin/calcom36.i.html Calvin, John, 2009). Commentary on Acts, vol. 1, enhanced version (Calvin's Commentaries) (Kindle location 111). Christian Classics Ethereal Library. Kindle edition.

11. Ben Witherington III, *The Acts of the Apostle: A Socio-Rhetorical Commentary* (Grand Rapids: Eerdmans, 1998) 126–27.

he will wait for the Spirit to come and the Spirit to speak and then he will know what he must do with the others for the sake of Jesus. If he is the right one then God has done to him what God does to all those who hear the words of Jesus—sits them down, fills them with hope, and asks them to join the others in prayer.

There awaits a destiny for the twelve, but the politics of representation—finding the right "man"—is about to be interrupted. Israel, new Israel is soon to be constituted by the Spirit, constituted in the opening up of lives to the world. Whatever ideas of leadership Peter and the other apostles were imagining, they could not anticipate what God was about to do. A common thing, a selection process, has been placed in an extraordinary setting, in the upper room before Pentecost. From this moment forward every common thing of the disciples of Jesus, every administrative act, every bureaucratic gesture exists in the posture of waiting and stands in the shadow cast by the Holy Spirit and within the necessary work of prayer.

2:1–13

The Sound of Intimacy

And I said: "Woe is me! I am lost, for I am a man of unclean lips, and I live among a people of unclean lips; yet my eyes have seen the King, the LORD of hosts!" Then one of the seraphs flew to me, holding a live coal that had been taken from the altar with a pair of tongs. The seraph touched my mouth with it and said: "Now that this has touched your lips, your guilt has departed and your sin is blotted out" (Isa. 6:5–7).

The Miracle of Pentecost is less in the hearing and much more in the speaking. Disciples speak in the mother tongues of others, not by their own design but by the Spirit's desire. The new wine has been poured out on those unaware of just how deeply they thirsted. This famous account from Luke is the epicenter of the revolution. Here is the unfolding moment that will define the drama of the Book of Acts. This is the beginning of the miracle of Pentecost, *the revolution of the intimate.* This is the beginning of a community broken open by the sheer act of God, and we are yet to comprehend the extent to which God acts and is acting to break us open. Indeed it will be a community created by the Spirit precisely in the breaking open. Now Israel, the new Israel, is turned out by the Spirit. Only the gracious work of God in creation matches this moment of prevenient grace. This is God's doing: no one helped, no one assisted, everyone only tarried. The waiting in prayer has not come to an end. It has only moved forward into an action fully of God.

God's direct action

The similitude of the wind to the Spirit's coming suggests not only its absolute power but its absolute uncontrollability. No structure is stronger than the wind, and there is nothing beyond its touch. How much greater is the reality of the Spirit than this weak metaphor? Wind and fire speak of ancient theophany in Israel, harkening back to Moses and Israel's beginnings in miraculous displays of divine power. This moment of divine power will be used to signify the full presence of the Spirit through one crucial reality of life: language. Here we must not draw back from what is being displayed in Luke's account. This is God touching, taking hold of tongue and voice, mind, heart, and body. This is a joining, unprecedented, unanticipated, unwanted, yet complete joining. Those gathered in prayer asked for power. They may have asked for the Holy Spirit to come, but they did not ask for this. This is real grace, untamed grace. It is the grace that replaces our fantasies of power over people with God's fantasy for desire for people.

God has come to them, on them, with them. This moment echoes Mary's intimate moment. The Holy Spirit again overshadows. However this similar holy action creates something different, something startling. The Spirit creates joining. The followers of Jesus are now being connected in a way that joins them to people in the most intimate space—of voice, memory, sound, body, land, and place. It is language that runs through all these matters. It is the sinew of existence of a people. My people, our language: to speak a language is to speak a people. Speaking announces familiarity, connection, and relationality. But these people are already connected, aren't they? They are "devout Jews from every nation under heaven" (*andres eulabeis apo pantos ethnous*, v. 5). They share the same story and the same faith in the God of Abraham, Isaac, and Jacob. They share the same hopes of Israel's restoration, even its expansion into the world freed from oppression and domination. They are diaspora, and diaspora life is already a shared obligation and hope.

God has, however, now revealed a mighty hand and an outstretched arm reaching deeply into the lives of the Son's co-travelers and pressing them along a new road into the places God seeks to be fully known. This is first a miracle of hearing. "… [E]ach of us, in our own native language" (*hameis akouomen hekastos tē idia dialektō hamōn en hē egennēthēmen.* v. 8). The homes of mothers are announced in the mouths of those who were far removed from those mother tongues. This is not generic speech, formal pronouncements, but the language of intimate spaces where peoples inside talk to one another. The hearers query a past that does not exist for these followers of Jesus. "How do they know my language and know my people? When did they gain that knowledge?" But their miraculous tongues are not about the past but about the future, a future shaped by divine desire. This is why we must see more than a miracle of hearing. Such limited seeing reveals our failure as readers to grasp God's unfolding of the divine fantasy to these early believers. It also exposes our modern failure to grasp the revolutionary intimacy that will give birth to a belonging that we will call church. This is a revolution of the Spirit always poised to unleash itself at the slightest moment of faithful waiting and yielding.

The miracles are not merely in ears. They are also in mouths and in bodies. God, like a lead dancer, is taking hold of her partners, drawing them close and saying, "Step this way and now this direction." The gesture of speaking another language is born not of the desire of the disciples but of God, and it signifies all that is essential to learning a language. It bears repeating: this is not what the disciples imagined or hoped would manifest the power of the Holy Spirit. To learn a language requires submission to a people. Even if in the person of a single teacher, the learner must submit to that single voice, learning what the words mean as they are bound to events, songs, sayings, jokes, everyday practices, habits of mind and body, all within a land and the journey of a people. Anyone who has learned a language other than their native tongue knows how humbling learning can actually be. An adult in the slow and often arduous efforts of pronunciation may be reduced to a child, and a child at home in that language may become the teacher of an adult. There comes a crucial moment in the learning of any language, if one wishes to reach fluency, that enunciation requirements and repetition must give way to sheer wanting. Some people learn a language out of gut-wrenching determination born of necessity. Most, however, who enter a lifetime of fluency, do so because at some point in time they learn to love it.

They fall in love with the sounds. The language sounds beautiful to them. And if that love is complete, they fall in love with its original signifiers. They come to love the people—the food, the faces, the plans, the practices, the songs, the poetry, the happiness, the sadness, the ambiguity, the truth—and they love the place, that is, the circled earth those people call their land, their landscapes, their home. Speak a language, speak a people. God speaks people, fluently. And God, with all the urgency that is with the Holy Spirit, wants the disciples of his only begotten Son to speak people fluently too. This is the beginning of a revolution that the Spirit performs. Like an artist drawing on all her talent to express a new way to live, God gestures the deepest joining possible, one flesh with God, and desire made one with the Holy One.

> **"My Faithful Mother Tongue"**
>
> You were my native land; . . .
> I believed that you would also
>   be a messenger
> between me and some good
>   people
>
> . . . .
>
> not born, as yet.
>
> —Czeslaw Milosz, "My Faithful Mother Tongue," in *New and Collected Poems, 1931–2001* (New York: HarperCollins, 2001), 245–46.

Yet here we can begin to see even more clearly the ancient challenge and the modern problem. The ancient challenge is a God who is way ahead of us and is calling us to catch up. The modern problem is born of the colonial enterprise where language play and use entered its most demonic displays. Imagine peoples in many places, in many conquered sites, in many tongues all being told that their languages are secondary, tertiary, and inferior to the supreme languages of the enlightened peoples. Make way for Latin, French, German, Dutch, Spanish, and English. These are the languages God speaks. These are the scholarly languages of the transcending intellect and the holy mind. Imagine centuries of submission and internalized hatred of mother tongues and in the quiet spaces of many villages, many homes, women, men, and children practicing these new enlightened languages not by choice but by force. Imagine peoples largely from this new Western world learning native languages not out of love, but as utility for domination. Imagine mastering native languages in order to master people, making oneself their master and making them slaves. Now imagine Christianity deeply implicated in all this, in many cases riding high on the winds of this linguistic imperialism, a different sounding wind. Christianity was ripe for this tragic collaboration with colonialism because it had learned before the colonial moment began to separate a language from a people. It had learned to value, cherish, and even love the language of Jewish people found in Scripture—but hate Jewish people.

Thankfully this is not the only story of Christianity in the colonial modern. There are also the quiet stories of some translators, and the peculiar few missionaries who from time to time and place to place showed something different. They joined. They, with or without "natural language skill," sought love and found it in another voice, another speech, another way of life. They showed something in their utter helplessness in the face of difference: they were there in a new land to be changed, not just change people into believers. They were there not just to make conquered Christians but truly and deeply make themselves Christian in a new space that would mean that their names would be changed. They would become the sound of another people, speaking the wonderful works of God. However these stories remain hidden in large measure from the history of Christianity that we know so well, which means we often know so little of Christianity.

The modern problem points back to the ancient challenge. We can sense that challenge even in this first experience of Pentecost. Those listening were amazed and perplexed. They asked the right question: "What does this mean?" (v.12). The meaning is not obvious because the event is unprecedented. As Luke Timothy Johnson notes, even if other oracles had spoken in ecstatic speech, normally the hearers would not be able to understand (as these hearers did in their most intimate language) because the words come from the gods.[12] But this need for meaning here reaches toward the future. The question bends toward its sister question: What is God doing here and now? Peter will soon speak and begin to give an answer to this question. Yet he is only at the edge of morning. The noon day of Peter is yet to unfold. The meaning of the speaking in tongues is so obvious, so powerful, that it was missed. The Holy Spirit has come. Joining has begun. This is the real meaning.

The same Spirit that was there from the beginning, hovering, brooding in the joy of creation of the universe and of each one of us, who knows us together and separately in our most intimate places, has announced the divine intention through the Son to reach into our lives and make each life a site of speaking glory. But this will require bodies that reach across massive and real boundaries, cultural, religious, and ethnic. It will require a commitment born of Israel's faith, but reaching to depths of relating beyond what any devotion to Israel's God had heretofore been recognized as requiring: devotion to peoples unknown and undesired. What God had always spoken to Israel now God speaks even more loudly in the voices of the many to the many: join them! Now love of neighbor will take on pneumatological dimensions. It will be love that builds directly out of the resurrected body of Jesus. It will be love, as Karl Barth says, that goes into the far country.[13] This is love that cannot be tamed, controlled, or planned, and once unleashed it will drive the disciples forward into the world and drive a question into their lives: Where is the Holy Spirit taking us and into whose lives?

This famous text has been the foundational text of so many churches that see themselves born of the Pentecostal experience, and rightly so, because here is the birth of the church. But *this child* was not expected. There has been in the last one hundred years in and among those churches born of the modern Pentecostal movement discussion about the importance of speaking in tongues as an essential sign of being filled with the Holy Spirit. There have also been and continue to be untold millions of Christians who claim

12. Luke Timothy Johnson, *The Acts of the Apostles* (Collegeville, MN: The Liturgical Press, 1992), 54.
13. Karl Barth, *Church Dogmatics*, IV/1, *The Doctrine of Reconciliation* (Edinburgh: T. & T. Clark, 1956), 175-298.

a charismatic experience, who believe that God has granted them holy tongues by the Spirit's uttering power. The controversy that grew up around Pentecostalism and later the charismatic movement has always been an unfortunate misplacement of focus, exposing our modern inability to grasp the desire of God revealed by the Holy Spirit. Neither concern for auditory evidence nor for linguistic authenticity brings us to the heart of the Spirit's signifying reality. The only real question is, Do we hear what the tongues mean? For this, we do not need interpreters. We need translators, people who will allow their lives to be translated, not just once, but again and again as the Spirit gives utterance.

2:14–36

Speaking in the Spirit

Peter again speaks. The only real difference in this second speech is the subject of the discourse. We have gone from Judas to Jesus and from replacement talk to talk about Israel's future. Peter's words are about Israel, in Israel, and for Israel. Our Christian readings of this text often fly past the iconic element found in verse 14 that shapes the entire speech. Immediately after the ears have heard the new, the eyes will see it. Standing in front of all those who had heard their tongues are the twelve disciples, now becoming apostles of Jesus. This is Israel speaking to Israel, calling to their own with the good news of the intensification of their election and of the personification of the free grace that shaped their existence from its beginning.

This is precisely where the scandal that was Jesus of Nazareth, Mary's baby with all the tensions he created and all the theological, social, and political contradictions that religious and civic leaders associated with his ministry, began to spread over many bodies. This is a strange image, an unappealing icon—twelve men, none with exceptional credentials, no fabulous educational pedigrees, none with reservoirs of immense cultural capital to draw from, all standing in front of Israelites with nothing more than a message. We live in times when images create and carry so much power. For us, image and word, body and text, are inseparable, merging together, mutually constituting. Yet in this primordial moment the image standing before these gathered does not carry gravitas. It can never match its message. Nor will it ever. This is the eternal imbalance that will mark preaching, a message far more powerful than its messengers. Indeed, image emerges here fully encased in witness.

If this is the first Christian sermon, then we must take note of several of its elements. First, it exists only within the Holy Spirit. It begins only after the Spirit has come. It is a second word after the words of praise have been given by God. Before the Spirit came, Peter had little to say. His words will now and forever be only commentary on what the Spirit is doing, and what God has done for us in Jesus. Second, he does not stand alone. As he stands, the other disciples stand. As he stands and speaks, Israel's prophets are echoing in his words. It is a life-draining deception to ever believe that one preaches alone. Of course, one voice speaks in the preaching, yet at every moment, at any given moment when a preacher speaks, many preachers past and present are speaking. The preacher is always a company of preachers.

Knowing that the one is bound to the many, that this one Peter is bound to these other erect figures, will not make matters easier. Indeed it will only clarify the risk of this moment. This first Christian sermon is born in Israel and shaped for Israel. To say that Christianity began as a reform movement in Judaism is correct but horribly sterile. This moment exposes what Bonhoeffer calls the power of the weak word.[14] Peter, along with these others, will now attempt to seize control of the narrative of a people, positioning themselves as its master storytellers, and render their witness the site of Israel's real history. Luke plays in the intertextual and gives us a Peter who travels back and forth from an ancient Israel to the one gathered there with him and stamps the current moment as the last days with an end, if not in sight, certainly in mind.

The famous Joel passage noted here could never be fully captured with our conceptions of egalitarianism. It proclaims a new world order energized by the movement of the Holy Spirit, breaking through on all flesh and destroying social orders that find slavery

---

14. Dietrich Bonhoeffer, *Letters and Papers from Prison*, Dietrich Bonhoeffer Works, vol. 8 (Minneapolis: Fortress Press, 2010), 479.

useful, stable, capable of making fundamental differences of identity between would-be masters and would-be slaves. These slaves, men and women, prophesy. God speaks through them and they are to be obeyed. This new world order begins with collapse. God shakes foundations, especially ones that wrongly claim divine imprint. However, it is only as Peter makes the christological turn that he connects the overturning of the social order with the new order of the Spirit. Only as he speaks of Jesus does he begin really signifying the present. Now Peter sets the template through which future preachers' words will be spoken about the real God in real time who is working in the concrete histories of people.

Jesus of Nazareth is the history foretold by Joel. We must not lose sight of the storyteller at work here, because this will become the legacy for the many that will follow Peter. He presents the life of Jesus as reachable, attainable, and one who has been among us. This Jesus was murdered, and in his journey toward death, Peter declares the sameness of Jesus with all human beings. Like us he faced the powers of empire and death. But now he has risen from the dead. Through an audacious act Luke binds the story of King David to this risen ruler Jesus. This Jesus reveals not only the destiny of Israel's God, but the divine identity as well. The cosmic, the universal, the great and mighty not only has revealed in this One, but more shockingly this Jesus reveals the great and mighty, the universal, the cosmic, the God who is greater than death. The Jesus you knew—crucified, dead and buried, and now alive—is both Lord and Messiah, the bearer of the divine image and reality. This is the great contradiction.

It is the contradiction inside of which all the disciples of Jesus will live forever. Life inside this contradiction means, as Samuel Proctor said, that we may now see the world for what it is: upside down.[15] The world, seen from the site of the crucified One, moving quickly from life toward death, is the real contradiction. Only from within the declaration of a God who was crucified will any words about God in this world, the real world, make sense. Whether Luke or Peter understood it, through the Holy Spirit they had turned the story of Israel toward life everlasting and had shown us the way to

---

15. Samuel Proctor, *My Moral Odyssey* (Valley Forge, PA: Judson Press, 1989).

our life stories and the stories of our peoples toward redemptive by drawing people to the victory of God in Jesus. Who would ~~'e~~ such a remarkable word coming from such unremarkable witnesses? There would be no chance of success unless the Spirit of the living God breathed on their witness. Thankfully, now the Spirit has appeared, living and breathing on and through unlikely voices, voices just like ours.

2:37–41

A New Response

A change is taking place among the people of God. Faith in Israel is taking a new direction. And it all begins with a simple but terrifying question: "What should we do?" These devotees of Israel's God have heard a message as disruptive as anything one could hear. It is a message that flows directly out of the divine propensity for interruption, first of Mary's life, then of Joseph, and then of these apostles, one by one, called away from home to a new direction in Israel. Now inside the explosion that is the coming of the Spirit, these who have heard Peter's message confront the reality of a more excellent way of faith in Israel. The question they asked Peter is indeed terrifying because it begs the question of religious necessity. Why should those who are already faithful in Israel, committed to its way of life, religious practices, and sensibilities need to ask the question, "What should we do?" Their lives already answer such a question.

The question itself is at the door of offense. Although the irenic is concealed within the question, nonetheless, it suggests a *necessary* change for those already of committed faith. We must hear in this question the astounding work of the living God who will not be relegated to Israel's past but will reveal divine faithfulness to ancient promise in the present moment. And in so doing, we see the precise way Israel's Lord alters theological frames of reference by demanding more of those who believe.

Here in Israel, God will seek after the elect, all of them. God will stand over against religious faith, as neither its friend nor its enemy, but as God. Here is the point of offense: all religious faith believes it already has God in its sight. It knows and seeks after; it tirelessly devotes time, energy, and resources to the Holy. Those who hear this message, however, encounter a difference born of the body of Jesus. He is a difference in Israel that will yield an intensification and alteration of the faith received. But he must be chosen. He will not destroy faith in God, only fulfill it. But he must be chosen. Thus Peter's response to the question instructs moving in a fresh direction. His response reveals language internal to the culture and theology of Israel. Repentance, forgiveness, and gift are all themes that flow through the streams of Israel's historical consciousness. Yet now a new point of entry and departure has emerged through a new stream that flows in a new direction. All must be baptized in the new stream, baptized into Jesus.

Baptism in his name signifies this new point. Indeed Jesus has seized baptism in Israel and merged it with the divine life. Just as he turned water into wine, he will now bring water into service to the Holy Spirit. By the Spirit, water will become a steady voice calling for the renewal of creation. Each baptism in the name of Jesus will say loudly and clearly, "Come, Holy Spirit, claim yet another part of your creation, claim yet another child of God." There continue to be churches that believe baptism in Jesus' name is the only legitimate form of baptism, and they would draw our attention to this crucial text as the beginning of this new ritual. I would suggest that they have correctly captured the newness, but where they envisage restriction and limitation, it would be more helpful to see expansion and openness. The trajectory of the text is not toward formula but formation. From this moment forward, life with God will be through Jesus, and this moment of baptism will yield life in a body turned toward the renewal of creation. The story of Israel has opened up, and God's body has been joined to Israel's body and will be joined to all who will come to the water. Luke signifies a redeemer who would bring all of Israel from death to life through these holy waters and draw them more deeply into divine desire.

Now divine hunger will be revealed. God is calling to Israel and its children and other children and their children. This calling will be *contra mundi*, against the world's calling, the world's desire for the children. It will be against this "corrupt generation" (v. 40). This will be the difference bound to a decision, God's calling or the world's calling, and at this moment the new word reveals the old tension for God's people between listening and thus obeying the voice of the world or hearing the *dabarim* of *Adonai*, the word of the Lord. Luke draws us into a pleasant result, a welcomed message and converts in large numbers. But even in this exuberant account we still see a shadow that will grow as the story moves on. Some did not welcome the message, even in the presence of the Spirit of God. We read past this reality at our own peril. The offensiveness of the message of Jesus, the message about Jesus, is a real problem for some, and they will not have their religious sensibilities challenged, even if the challenge is a word of good news that the God who created them seeks after them in Jesus. For such folks, God's real body will not be allowed to eclipse their vision of the Holy.

For those, however, who heard this message a new social reality begins to take hold of them moving between three wonderful points of reference, the apostles' teaching and communion, the sharing in meals, and prayer. As Jaroslav Pelikan notes, the emergence of these characteristics will mark this new community and create the lens through which such communities may be identified and even judged.[16] Equally significantly for us, the marks of divine disruption are witnessed in these actions. These actions mark those baptized as having entered a contrast society, as Gerhard Lohfink calls it, a radical cell bound to the ministry of Jesus through his disciples.[17] The words of Jesus that defined those disciples' lives will now give direction to these who have been filled with the Spirit: follow me as I follow my Father. What follows from this moment is neither utopian nor unrealistic, but a clear trajectory born of the sure exposure to the divine life.

2:42–47

A New Reality of Giving

Life with Jesus must give shape to life in the Spirit. The Apostles were yet caught in the echo of a life fully dependent on God, a life yielded

16. Jaroslav Pelikan, *Acts* (Grand Rapids: Brazos Press, 2005), 58.
17. Gerhard Lohfink, *Jesus and Community: The Social Dimension of Christian Faith* (Philadelphia: Fortress Press, 1982), 31–60.

to the Spirit, and one that did not reject the weakness of flesh. As such they carried forward the reality of divine power clothed in the common and the miraculous flowing through weathered hands. It would makes sense therefore to see in this moment the power of Jesus' life pressing into the normal, the daily, the routine and drawing God's people into the new. Now at this moment they were together and "had all things in common" (*kai eichon hapanta koina,* v. 44).

The space of this common was where life stories, life projects, plans, and purposes were being intercepted by a new orientation. This common is created by the Spirit. How could the things they held dear not be drawn toward the common, this new gathering, this *ekklēsia*? Time, talent, and treasures, the trinity of possessions we know so well, would feel the pull of this holy vortex. We could certainly imagine that Luke is painting a sunny picture at this moment not because these things did not occur but because they were indeed tentative and fleeting due to the immense implications of living according to the life of Jesus. The real questions are not whether this holy communalism, this sacred sociality, could or would be operative, be practical in this ancient world or any world, but what must it have been like to feel the powerful pull of the life of our savior, and what energy did it take to resist the Holy Spirit, to slow down this pull enough to withhold themselves and their possessions from divine desire.

It is not a new thing that people would offer up their possessions to a noble or religious cause, nor withhold their possessions from such causes. A different order of sacrifice is being performed here, one that reaches back to the very beginnings of Israel. Their God does not need possessions and has never been impressed by their donation. The divine One wants people and draws us into that wanting. This is intensified giving, feverish giving that feels not only the urgent need but the divine wanting. A new kind of giving is exposed at this moment, one that binds bodies together as the first reciprocal donation where the followers will give themselves to one another. The possessions will follow. What was at stake here was not the giving up of all possessions but the giving up of each one, one by one as the Spirit gave direction, and as the ministry of Jesus made demand. Thus anything they had that might be used to bring people into sight and sound of the incarnate life, anything they had that might be used to draw people to life together and life itself and away from death and end the reign of poverty, hunger, and despair—such things were subject to being given up to God. The giving is for the sole purpose of announcing the reign of the Father's love through the Son in the bonds of communion together with the Spirit.

Luke gives us sight of a holy wind blowing through structured and settled ways of living and possessing and pulling things apart. People caught up in the love of God not only began to give thanks for their daily bread, but daily offered to God whatever they had that might speak that gracious love to others. What is far more dangerous than any plan of shared wealth or fair distribution of goods and services is a God who dares impose on us divine love. Such love will not play fair. In the moment we think something is ours, or our people's, that same God will demand we sell it, give it away, or offer more of it in order to feed the hungry, cloth the naked, or shelter the homeless, using it to create the bonds of shared life. This will be the new direction born of this moment. The salvation of Israel is sure and now intensified through the Spirit, who tightens God's claim on them by announcing a new order of things that will not pass away.

3:1–11

A New Gaze

The gate of the temple becomes the entrance to a new future. Peter and John have entered that future, and now they perform it. There is absolutely nothing wrong about this religious practice of temple and prayer, almsgiving and worship. This scene shows us the faithful following life-giving tradition. There is, however, also here present the repetition of pain, the sight of suffering. There is a man "lame from birth" (v. 2); from the womb of his mother he has carried this wound. And he is carried again and again to the temple's gate. This is unanticipated infirmity that resists the cause and effect, thinking of sin and then suffering. The scene reminds us of the episode of Jesus in the presence of the man born blind (in John 9). There in John's Gospel, Jesus bring the disciples to a place where their questions about suffering flesh and infirmed bodies collapse in the face of a single encounter, Jesus and his disciples with this man, the blind man.

At the temple gate this collapse happens again. No questions about the how, who, when, or why of this infirmity survive in this space where inexplicable hurt meets faithful witness. The only thing that matters is the meeting. At the doorway to worship are those whose very presence should discipline praise and guide hope. Before praises go up to God the poor and lame, sick and pained must be seen. This lame man lay in the path toward praise which is also the path of the disciples. This route was established by Jesus. This man is precisely the person Jesus will see and demands his disciples see. Peter and John find themselves without an option: time to see with the eyes of Jesus.

This man was a daily reminder of the need of Israel itself, for miraculous healing, and for yet another moment of divine revealing. Before we turn to the many of Israel we must see the one moment unfolding. As this man follows his desperate pattern of begging, it is interrupted with the words of Peter, "Look at us." Eyes meet at this moment. Peter and John gaze at this man (v. 4) and the man looks attentively back at them. This man anticipates receiving the signs of an economic relation, the symbols that indicate that ever-present imbalance between the haves and the have-nots. This gaze between them suggests the usual, but its intensity soon opens to something much more. Here the poor and needy will not be overlooked. Here at the beginning of the post-Pentecost ministry of the followers of Jesus, people will be seen fully, strongly, clearly. Equally important, Peter speaks a necessary optical reciprocity. Disciples are watched, especially by those in need. Disciples must be seen, especially by those in need. Even more fantastic, disciples must call attention to themselves, not as an act of religious hubris, but as the absolute mandate of a witness. As all eyes were fixed on Jesus in the synagogue (Luke 4:20), so in this scene the gaze invites fresh anticipation, unexpected by the lame man but imagined by those of faith: God will move and God will speak.

Only such divine action could

> Disciples are watched, especially by those in need.
> Disciples must be seen, especially by those in need.

break open the power of the economic relation that binds financial hierarchy to life, concealing the true vision of our deep interconnectedness. Peter has no riches to give. He has something else to offer. The contrast of gifts introduces the truth of belonging. There is silver and gold, the gifts of the Caesars of this world, and there are the gifts of God. Both carry power and both lead to worship. Peter and John witness the greater claim on creation itself and thus a greater reality of gift. In the name of Jesus, this disabled human being is touched by his creator and given strength to his limbs. God yet claims the creation and the creature, Israel. The sight of this man imagined as forever sitting and begging, now leaping and praising God rightly turns all eyes toward him and draws a crowd to see and understand. Now he will be truly seen, yet before the hurrying crowd turned to see, the work of the witnesses was to see.

I pointed out to the good people of the NAACP that although many of us were doing fine, the poor people we'd met in the neighborhood surrounding our church in Goldsboro had a different story to tell about the state of justice in America. . . . If a room full of black folks knew they were doing better than they had been doing fifty years before, then simple math made clear that, somewhere, there was another room full of black folks doing worse.

William Barber II (with Jonathan Wilson-Hartgrove), *The Third Reconstruction: Moral Mondays, Fusion Politics and the Rise of a New Justice Movement* (Boston: Beacon Press, 2016), 46.

3:12–26

History in the Making

As the crowd begins to gather Peter begins to speak. Another icon stands before the crowd, Peter and John and with them the healed one. The miraculous is not only the one healed but Peter and John, who now live on the other side of the journey of Jesus as his true witnesses. All are miracles. Peter offers words that would guide sight. He and John are not the source of this blessing. No one is healed by the power or holiness of witnesses, but only through Jesus of Nazareth. Peter's words then move into the profoundly dangerous arena of accusation and guilt. Peter speaks to a specific crowd, the children of Israel, and invokes the same behavior seen in Jesus. They killed the prophets before him (Luke 11:47). We know the danger here, which is registered in a history of misuse. The killing of Jesus mutated over the centuries into an unrelenting accusation against Jewish people. But Peter speaks to *his* people. This is an in-house conversation. We have lost the sense and struggle of this family argument, this cultic contention. But what he speaks captures a reality for all peoples and their leaders. Peoples often do act in ignorance or malice, killing the innocent and allowing murderers to go free.

Told from this angle the story of servant Jesus highlights the weakness of the many, the ease with which the crowd could be deceived to choose against their own well-being. If the many can be deceived, then what must it be like to see their deception? Luke positions Peter in that painful position of seeing and knowing what others don't fully see. Such a position does not reflect a heavenly vision but is a door that easily leads to despair. How many intellectuals, activists, scientists, or sages have found themselves precisely in this position wishing for a more enlightened multitude (a smarter crowd) that would always will and do the common good? Yet such seers are tormented by the knowledge that the many have yielded themselves agents of death and may do so again. Peter and John carry the memory of a crowd that called for Jesus' death. But now Peter's speech marks the path through such agonizing knowledge with its temptation toward self-indulging intellectual narcissism. The point here is not the actions of the many but the actions of the One. The man healed is now a sign of the man resurrected from the dead, the author of life itself. Now the actions of the One confront the wayward propensities of the many. If peoples are often seduced by the power of violence and take up the weapons of death, here is Jesus the Messiah who has overcome the effects of violence and the pull of death. If peoples are prone to choose against their own well-being and life, here is the Messiah who heals, restores, and gives life. We need not be mystified by the crowd or frustrated by their failures to act for the common good; Jesus has acted for them and offers his body as a way out and a way to be together.

Luke turns his readers to the outrageous view of a providential act, of a God who knew suffering was unavoidable for this prophet called to save his people. Indeed all the words of Israel's suffering prophets pointed to this one final prophet, Jesus. Peter declares that Israel's history has been turned toward the body of Jesus. Luke has entered into a radically subversive historiography. The story-teller has appeared in outrageous presumption declaring that Jesus has begun the end of time. In him, time has been confronted by its maker. Marked from his ascension, the followers of Jesus now know and feel the great expectation. The Son of God in heaven will soon return to earth. The Son of God in heaven means that the unfolding of history will be a marked by a decision, to follow Jesus or not. Yet the simplicity of this decision in Israel points to the faithfulness of their God. Luke is doing things with words. He is playing with history and historical consciousness, drawing it down to its properly creaturely realm and pulling it without remainder into the body of Jesus.

Luke at this moment gives us guerrilla history-making and insurgent strategies that will travel with the faith. Every witness to Jesus now has the possibility of drawing the stories and histories of people to Jesus as their *telos*, that is, their fulfillment, their meaning, and their end. Yet the idea of *telos* points to the awesome danger and troubled record of Christians who messed with the histories of people. Some would-be evangelists presented Jesus as the destruction of people's histories, negating their stories and killing their storytellers all in the name of eradicating the demonic and the heterodox from their consciousness. Others have treated the histories of peoples as naive hagiography or intellectually deficient accountings of historical truth and therefore presented Jesus as the ground clearing beginning point to enlightened history. The Jesus presented by Luke, however, has overcome death so that peoples' histories no longer face the silencing power of death that can erode and ultimately destroy the memories of all people. Now Jesus eagerly wants to take hold of the histories of people and bring them to a good end, which is a new beginning. He can take hold of their ambiguity, their pain, and their memories of horror and weave their stories together with the stories of others and give all people sight of a new creation and life eternal. This is the spilling over of the restoration of Israel and the explosion beyond its borders of historical expectation. All peoples may have a new future in Jesus, and each one of us have a new story to tell that changes the end we previously expected.

4:1–37

The Criminal-Disciple Emerges!

Christians of the modern West have never really grasped our deep connection to the criminal mind, our mind.

Speaking holy words has serious consequences. These are not words that simply speak of God. There is nothing inherently serious, holy, or dangerous in God-talk. The holy words that bring consequences are words tied to the concrete liberating actions of God for broken people. Such holy words bring the speakers into direct confrontation with those in power. Jesus not only spoke such words but he was such a word. He was predestined to challenge those in power and confront the powers, spiritual and human. This moment was inevitable. The disciples knew this confrontation was coming. The struggle against those in power that marked the life and death of Jesus was coming for them as well. The great illusion of followers of Jesus, especially those who imagine themselves leaders, is that they could live a path different from Jesus and his disciples. They believe somehow that they can be loved or at least liked or at least tolerated or even ignored by those with real power in the world.

This illusion is born of the forgetfulness of location. The disciples are among common people proclaiming liberation and that violence and death are no longer the ultimate power. Jesus is risen! There from the site of the common, holy words touch two intersecting nerves, the religious and the political. For some in power, these disciples speak heresy (Jesus is the power of God) while for others in power, these disciples speak sedition (Jesus is the power). Only criminals touch nerves at this level and receive the consequences: "So they arrested them and put them in custody" (4:3). Real preaching and authentic teaching is inextricably bound to real criminality. Christians of the modern West have never really grasped our deep connection to the criminal mind, our mind. We should always understand ourselves as what Edward Said called secular critics who unrelentingly call into question the gods of this age, that is, the prevailing social, cultural, political, economic, and academic logics that support or are at ease with the status quo of grotesquely differentiated wealth and poverty, uneven access to the necessary resources for life and health, and forms of sublimely stubborn oppression masked inside social conventions.[18] Yet a status quo is always embodied in people with real power, the power to imprison and torture us.

So Peter and John entered the moment of judgment when the eyes of the powerful are trained on them and the questioning begins. Jesus tried to prepare his disciples for this moment, but not simply as a moment but as the revelation of the dividing line between two distinct ways of seeing human life. On the one side are the judges and on the other side are the judged. The legal view is only one angle of this divide that reaches into the depths of people's life projects. The judges are accomplished. They finished their education, benefited from social advantage, believed appropriately, and followed the right confessions, theological, social, and economic. The judges understand political realities and can work with the given situations in order to gain a profitable result. This particular group of judges might have been the Sanhedrin or it might be better to simply see them as the religious and social elites who are in the position to judge.

The judged are Peter and John. Their lives took turns that they had not anticipated or wanted. This is what happens to common people. The life currents they face are strong and very unpredictable. Sometimes they catch a branch or a rock that allows them to move against the currents, angling their bodies toward calmer waters. Other times they become very powerful swimmers who can battle the currents and find dry land. But most of the time they flow with the currents wherever they may lead. The difference for Peter and John and many others like them is Jesus. He entered the waters just like them. Another John would have prevented him, but he insisted on the currents (Matt. 3:14). Once in the water, Jesus stretched out his body like a swimmer and allowed the currents to take him. Even with the help of the Spirit guiding the winds of the currents, Jesus'

18. Edward W. Said, *Representations of the Intellectual* (New York: Vintage Books, 1996), 88–89.

end was inevitable. He ended up in exactly the same kind of place that now his disciples Peter and John stand, the judged. But he got there before them in order to meet them there when they arrived and to guide them precisely from that place of being judged. Jesus never sought to escape the place of judgment. He planned to seize it.

The judged are questioned (the judges are not). The judged must give account of their power and authority to speak, to believe, to suggest a different world order. The judged must show connection to the powerful, to names that are recognized by those in power. Power only sees power. The judged are evaluated (the judges are not). A scale is unleashed against the judged. Their education, social pedigrees, elocution, and bearing are all measured against the judges. Now the dividing line is exposed. Now the moment of judgment will begin, but not as the ruling religious and social elite imagine. They misunderstand this moment just like Herod and Pontus Pilate misunderstood it with Jesus.

Peter spoke again. He has become like the great jazz master, Louis Armstrong. He states the melody and reveals the primordial blues structure that will become the home for endless variations, ever new but always familiar. "Jesus Christ of Nazareth, whom you crucified, whom God raised from the dead" (v. 10). The table is being turned over, an upside down world is being turned right side up in these words of Peter. Peter stands next to the man God has healed not by the power claimed by the elites, by the judges of this world, but only through the Holy Spirit. The first word of judgment to the elites has come: You do not have the power of God to heal the broken. You cannot raise the dead, only Jesus can. There is a second word that comes from Peter: "This Jesus is 'the stone that was rejected by you, the builders; it has become the cornerstone.'" (v. 11). What Jesus stated indirectly to the elites who persecuted him, Peter comes right at them. Peter comes correct!

The judges are in fact builders. This is the great dilemma of the advantaged in this world. They institutionalize life. They are socially ordered and they enact social order. They are inside what they create and they create what they are inside of and from within this circle they often cannot see a divine judgment being brought on them, brought against them. God judges them from the position of the judged. As Karl Barth said, Jesus is the judge judged in our place. God waits in silence with those brought in courts, standing in front of tribunals, juries, and officers of the law and listening as the judges of this world, not only in courtrooms but also in boardrooms and legislative halls, decide on their future and plan their destinies, and God reminds all those in power that a judgment is being brought on their decisions and their lives. They will not escape the true judge. Peter in this moment offers a truth they desperately need to hear: Jesus is the cornerstone of any building effort that would move toward life. Jesus enacts a new social order that saves. No one else can do this.

Peter's speech again creates silence, but not for long. After serious political deliberations, the elites retrace the line that divides the judges from the judged. This is a tragedy, because it did not have to be. The judges could have crossed the line and joined the judged. They could have built anew, rebuilt their own lives with the good news that God in Christ raises from the dead and life can be lived differently now. Instead they threaten Peter and John with the power they have at their fingertips. They called them and ordered them not to speak or teach at all in the name of Jesus (v. 18). Now the weapon of choice is fear, fear of imprisonment, torture, or worse. It was one that had proved effective against Peter in the past, but now this was different. The judgments of the elites now stand in the sight of a judging God, and Peter and John will force the judges to face the full ramifications of their actions. They are judging God (v. 19). Of course, these leaders did not imagine they were judging God. But make no mistake, the decision for or against these disciples, and the decision for or against the words of Jesus of Nazareth, and the decision for or against the resurrection from the dead made real in Christ that rewrites all histories, is in fact judging God. The elites of this world are exposed in the hubris and honor of being judges exactly at the moment when they must decide for or against Jesus. This is not a moment of aggressive evangelism. It is the predicament of the elites who have made it to the top and now look down on a God who actually sits above them.

Peter speaks boldly, but this boldness is not the result of character refinement or moral formation. Peter has not become the great man who stares down his enemies with epic courage, the kind that creates an odyssey or a heroic tale. Indeed there is no such thing as individual boldness for the followers of Jesus. Of course each disciple can and must be bold, but their boldness is always a together boldness, a joined boldness, a boldness born of intimacy. The modern lie of individualism is most powerful when we imagine that boldness comes from within. It does not. It comes from without, from the Spirit of God. The disciples gathered together to ask for what comes from without: "now, Lord, look at their threats, and grant to your servants to speak your word with all boldness . . ." (v. 29). They see the threat, they pray, and they ask for boldness. This moment sets the template for the movement, for any movement that is of Jesus. We saw it in the civil rights movement. We see it in movements today. There will always be threats because they are the central currency of this world. Threats reflect the anxieties of the powers and principalities having migrated in the hearts of those who believe that they must control religious and political movements, rendering them innocuous or exploitable. We should never marvel at threats. We should marvel here at the action of God witnessed in this template-setting moment.

> It is our basic sin to take the place of the judge, to try to judge ourselves and others. All our other sins, both small and great, derive ultimately from this source . . . [Jesus] took our place as Judge. He took our place as the judged. He was judged in our place. And He acted justly in our place.
>
> Karl Barth, *Church Dogmatics*, IV/1 (Edinburgh: T. & T. Clark, 1961), 235, 273.

They prayed and God shook the place. Again the Holy Spirit comes and fills the disciples and they speak, but this speaking is already a joined speaking, a chorus of faith. They speak the word of God with boldness. This shaking of the Spirit is not simply a sign of power, but of pleasure. God's excitement is evident here. Here and now God's people are one—calling on the faith and boldness of Jesus to do the divine will. Here and now the new order confronts the old order and God sees the unfolding of divine desire in and among God's creatures. This is the Spirit's quivering joy exposed in the impartation of holy power. Yet what comes to the disciples now is not simply boldness. In fact boldness is not the ultimate gift but the intensification of the common. The common is the gift realized in the Spirit.

This part of the great drama confronts us again with the new order of giving rooted in the divine wanting, rooted in the divine desire to join us together. These followers of Jesus released themselves to one another, making themselves responsible for and accountable to one another. Matters of money are inescapable. They are at the heart of discipleship, but they are not the heart of discipleship. Money here will be used to destroy what money normally is used to create: distance and boundaries between people. Distance and boundary is not merely between the haves and have-nots, but also between the needy and the comfortable, and between those who testify to Jesus and those who, like Jesus, help those with little or nothing. Jesus will join us and he will use whatever we have to make the joining possible. We are yet to hear clearly this ancient strategy of the Spirit. Too often in our reading of this story our view is clouded by the spectacular giving and we miss the spectacular joining. Now these followers of Jesus will become the bridge between uneven wealth and resources, uneven hope, and uneven life. Those who have must join those who do not, and those in the middle, having neither a lot nor just a little, must find their home in the space at the apostles' feet. There they must hear the call to offer themselves for the sake of a God who feverishly seeks to create the common.

So like an ancient altar but now made of human bodies, the apostles' feet become the place of sacrifice and giving. We cannot escape so awesome and frightening a reality made present at this moment. Israel's ancient gesture of obedience—sacrifice and giving—appears outside the temple, and God is present watching, noting faith found in giving. Every disciple of Jesus who will follow this moment, standing at the altar to receive the gifts of God's people, should remember what takes place here. Here God watches and waits to see faith that connects resource to need, echoing the divine love for creation found in the gifts God gives to the just and unjust. Those who stand at this fleshly altar always face the temptation of corrupting the connection by taking resources meant for need or ignoring need altogether. Many have yielded and yet yield to this temptation and, in so doing, conceal from many people the sight of a God who never withholds, not even a beloved Son. The church only lives at the site of this connection of resource to need where God waits to receive and promises to give. On the horizon of these gestures of donation, there appears someone who will announce an unanticipated future. Barnabas appears. This one, this Joseph of Cyprus, who comes from a distant land and culture, and who has sold what he had and laid it at the disciples' feet, will be changed in name and destiny and in turn will help change the name and destiny of the disciples of Jesus. He will help them to become Christians.

5:1–9:43

The Struggle of Diaspora

5:1–17

The Death of the Sovereign Couple

Standing in front of the apostles, at their feet (as it were) is a dangerous place. Anyone who truly believes their testimony and follows their teaching and that of their Lord, Jesus the Messiah, will be caught in the powerful wind that moved around their bodies. Bodies matter, and this revolution of the Spirit will not be ephemeral or ideological. It will be a new order of bodies joined to the Holy One of Israel. We saw this radical new order in the holy work of giving where possessions are broken of their boundary-making power and people are drawn toward one another in and through mutual and interlocking needs. Yet now the new order will be seen on the site of the old order of violence and death. The demise of Ananias and Sapphira (husband and wife) is not glorious. Their deaths should never be celebrated or treated flippantly as some morality test case against lying to God. Luke has entered the frightening space where the name of God is mentioned in relation to violence and death. He may have been alluding back to the tragic story of Achan in Joshua 7:1–26, where similar events join these stories.

The couple, Ananias and Sapphira, had agreed to hold back part of the money they received from the sale of their property. Like Achan they held back things that should have been offered up to the Lord. The withholding is indeed the offense, and it signifies resistance to the new order where possessions will no longer divide and establish social hierarchies and where living by faith overcomes the worship of the other gods: money and possessions. Yet the new is at play here in astounding ways. God is continuing the work the disciples saw in the body of Jesus. God is encircling violence and drawing down its access. Unlike Achan, who is killed at the hands of God's people (Josh. 7:24–26), the apostles' hands are not free to kill. There is no justification for killing in the name of Jesus. Indeed they speak no curse. They conjure no evil force. They give themselves no right to take life. Such will never be given to the followers of Jesus. But there is violence.

Readers of this revolution must never run from the violence in it. God takes from Ananias and Sapphira what only God gives: life. If God had given to others this power to take life, God is certainly now reclaiming its rights and keeping it from the apostles. We could read Luke here as deploying God to do what the apostles want done. That would make this moment ideological indeed: God used as the justification of violence within the community. Christians at many points in the history of the church have read this moment precisely as one set of indistinguishable actions: God and the apostles discerning deception, God and the apostles rendering judgment and doing violence, God and the apostles setting in place the disciplinary reach of this new community. However, such a conflation loses the newness. The Spirit is moving. At this moment of full divinity identified, God the Holy Spirit is giving discernment of deception and bringing judgments on unfaithful actions. But God then turns the hands of Israel away from ancient killing gesture. There will be no stoning in the community of Christ. Only the Holy Spirit may draw back the breath of life. A line has been drawn that the followers of Jesus may not cross over. We are the people of resurrection, not death.

There is, however, a death here, a killing that we have failed to see in its full power. It is the death of the couple. Although Ananias and Sapphira do their actions *as a couple*, we read past the malice lodged in coupling and turn each of them into singular sinners standing before an angry God. This, no doubt, is the continuing problem of our internalized individualism that distorts our understanding of this great drama, but it is also the problem of an idol or fetish, an object of worship lurking inside even the would-be followers of Jesus. It is precisely as a couple that they planned their deception. It was precisely as a couple that they engaged in their economic calculations, and it was precisely as a couple that Satan filled their hearts and they lied to the Holy Spirit (v. 3). The couple agreed together to put the Spirit of the Lord to the test (v. 9). This is not the first couple to test God. Indeed from the first couple made one flesh by God, God has had to contend against its plans that would resist the divine will.

Here is the energy that drives the most powerful forms of cultural, social, or economic boundaries. Here is the fortress that resists the new order most consistently. Here is where the worship of possessions and money come fully to life: in the two made one flesh. Together they imagine they can do anything. Together they believe in their sovereignty. After all, were they not made by God? Were they not the plan through which the future would be secured? Are they not an unbreakable bond made so by God's will? Yet God will now do what no one else can actually do: pull asunder, take apart, and break

> The community of Jesus must confront the couple, whether heterosexual or homosexual, with a new truth: you belong to us. We do not belong to you.

open. The Holy Spirit will take back from the couple what rightly belongs to God and to the community formed in and through the resurrected Jesus. No longer will the couple be the keeper of the secret, the owner of the intimate, or the custodian of the closed field of dreams, both personal and private. The community of Jesus confronts the couple with a new truth: you belong to us. We do not belong to you.

Jesus, in an act of utter terrorism, tore open ancient kinship networks, and now the Spirit will complete that work by forming the new family. The new family, however, is not a bigger version of the old. There is no gentle analogy that flows easily from earthly family to heavenly vision, from earthly couple to heavenly life. "For as the heavens are higher than the earth, so are my ways higher than your ways and my thoughts than your thoughts," so said the Lord of hosts (Isa. 55:9). The new family of God kills before it makes alive, tears open before it puts together, and returns to the shared life of the common, born of baptism and confession, the intimacy stolen by the obsessive power of coupling. Modern coupling is especially dangerous because it claims to be the home of what Elizabeth Povinelli calls the intimate event.[1]

The intimate event is a mode of organizing intimacy that invites us to imagine love as an act of choosing that exfoliates social skin and abstracts each of us from all other forms of connection in our loving and choosing love. At its most powerful, the intimate event "opposes all other modes of organizing intimacy."[2] Modern coupling is an energy-draining vortex that seeks to capture all our imaginative capacity for intimacy. As such it is a vortex fully exploited by corporations and nation-states who wish to channel our desires toward the ends of the market or the nation. Yet the power of coupling to carry our hopes and dreams of life together and a prosperous future dies at the apostles' feet. There will, however, be a resurrection, but the new life together will forever change the old. Soon the drama will unfold, and a people will know itself inside one all-encompassing reality of intimacy that enfolds many forms of intimacy. We will be one with the triune God.

We have not had the courage to face the idolatry of the couple because it contains our fear and controls our faith. It encircles our fear of bare life, life vulnerable and subject to wind and force, chaos and death. The couple gives us the illusion of manageable life. It narrows our vision of intimacy to the joys a couple rightly shares and turns us toward the narcissism of the two made one. The horror the couple creates is to turn love into its possession. It believes the call to the community of Christ belongs solely to the two made one to believe all things, endure all things, and hope all things (1 Cor. 13). And from its temple erected inside the church it seeks to guide faith, direct our prayers, and shape our hope. Too many churches understand themselves as in service to the couple, its high priest and holder of its flame. This couple believed it may lie to the Holy Spirit, and couples now are often led to believe they may do the same, because too many churches have told them that their life supersedes our life together.

---

1. Elizabeth A. Povinelli, *The Empire of Love: Toward a Theory of Intimacy, Genealogy, and Carnality* (Durham, NC: Duke University Press, 2006).
2. Ibid., 177.

So people called by Jesus learn that they had lived an illusion in their relationship to the world. The illusion is immediacy. It has blocked faith and obedience. Now they know that there can be no unmediated relationships, even in the most intimate ties of their lives, in the blood ties to father and mother, to children, brothers and sisters in marital love, in historical responsibilities. Ever since Jesus called, there are no longer natural, historical, or experiential unmediated relationships for his disciples. Christ the mediator stands between son and father, between husband and wife, between individual and nation, whether they can recognize him or not. There is no way from us to others than the path through Christ, his word, and our following him. Immediacy is a delusion. But because any delusion which hides truth from us must be hated, immediacy to the natural given things in life must also be hated, for the sake of Jesus Christ, the mediator. Anytime a community hinders us from coming before Christ as a single individual, anytime a community lays claim to immediacy, it must be hated for Christ's sake. For every unmediated natural relationship, knowingly or unknowingly, is an expression of hatred toward Christ, the mediator, especially if this relationship wants to assume a Christian identity. Theology makes a serious mistake whenever it uses Jesus' mediation between God and human persons to justify immediate relationships in life.

Dietrich Bonhoeffer, *Discipleship*, Dietrich Bonhoeffer Works, vol. 4, trans. Martin Kuske and Ilse Tödt (Minneapolis: Fortress, 2001), 94–95.

God is present in the new community—untamed, uncontrollable, but desired. So the apostles now exist in the complicated space of avoidance and compulsion. Like the people of Israel at the foot of Mount Sinai, where holy space was touched and someone died, so too now fear grips the followers. Yet much like life at the foot of the mountain, so too again we find crowds of broken and needy people looking for the power of God to touch them. So more desperate people come believing and needing, and the apostles are brought back to the revelation of the creation first shown to them by Jesus. The creature is sick and tormented and in the presence of God cries out for help from a God who hears and helps. The apostles live and move in that sacred meeting space between wounded human cry and outstretched divine arm. Their actions again draw the attention of the politico-religious caste in Israel who will now move against them, motivated by one overarching reason—jealousy. The great irony of political struggle once again shows itself. Those who want control

over people become insanely jealous of those who want to help people. Yet beyond this irony of political struggle is a deeper theological truth. God, through these apostles, announces that creation has
been taken back from the powers and principalities.

FURTHER REFLECTIONS
Marriage, Money, and Discipleship

Christians often turn marriage from an act of worship into an object
of worship and turn the couple from a shared journey of disciples
into the end and goal of discipleship. The problem we face is not the
couple, but its claimed sovereignty over intimacy and life together.
The story of Ananias and Sapphira is about money because it is
about their life as a couple. The couple now exists for us as a stronger and more compelling reality of life together than the church,
any church. Whether this has always been the case is a question
for historians, yet in the West and in a growing number of other
contexts our capacities to imagine the joy of any form of intimacy,
and the pleasures of everyday life, have been fully captured by the
fantasy generating power of the idea of the couple. Economies and
financial cultures increasingly circle around the energy-generating
vortex of the couple. This is why matters of money for disciples of
Jesus must be thought freshly through the actions and activities of
couples, and the couple itself must be seen through the shattering
reality of the body of Jesus (Luke12:51–53).

Jesus has seized the power of coupling and drawn it toward his
own life. Now a marriage of disciples, any disciples, will witness the
church and her lover, Jesus Christ. Yet this witness is not revers-
ible—the church and its lover do not yield their spotlight, their center of attention to the couple, because in the light of this true love
is found the love of God for the creation and for the creature. The
witness of the love of God for all creation and creatures is always at
risk in the attention-stealing reality of modern coupling. Too many
churches have yielded the spotlight to the couple and have weakened local church life as a site of loving and belonging and turned
those who are not coupled or married into resident aliens inside the

church. They have turned them into a strange non-creature of God, a single. The question we must ask is whether singleness as a state of being makes any theological sense. It does not. All disciples of Jesus are caught up in a life of unfolding intimacy with the triune God and with each other. This is the coupling that makes intelligible our coupling, where two seek to be one with each other *as disciples joined in a shared journey with others.*

Coupling in this regard is a wonder to be shared by all who wish it, whether heterosexual or homosexual, and marriage should be grasped by all who would mark their life together as a life inside the way of disciples. Yet we must end the burden placed on couples to be the container of all intimate life, and the heresy that the couple is the only safe and sanctioned place where the honesty, safety, and joy of being vulnerable creatures may be touched and celebrated. That heresy has allowed the couple to bend the life of the church toward itself, enfolding ecclesial existence in its wishes and dreams and defining the quality of life by its own lights.

The church continues to struggle over whom may be married as well as how to claim a vision of intimacy for our common life. Our obsession with coupling has served as a way to avoid the ecclesial work of forming intimate community, and it has drained the church of the deep riches of its own erotic and intimate life born at a table where the body and blood of Jesus calls us continually to partake. God says to us, "Here and now—please take, touch, and handle my body. I offer it all to you, every cell—all my flesh and blood. Please eat and drink my very life." For too many people intimacy means only sexual intercourse, and their bodies are rendered in this vision of intimacy into dumb machines activated only by and through narratives of sexual consumption. Such a narrowed understanding of intimacy has clothed our bodies in relentless anxiety over its desires and forced us to equate our longings and hungers with the sinful condition of the human creature. For those who long for a home beyond feverish coupling or the anxiety over their desires as well as for those whose sexual identity does not rest easy with a stable orientation, there remains a call of discipleship not away from intimacy but toward it, not in concealment of hungers and longings but in their full and complete exposure—into a God who not only receives us without shame but also *celebrates* our life in all its complexities.

The church should be *the* intimate reality of a disciple's life. From its depth of closeness comes the logic of joined disciples, those who have chosen to live together in a bond of marriage that echoes the communal life of faith. Only as churches begin to grasp their space as safe and erotic space may the bloated expectations and idolatrous intimations of coupling be taken off the backs of would-be couples. Churches should draw on the rich reservoir of Christian contemplation and mysticism to articulate a sensuous language of life in the Spirit that receives the body's passions as gifts of grace and not obstacles of faith. Unfortunately, because of our ecclesial failure in this regard, we constantly ask couples to create what they cannot—a space of safety and freedom. No couple can create only what God gives. A couple *can be* a space of safety and freedom *only as it participates* in a space of safety and freedom for a gathering community. Only in a space of shared intimate life may a couple be spared from its own idolatry and its use as a destructive power.

The couple has become one of the greatest tools to sustaining the realities of oppression, economic injustice, racism, sexism, and sexual violence by becoming a citadel of ultimate concern for people. The life and well-being of a couple and their children easily command our greatest loyalties and constantly draw us toward supporting polices of governments and the practices of corporations that destroy life and are harming the planet. The actions of Ananias and Sapphira in withholding part of their resources is precisely the gesture that seems sensible but opens them to falsehood and resistance to the Spirit of God. This gesture of withholding connects easily onto our current condition, where couples are invited and invite us to selfishness. Not all couples are equal, and those with resources and influence in this world are tempted to collapse their energy into enabling, supporting, protecting, and enhancing what they have and standing idly by enjoying economic, social, and political structures that benefit their life together and drain the life out of others. The church in this world will speak more powerfully and act more clearly for the sake of the gospel and the reign of Jesus if it can overcome its worship of the couple and finally and completely make them disciples.

Christians who couple should allow their coupling to be a witness of discipleship not by how they display an obsessive commitment to each other and their offspring but how they help a community enter into a greater reality of vulnerability, sharing, and intimate life. Every Christian couple should become iconoclasts of the couple, helping to break all the idols of a community that constantly hold up the couple as the center of its missional activity, its entertainment, and its joy. There is joy in coupling that should be celebrated and shared by all who wish life together, especially for gay sisters and brothers whose lives of love are yet to receive the celebratory embrace by the church that they greatly deserve. Even among churches that affirm homosexual marriage, the sound and songs of celebration ring much too quietly and sometimes not at all.

A marriage folded into discipleship always becomes more than the world imagines, more than the state envisions, and more than those so joined understand. It is two who have allowed the desire of God to flow through them on all sides, like a light shining uncontrollably into formerly shadowed places. This is why calling gay marriage a civil union is a denial of Christian discipleship of the two. When disciples marry, their love becomes the site of God's outrageous joy. There, in these two, divine desire will be magnified beyond the two into the many. Their love intensifies God's aim and reach into a community being gathered to know and experience God's strong embrace. This is why gay marriage must be celebrated just as strongly, as loudly, and as intensely as any marriage of disciples, because what begins in civil toleration when touched by the Spirit of the living God becomes joyous and extravagant celebration. Yet the joy of coupling is not only for the couple. That joy is a line of pulsating life reaching from the triune God through the incarnate Son to his disciple through the Spirit. The couple enters that line not at the beginning but in the middle. They have taken hold of a line that reaches through them and through the church into the world where it moves through the creation and returns to the life of triune God.

This couple, formed in discipleship, knows that their love belongs to God and exists only moment by moment in the grace and mercy of God's love and not by their own energy, cunning, or even desire. They believe in the daily marriage, not the principle of marriage, or the sanctity of marriage, or even the institution of marriage, and certainly not the cult of the wedding. They believe in the everyday oneness, the newness of awakening in hope and in prayer that today, and just for today, God will give each of them the strength to love the other in precisely and exactly the way God would have them love each other. With that love they will turn their attention to a widening circle beyond children and extended family toward a world that must know the exact same daily love. How could such a couple withhold their time, talents, or treasures from the needs of a community and a world that God has bound them to by love? They cannot. They will never be a sovereign couple.

5:18–42

The Unity of Suffering

The apostles are arrested. The apostles are whipped. This is the ever-present consequence of obedience to God—capture, incarceration, and whipping. The church has rarely remembered these other characteristics of the apostles' unity. They are united in proclamation and in power, but they are also apostles precisely because they are incarcerated, and exactly because they are threatened and whipped. These actions of torture are bound to the actions of liberation as the full-orbed reality of following Jesus. These actions sandwich the actions of the religious leaders who believe less in the power of God and more in the power of violence and prison to accomplish their goal of silencing these upstart preachers in Israel. Once again, however, Luke shows us that the new order will challenge even the power of the prison.

The prison, like the couple, claims a God-given right to exist. It claims a right to establish order and control as a fundamental tool of worldly authorities and governments. God at this moment in the drama will again take back what God had given. The power to incarcerate will be trumped by the power to free. The power to free people from bondage is of the new order just as the power to imprison is of the old order. As such incarceration is shown in all its horror as a tool of interests—political, economic, social, religious, and deployed in the arbitrariness of law and policy, threat and jealousy. If the apostles in prison represent social malcontents, disruptively bad people, then the angel of the Lord comes to such people. That we know that these apostles are good people is beside the point. The true hearts of the incarcerated are hidden behind the mechanisms that locked them away, and only when we follow the angel of the Lord into those spaces of captivity will we see what has been hidden from us: a system that kills, steals, and destroys lives while claiming to keep order and protect the innocent.

The apostles are then freed by divine action, by a God accustomed to moving through locked doors. They are free, but they are not safe. They are never safe. Safety is not the inheritance of Jesus' disciples, only witness. So after release, they are arrested again. These repeat offenders are brought before this religious court and with clear discerning political eyes the religious leaders speak to the heart of the matter. The apostles will make them guilty of murdering Jesus, destroying their moral authority and social clout and positioning themselves as the new leaders. The apostles' response to this trenchant assessment can be only one of witness and obedience in truth telling. Yes, there was a murder on a hanging tree (*kremasantes epi xylou*, v. 30), but the power of assassination has been broken because a new leader has emerged on the other side of death, a leader who is also a savior. The apostles are speaking of the new order, of repentance and forgiveness of sins, and of a joined witness with the Holy Spirit who has been given to us. The religious leaders speak of guilt, but the apostles speak of gift. There is in this drama no greater moment of failure for these religious leaders than this moment. Rather than joyful relief and curiosity at these groundbreaking words, they give into their rage and long for the intoxication of violence. They desperately want to kill them.

It is precisely in this moment of failure and of the old order that we must understand Gamaliel and his counsel. As Luke Timothy Johnson suggests, it would be a mistake to read Luke as a

pro-Pharisee writer or read Gamaliel in positive terms.[3] Gamaliel
is the quintessential compromised intellectual who reads history
from the wrong side and politics from the sidelines. The frightful
reality at the heart of his words is that they reflect a properly formed
and supremely trained scholar who, like so many others, cannot
see the day of divine visitation because it has come in unimpres-
sive flesh. It has come in the common. Gamaliel is exceptional, and
the exceptional in society look for their own, the exceptional. God
must appear in the exceptional to appear as God to this Pharisee.
So he reads history with keen analytical skills, but from the wrong
side. By placing Jesus and the apostles next to other revolutionaries and their followers, Gamaliel confirms his class formation and
betrays his formation as a teacher in Israel. He believes in Israel's
God. He believes that same God can move in history, he simply
does not yet see that God is making history in Jesus. Gamaliel is
the politically astute casual observer who did not actually hear
what the apostles were saying even though he listened carefully,
and so he did not hear the voice of God speaking through them to
him, saying, "Come and follow me." Yet Gamaliel shows us the way
of compromised intellectuals (even among the faithful) whose
politics always end in observation from a safe distance. Gamaliel's counsel is simply to leave them alone and wait and see if they
amount to anything. But how would he or the other religious leaders know if God is at work in these disciples of the Nazarene? They
cannot imagine God's own political action embodied in the common and consequently they cannot hear God calling them to come
and join this movement. So they watch as apostles are whipped
and wonder what will become of them.

It is precisely this inability to see God's own political action
in the concrete actions of the common that enables us to watch
casually the perpetuation of violence without being moved to
action. In our time, we have been inundated by the fantasy of
violence through ubiquitous media. The fantasies of violence
are mapped across real violence so that our responses have been
made into one and the same: we watch. A show that portrays

3. Luke Timothy Johnson, *The Acts of the Apostles* (Collegeville, MN: The Liturgical Press,
1992), 101–3.

violence merges with news reporting that shows violence, and as the philosopher Jean Baudrillard suggests, we learn to entertain ourselves with both, both become sites of sensation and not mobilization.[4] Gamaliel's dilemma confronts us daily and ever raises the question for us: Will we see and respond to the Spirit at work in the world?

6:1–15

The Pain of Diaspora

6:1–7

Chapter five ended with absurdity. The apostles who were incarcerated and whipped afterward rejoiced. They were treated like criminals and disobedient slaves and yet with perfect clarity they understood that their lives were now fully joined to the life of Jesus, a life of glaring dishonor. Something utterly path-breaking was taking place in and with them. Honor systems were being turned upside down and torn apart, freeing people from their caste-making power, and criminality and slavery were being collapsed onto God and those who preach Jesus the Christ, freeing people from their identity-constituting power. The apostles follow a God who has broken open the binaries of honorable and dishonorable people, criminal and good citizen, master and slave. Their difference and distance were collapsing in a community born of the Holy Spirit and shaped through witness. A new way of understanding and living life was emerging around these apostles, and now a primary site of struggle for the new order would begin to appear—diaspora.

Diaspora was both of the body and of place, of exile and return, of sameness and difference, and of fear and hope. For Israel, diaspora existence was faithful existence shaped in unrelenting determination to follow the way of Israel's God in lands far from the land of Israel and in a time of Jerusalem's foreign occupation. The diaspora was Israel in the raw, in the real contexts of struggle to hold authentic

4. Jean Baudrillard, *Simulacra and Simulation* (Ann Arbor: University of Michigan Press, 1994).

identity by remembering covenant, law, and temple. Diaspora people are always on edge, because they know the stakes. They understand that life together as a people is not a given. It must be won again and again against those alien forces that would undermine it, drain it of life, and leave it sickly and dying. Those who came to Jerusalem were diaspora, of different tongues and cultural knowledge(s) but of same commitment against the threats to Israel's life.

As Luke tells it, Jews of the diaspora, Hellenistic Jews saw their own widows slighted, overlooked in the daily distribution of food to the weak and most vulnerable, and complained about it. That complaint confronted the apostles. This is, however, no simple matter. Here the sub-textual is the textual. Now the apostles must be confronted by those who really mattered, diaspora, and the situation that made things matter, care for the weak and disadvantaged in Israel. If the gospel was true word from God, light from light, and a gift to the people of God then it would of necessity have to be confronted by these faithful from outside of Jerusalem who are at this moment in Jerusalem. The complaint comes to the heart of the community—who will care for us and our most vulnerable? The complaint carries the divine command to serve, and the apostles understand the weight of this command. Their response offers an interesting division of labor. They will continue to devote themselves to prayer and teaching, and others must be elected to serve and answer the concerns of diaspora.

> Exile is a jealous state. What you achieve is precisely what you have no wish to share, and it is in the drawing of lines around you and your compatriots that the least attractive aspects of being in exile emerge: an exaggerated sense of group solidarity, and a passionate hostility to outsiders, even those who may in fact be in the same predicament as you.
>
> Edward W. Said, *Reflections on Exile and Other Essays* (Cambridge, MA: Harvard University Press, 2003), 178.

Luke is here exposing us to more than the overwhelming realities of survival and support in patriarchal agrarian cultures where widows and orphans hang on only by threads of mercy. He is also showing a connection—the apostles joined to diaspora and the new order joined to the existing order of survival. Seven people of exile and return, of hope and fear will be elected to serve. The apostles will pray and then lay their hands on seven who are already filled with the Holy Spirit and wisdom, and at that moment they will be joined to the apostles' mission and to the ministry of Jesus the Christ. These seven will now stand in the intimate space created by the Holy Spirit where many bodies are moving toward becoming one body. This is the heart of apostolic succession in which a joining happens in the Spirit that binds hope to struggle and the common to resurrection. They will be deacons (*diakonia*), that is, signs of the many becoming the one servant of all. Yet service in the name of Jesus in Israel leads to contention in that name. The seven are of the diaspora, their bodies already bearing both difference and sameness, both foreign and home. They are of Israel and of more than Israel. Now they will be angled by the Spirit of the living God into a living, breathing struggle for Israel's future, for its identity and life.

6:8–15

Stephen appears as the agent of the new order. He is a servant with grace and power who will perform Jesus. He will gesture so deeply of the divine life made incarnate that he will expose the complex pain of Diaspora. That pain grows out of the ever necessary work of securing a people's identity against the constant threat of dilution or destruction, especially in those far off places where covenant, law, and temple are strange words, even words of possible sedition against the empire. Maintaining faithfulness is difficult and painstaking sociopolitical and economic work, and those of the Diaspora know this down to their bones.

It is in this tortured context that we must read Luke's account of this confrontation, of discipleship existence with Diaspora existence. Stephen's words and ministry are opposed not by evil God-haters but by faithful Jews who understood slavery, that ancient yet contemporary horror that reduces humans to utility-bodies and nameless tools. These were those who knew slavery either personally or of parental memory, and their commitment to Israel and its way of life was woven into their legacy of hard-won freedom (v. 9). These men were faithful to God and faithful to their covenantal identity formed in foreign places. Before we turn this story into the heroic, into the moment of Stephen's witness, we must see the tragic unfolding here. These faithful of Israel's far off places perceive Stephen as a threat. Like the religious leaders who interrogated the apostles earlier in our story, these anxious souls cannot hear and see the new order coming from Stephen. They only hear one who would take away hard-won freedom to be true to the ancestors and one who would render unrecognizable the identity of the faithful to God.

What would you do to protect your people and your faith from a threat to their existence? The church has often failed to see in this moment not an analogy but the reality out of which it comes to be church. We will be born in the tight space between faith and fear and forever live in that space. Only the Holy Spirit keeps that space from collapsing in on us. When and where the church resists the Spirit we see again and again that mournful collapse. The freedmen saw their fears collapse onto their faith, and they descended into worldly captivity by taking on themselves the same political operation that brought on the torture and assassination of Jesus. They will get others to lie for them, leaving their hands clean. They will get others to grab Stephen and drag him to the religious authorities, leaving their hands free to worship God uninterrupted by Stephen's witness.

Once again we see the contradiction of the faithful acting against their faith, but now that contradiction unfolds inside the painful failure to see the very help Israel needs to maintain its identity and deepen its faithfulness shining out in the face of Stephen. But we must not be too judgmental of these men

> The church was born in the tight space between faith and fear and forever lives in that space. Only the Holy Spirit keeps that space from collapsing in on us.

because the new order that surprises them requires a step of faith that can only be taken by yielding to the Holy Spirit. Only through the Spirit could a people imagine the embrace of Jesus to be the embrace of their own deepest and most beautiful life that will also be the deepest and most beautiful embrace of a new way of life, one that will be shaped by expansion, and growth, and joining.

The stakes are high, very high at this moment, but this is where the laying on of hands leads us, and the church in our world is yet to grasp fully the cost of believing. It costs our hopes for the survival of our peoples. Here with Stephen we will soon see that a divine exchange must be made, our hopes for God's hope for all peoples, our mechanisms for securing faith and identity and authenticity for God' way of holding our peoples together as peoples and yet becoming a people. It all begins and ends with Israel. They are the one incredible and stunning site of joining and mixture. No other people can take their place and no other people can draw together exile and home, returning and leaving, not by ability but by the sheer grace of divine presence. Stephen will soon speak, but the question is, can anybody hear him? Can anybody hear what he is doing with Israel's story? Stephen will make Israel's story our story and, in so doing, repeat his Savior.

7:1–8:2

A New Storyteller

Storytellers rule this world as they have always ruled. Yet Jesus challenges the storytellers. Which ones? All of them.

7:1–53

It is story all the way down. There is no life without story. We enter story from the time we are born and never exit story even in death. Stephen has been brought to this moment in his life because of a new story. That new story has Jesus at its center, and from that center a radical reordering of Stephen's life began, and now that radical reordering has taken hold of him. His accusers saw him as dangerous, and they were right. Stephen has become a storyteller. There is no more powerful embodied reality in the world than a storyteller. They conjure reality, capturing in word and sound, in songs and deeds, in pictures and diverse renderings—past, present, and future. Give me storytellers, and I will rule the world. Indeed all worldly power begins in storytelling and reaches its greatest leverage in story believing. Even more amazing is the work of story on the body. The body, even if fully clothed, is naked without story. In fact, no body moves and breaths, lives and grows without being completely covered in stories. The stories unleashed on us by the storytellers greet us in the morning and follow us through our daily journey. They stare out at us through our eyes, constantly teaching us how to see ourselves and others. Storytellers make our bodies for us, forming narrative fabric so tightly aligned with our skin that it becomes our skin.

If storytellers rule—and they do—then Luke tells us of an unprecedented intervention in and usurpation of their power. Jesus challenged the storytellers. Which ones? All of them. Only God can overcome the storytellers, and in the messiah he did so not by denying story its power, or destroying story, but by drawing it back to its creator. Jesus spoke in story and entered story, allowing its winds and currents to take him up. Yet while in story he seized its flow and drew it into his own body. This happened in Israel, and now Luke will show us through Stephen and his speech what it means for God to be both in story and yet storyteller. The accusations against Stephen are false, but they are also angled. They push Stephen's words and actions into the most damaging narrative that one can have as a Jew: he walks a path that denies the power of Moses the lawgiver and would destroy both the efficacy of our faithful obedience to God and the majesty and centrality of the temple. This is, however, exactly the power of storytellers who through story, either stated or implied, can create the conditions that call forward praise or accusation and life or death.

Stephen stands before the Sanhedrin and the chief priest, and there he must answer the question, "Are these things so?" But another question is there with that question, right at the surface and easy to see. It is simply, "Who are you?" Are you one of us, one with us, or are you an enemy, bound to false teaching and a false teacher? This is the same line of inquiry that was drawn around the body of Jesus, and now it encircles Stephen's body. Stephen presses against their line of inquiry by redrawing the lines of Israel's story. His response, however, is not just his speech but his body as well. We will miss the full power of his response if we forget that a body known but unknown, familiar yet alien stands before the powerful religious rulers of Israel. Luke makes this clear when he tells us that the rulers gazed attentively at his face, which was like the face of an angel (*to prosōpon autou hōsei prosōpon aggelos*, 6:15). What does an angel's face look like? We don't know, but could it be that the particular characteristics of his face are not at play here, but rather its orientation? Stephen looks as though he is now inside a new reality of heaven and earth, one that can only be imagined as being of angelic body. Stephen in fact looks out at the Sanhedrin from inside a reality that has captured them, but they refuse to see it. So he will make it plain.

Stephen speaks of the greats of Israel's past, Abraham, Joseph, and Moses. This is a simple but elegant line, but like the great Jazz tenor saxophonist John Coltrane, Luke will take this line and expand it through the body and words of Stephen until it travels into uncharted places of soul and mind, devotion and rebellion. We read this text poorly if we read it like a theological jigsaw puzzle, or a historical recitation, or even Luke proving a point. It may be all of those things, but it is first a performance. It is a storyteller at work inviting his listeners to move from death to life. So Stephen, with his life hanging in the balance, demands to be heard. This is improvisation, and as the Jazz critic Stanley Crouch has said, the moment of improvisation is always a moment of crisis.[5] For Stephen, even if situated in a speech prepared by Luke, this is the natural condition of crisis carried to its absolute extreme, but Luke has already told us that such an extreme moment was anticipated by Jesus for his followers.

> When they bring you before the synagogues, the rulers, and the authorities, do not worry about how you are to defend yourselves or what you are to say; for the Holy Spirit will teach you at that very hour what you ought to say (Luke 12:11–12).

This moment of death-facing improvisation is also a moment of joining. The Spirit will be present. The Spirit will speak as Stephen speaks, and the Spirit will guide Stephen even with the threat of death hovering over him. So this storyteller will give witness to the truth. The story Stephen tells begins not with the line of patriarchs but with God. God is the central actor of the story of Israel.

God took hold of Abraham and made him new by turning him

---

5. I heard him say this in a lecture he gave at Duke University in 2011. See Stanley Crouch, *Considering Genius: Writings on Jazz* (New York: Basic Books, 2006).

into a sojourner and making in him something new by creating a people who were sojourners. Imagine a people created only by a promise from God and who will live only in and through that very promise. This promised people would carry the vulnerability and fragility that comes with waiting. The waiting is everything. It is the time and place for meeting with God. There in the waiting God will reveal the divine name, expose holy mood and manner, and constantly give gracious word. Lives will be formed in the waiting, like Isaac who is the child of promise, and Jacob, his son, yet echoing the promise, and the twelve patriarchs, the flowering of the branches of that promise. Then there was Joseph, so overwhelmed by promise that he dreamed in it and offered it to his jealous brothers, who could not see their hope and future in Joseph or his words. Joseph was revealed to his brothers and the dream was fulfilled and deliverance was given, yet the waiting continued.

The promised people sojourned in Egypt as resident aliens (v. 6), that is, insiders who are outsiders, bearing the vulnerability that comes with life at the political and economic margins and bearing always the vulnerability that comes with waiting. What came to this people was oppression and slavery. They were slaves, but God was with them. God is always with the slave. Moses too will be born in the waiting, finding in it a future for his people who through him might again know deliverance. Yet like Joseph with his brothers, Moses found a people who could not see in him embodied divine word. Joseph the prophetic dreamer and Moses the prophet were sent by God as signs that the promise was alive and well and ready to carry its people forward toward God. The waiting *is* everything, because it will be the stage of the divine wooing of this promised people, calling them to a life of love and intimacy with God. God will wait, and in God's waiting there will be pain, frustration, and difficulty as this promised people resist divine love and reject embodied divine word.

From Abraham to Moses, Stephen is telling a story of two, of God and God's people and the drama of divine desire where God, like a feverish lover, navigates at the site of their resistance and rejection, waiting, always waiting for the result that only comes from yielding to love. God waits for covenant to take root in hearts and flower into desire. This loving God is less concerned about the house of meeting that they have made (the temple) and more interested in the time for meeting made by divine longing. And then at that moment in his speech when he takes his listeners from God's temple to God's time, Luke's Stephen moves from flight to soaring, climbing upward until the voice of God is heard in his speaking. God steps forward out of the story being told into the story being lived, repeating the ancient divine complaint, "You stiff-necked people, uncircumcised in heart and ears" (v. 51). These are not killing words in the mouth of a lover, but words that reveal divine presence yet caught in the drama of resistance.

> I love to tell the story
> of unseen things above,
> of Jesus and his glory,
> of Jesus and his love.
> I love to tell the story,
> because I know 'tis true;
> it satisfies my longings
> as nothing else can do.
> I love to tell the story,
> 'twill be my theme in glory,
> to tell the old, old story
> of Jesus and his love.
>
> —Katherine Hankey, as quoted in Jane Stuart Smith and Betty Carlson, *Great Christian Hymn Writers* (Wheaton, IL: Crossway Books, 1997), 77.

God's harsh words can never be separated from God's unremitting love for Israel. Nor may they ever be used by another. Only God may speak in this way to Israel and of Israel. Christians have struggled through the centuries to see and remember this space of intimacy that always surrounds anguished divine word to Israel, choosing to focus on such words as these words as though they stand alone and are self-interpreting, forever defining the identity of a people. The Holy Spirit is speaking through Stephen, and prophetic voice permeates the storyteller. A new story is being told, but an old story is being lived at that very moment. Another prophet will soon die.

7:54–8:2

Stephen performs what he speaks, and so do the religious rulers in Israel. Prophets were killed before, and now with anger turned up to its highest level, the faithful will take hold of affordable weapons and yield to violence, that ever-present power circulating in the wrong hands, human hands. Something else, however, is happening that could easily be missed in the rushed judgment to death and the silence engendered by closed ears and grinding teeth. Stephen is being joined to God. Luke has flashed forward to a future that waits for those who follow the prophets, the apostles, and finally Jesus. God, the Holy Spirit, fills Stephen and will face death with him. This will always be the case for believers. No matter how hard they are thrown, the stones cannot separate Stephen from God. Nor can any stone, no matter its velocity, its surprising angle, or its accuracy in hitting our vulnerable places, ever separate those who know the savior from God.

The joining has happened. But the performance is not finished. Stephen yields the stage to another player, whose performance, forever finished, can now only be echoed. Stephen looks up and sees the Son of Man, the bringer of the new age, standing. We lose the moment if we focus singularly on a standing Jesus and forget the speaking Stephen. Now Jesus and Stephen act together. Jesus stands and again gestures his journey's end in God, and Stephen repeats his savior's journey in deed and word. The thrown stones roll away and reveal words, simple human words but now with divine weight. "Lord Jesus, receive my spirit" (7:59). "Lord, do not hold this sin against them" (7:60). This is witness joined at the site of death. This is witness that cannot die.

Luke repeats a crucified God, acting out divine and human suffering imbued with love. It may be premature to invoke this christological conclusion, but the story and the storyteller lay bare such a trajectory for our thinking, because they make this suffering death not about Stephen or even about Luke but about God. If Luke allows us to imagine that the significance of Stephen the storyteller's performance may have been overlooked by that killing crowd, he certainly will not allow us to miss its possible organizer, Saul. Saul seems to be a shadowy presence in this whole affair only to appear fully at the moment of assassination.

For Saul, this is a righteous act. Killing in the name of God can be approved. But this approval is of the old order, not the new. Now its absurdity can be exposed. There were no doubt evil people in Israel worthy of death, but there was no one, without doubt, who was innocent enough to kill them. It is in this tension between the new order and the old that the old will assert its power in and among the faithful. Stephen has been seen as the first Christian martyr, but we must see more than a faithful witness unto death. We must also see the way faithful people can yield to the old order and kill if they believe they or God are threatened by a different witness. Stephen was executed, and his execution was approved. How often have Christians given their approval of executions, religious and political, but how often have we seen this as giving into the old order and resisting the Holy Spirit? Stephen died inside a wider moment. Indeed his death triggered it, like a sign to an army to attack. Severe persecution began, which is to say people who followed Jesus were being taken and imprisoned while others found themselves on the run.

A scattering has begun. Disciples born in Jerusalem and by the Spirit flee the city and head to the country. But before that scattering takes center stage, Luke invites us to say goodbye to Stephen and, in so doing, he reminds us that pain and tears, sorrow and mourning, are yet within the new order. "Devout men buried Stephen and made loud lamentation over him" (8:2). We must not rush past Stephen's tragic end to secure his glorious victory. This death should not be, and the work of lament must go on and give witness to death's intrusion into life. Men lament loudly. There is no gendered division of labor here. Devout men, like holy women, carry forward the work of mourning until the bright day of its end. Luke joins these mourning men to the circle of tears of crying women who looked on the suffering and death of Jesus (Luke 23), yet Luke pauses at the burial of Stephen as if to hold us there for a moment to clarify an aspect of our calling as the community of Christ's witness. Christians must lament loss, never brushing it aside and never normalizing martyrs' blood as an assumed and necessary aspect of the church's growth. Christians should in fact lament the loss of all those whose courageous voices pointed toward life and in so doing were the friends of God. Ossie Davis, the great actor, activist, and Christian, joined the many mourners who discerned the horror of loss in the untimely death of Malcolm X and in the final words of his eulogy caught hold of a hope embedded in such courageous sacrifice:

> Consigning these mortal remains to earth, the common mother of all, secure in the knowledge that what we place in the ground is no more now a man—but a seed—which, after

the winter of our discontent, will come forth again to meet us. And we will know him then for what he was and is—a Prince—our own black shining Prince!—who didn't hesitate to die, because he loved us so.[6]

This is finally a moment of transition for Luke's narrative, a transition registered in lament and seen in two men passing by each other, Stephen and Saul. Stephen found his way to love. Saul was yet to find his way. There was, however, another character whose emergence would soon also mark this moment of transition and expose more to us of the desire of God. His name was Philip.

8:3–25

The Scattering and the Saving

God's providence is always characterized by God's improvisation, which tirelessly turns us away from death and toward life.

8:3–13

The brutal image here tempts us to turn away quickly or become voyeurs, but neither action will help us reckon with its horror. Saul is a man convinced of his cause and ready to destroy lives to accomplish his goals. The fact that all of this takes place among God's people makes it all the more surreal. The danger here is to see providence poorly, that is, to imagine the divine will executed through Saul's full-throttled anger and unmitigated power. That would be a mistaken reading that positions us in the comfort of an illusory triumphalism that does not take seriously this struggle of faith. Here we are faced with two realities that are yet with the followers of Jesus.

First, some who believe live constantly in life-threatening danger and unrelenting humiliation because of that belief, and some disciples are spared such troubles. Again we see the prison deployed as a dividing line and a tool of oppression. Saul knows how to make

6. Ossie Davis, "Eulogy Delivered at the Faith Temple Church of God, February 27, 1965," http://malcolmx.com/eulogy/.

use of the technologies of incarceration to accomplish his theological and political ends. The scattering is always uneven, and we must
never resolve this tension with euphemistic slogans that summarize
the suffering of disciples to varied and diverse burdens. The deeper
question here is, What are the conditions that create this unevenness? The apostles are spared the scattering. It could be that their
considerable reputation as people touched by God and endowed
with healing power has made them untouchable. Or it could be that
the scattering was a matter intensely shaped inside the politics of
Diaspora and the sense that these Hellenistic followers of Jesus represented great betrayers of Jewish faith and an immediate threat to
Israel. However, the text does not show us fully Saul's logic of who
is targeted and who is spared, only his single-minded focus. The task
of discerning the reasons for the unevenness of scattering remains
for us. How is it that the faith of some disciples is rightly seen as a
threat to the social order while the faith of others may be seen as too
inconsequential to merit attention, or so closely aligned with the old
order that it is indistinguishable from it?

The second reality that confronts us here is that the disciples are
yet faithful in the midst of the scattering. The scattered preach the
word (v. 4). Here we can now take hold of a doctrine of providence,
seeing in the actions of these disciples the divine enabling and equip-
ping of the saints for ministry and for living life in hard times. The
Spirit of God yet works, and persecution will not stop that working. Indeed here is divine improvisation, God moving in, with, and
against the actions of injustice and the technologies of oppression.
Death and the forces of evil need silence and quiet acquiescence to
the old order, but God will deny them what they need. Through the
mundane voices and communicative gesture of disciples, God has
created weapons of righteousness that will announce divine presence and a providence that matters: God is with us now, working
out the good in and through us. Divine governance of the world or
the mission of the gospel cannot be seen from the safe distance of
history or the comfortable sites of being spared real persecution, but
only from the places of scattering and suffering where disciples yet
believe and will speak and perform their faith. But can those who
suffer differently a suffering not born of persecution know divine

providence? Of course, and their knowledge is born of this knowledge of the scattering. The scattering unfolds inside the command of Jesus to his disciples to be witnesses in this world in the places we find ourselves and where God sends us, and there is little need to parse the difference. The Spirit promises to guide the going if we but yield to divine desire. If God can sustain us against Saul, God will also do so against all enemies of body, soul, and mind.

> **"One-Way Ticket"**
>
> I pick up my life
> And take it away
> On a one-way ticket—
>
> Langston Hughes, "One-Way Ticket," in *The Collected Poems of Langston Hughes* (New York: Vintage Classics, 1994), 361.

Philip was scattered and now he was sent. What we glimpsed in Stephen we will see more with Philip, divine desire. Luke always shows us an active God, but here is more than the actions of God. We see a God who waits no more. Now is the time of salvation, and God will take hold of what God has always wanted, beginning with the Samaritans. The theological border dispute between Jews and Samaritans was about to be obliterated as Philip proclaimed the Messiah. This was the reign of God now covering Samaritans. The signs of the new order, of a world reclaimed by a God made flesh, flowed into Samaria, and once again the life of Jesus was revealed by the Holy Spirit. The signs that announced the new order also exposed the captivity created by the old order. People who were sick were healed, and those who were held in bondage to demons were freed.

Philip lives and moves in this space between word and sign, watching God gather in wayward creatures and freeing them from death's pull. Many in Samaria believed and were baptized. Even one Simon the magician believed and was baptized. Even Simon could see a power greater than him. Yet what some Christians have sometimes imagined they see in this text has been deeply troubling. Some have turned this moment into a lens through which to see the entire world as caught under demonic control and every indigenous miracle worker or local practitioner of healing arts as an evil trickster. The Jesuit theologian José de Acosta, missionary to Peru in the 1570s, imagined that rule of Satan was so comprehensive that only a hermeneutic of idolatry and demon possession would make sense of every ritual and gesture in a world outside of early Europe and Christendom:

> And, employing the same tyranny, after the might of the Gospel defeated and disarmed him . . . he attacked the most remote and savage peoples, attempting to preserve among them the false and lying divinity that the Son of God had wrested from him in his church . . . once idolatry was rooted out of the best and noblest part of the world, the devil retired to the most remote places and reigned in that other part of the world, which, although it is very inferior in nobility, is not so in size and breadth.[7]

Acosta's reading of the outside world is part of a wider tragic Christian history of poor mapping of the demonic in the world. That poor mapping taught Christians to approach the unknown with suspicion and what they perceived as strange was demon-imprinted or at least completely vulnerable to demonic attack and possession. As Christians became less comfortable with the language of demonic possession, they developed a new way of reading the unknown and the strange. It was culturally deficient or backward. Philip in Samaria, however, is not the story of Satan's rule, but of God's reign. This story offers us insight into God's love for those at the imagined limits of Israel, and yet with the Samaritans we are inside Israel. These are God's people, and God frees them from the demonic. Luke, like the other evangelists, has already shown us that the work of the demonic is first exposed as an operation *in and among* the people of God, not first *outside* them (for example, Ananias and Sapphira, and with the stoning of Stephen). To say that Christians have mapped the demonic poorly in the world is an understatement. We have failed to follow the trajectory of freedom witnessed by this and other texts of deliverance and exorcism. Freedom from captivity has come first to the faithful in Israel, even at its supposed edges. God will first cast out the demonic at work in those who believe! The world outside the

---

7. José de Acosta, *Natural and Moral History of the Indies*, trans. Frances López-Morillas (Durham, NC: Duke University Press, 2002), 254.

gospel is not first a world possessed by Satan but a world loved by God. Thus this story shows us not where the demonic is to be found but how the demonic is exposed between words and signs that speak of God's extravagant embrace.

Simon was caught up in the reign of God. He is no villain and no evil interloper, quietly waiting to reveal himself as a double agent for the devil. If we fault Simon for anything it should be for his intoxication with and addiction to power. Simon flowed in the currency of the crowd where attention and power circulated between the one and the many. Attention begat power as power yielded up greater amounts of attention. Simon saw power and was drawn to it. As John Calvin stated, Simon "was touched with wondering."[8] Simon followed Philip, and where we find Philip in Samaria there we will also find Simon. They go together. Yet Simon is no tare bound to Philip the wheat. This is no simple matter of a true teacher bound to a false one. Simon, there with Philip, is one who longs for power. The gospel draws such people who have not yet entered fully the space of redemption. They live in the space just outside redeemed space where their energy and time are caught up in chasing the crowd's attention and seeking power.

Simon mistakes God for power, and many who will come after him will make this same mistake. But this is an easy one to make because having some measure of control over people and being able to draw a crowd is the closest thing to being with God without God's help. Having power and attention, influence and regard is the closest thing to sensing God's will without knowing the divine will. Simon is not the quintessential prideful person. He is the ordinary power-broker in this world who has learned to live in the substitutes for life with God.

Even if such a person stands with disciples, and even if such a person is in fact a believer and ready to be a disciple, they have not yet entered in, and the question they raise for us is whether they ever will? This is our history, one where people who lust for power and attention circle around the work of discipleship, of preaching

8. John Calvin, *Commentary on the Acts of the Apostle*, vol. 1 (Grand Rapids: Christian Classics Ethereal Library, 2009), https://www.ccel.org/ccel/calvin/calcom36.i.html.

and teaching and healing. Their longings for recognition and power interlace the miracles of divine showing.

8:14–25

Philip and Simon wait for the Spirit to come to the Samaritans. This is a beautiful moment orchestrated by the Spirit. The journey begun in baptism will now continue with the Spirit. A processional has begun. Peter and John travel to Samaria from Jerusalem, and now gifts will be given. The delay of the Spirit was not for a defect of faith or of life for the Samaritans. Could it be that God waited for Peter and John so that they could watch the intimate event? Here and now these disciples, especially Peter, will see a love that extends into the world. They will watch as God stretches forth divine desire over the Samaritans. They must see again the Spirit descend and sense afresh the divine embrace of flesh. Disciples of Jesus must be convinced not only of God's love for the world but also God's desire for people, especially peoples we have been taught not to desire.

John Chrysostom says of this moment that it was meant as a twofold sign signifying the giving of the Spirit to these longed-for Samaritans and the *not giving* of the gift to give to Simon.[9] Chrysostom is on to something crucial here because this giving requires not only bodies touching but bodies yielded, bodies given to God. In this moment of waiting, like the other (Acts 1), God will draw near and give lavishly in an intimate space created by bodies and created for bodies. God's drawing and claiming of the beloved creation continues, reaching through the apostles and through Diaspora prophets, from Peter and John through Philip and now to the Samaritans. The Holy Spirit has come.

Simon could have no part in this because he does not understand what he sees. All he saw was power, raw power in the hands of the apostles, which for Simon circulates like all currency. The exchange of money for this power makes sense in the space just outside of redeemed space where the intimacy of faith remains hidden by its obvious utility. There are people the world over who live

9. John Chrysostom, *Saint Chrysostom: Homilies on the Acts of the Apostles and the Epistle to the Romans* (Grand Rapids: Eerdmans, 2010), Kindle, Homily 18:420.

and breathe and envision Christian faith only in its utility and only through exchange. Though they stand near its intimate space they are not in it. "Give me this power" (*dote kamoi tēn exousian tautēn*, v. 19). This is Simon's specific request for this specific item, and the apostles rebuke him. The rebuke is redemptive because through it Peter exposes to Simon his distance from God even while he stands in the divine presence, even as the Holy Spirit is being poured out again on all flesh. Simon is yet to be touched. So Simon is invited to enter the intimate space of waiting through repentance and prayer. It could be that only such rebukes can help those *believers* still captured in the optics of exchange and the currency of the crowd where money and recognition is just as valuable as the Holy Spirit. It was no small step for Simon to agree with the assessment of the apostles and ask them to pray for him. His response should give us hope that the new order can indeed break open the old order and cause those addicted to power to ask for help.

8:26–40

A New Sight of Love

The apostles are in Samaria, and their voices are being heard in unusual places. This is extraordinary. They are there, not because they want to be there, but because they are now subject to God's asserting love. The Holy Spirit is pushing them toward the Samaritans and beyond, drawing out the gospel from them into the villages of Samaria. They will soon turn back to Jerusalem, but little do they know that they can never fully go back. Their world turned upside down by the Spirit is yet turning, and the Jerusalem they know and the home they understand will soon become very complicated. They too will be altered by the scattering. Luke is laying out the cartographic vision of Jesus where witness will spread from Jerusalem, through all Judea, into Samaria, and to the ends of the earth (1:8). But he is also slowly exposing what that spreading will mean. There is an intensity building in this drama. God is overwhelming, and Philip will now experience what it means to fall into the hands of a desiring God.

Philip must move forward at the demand of the Lord. This is not precise direction, but Philip's obedience is clear and that is all God needs to direct disciples—imprecise direction and clear obedience. His destination is a desert road, that place that is no place. It is the in-between space that constitutes diaspora. Diaspora is road-embedded life born of old or fresh memories of migration, mobility, transition, upheaval, and hope. Roads are about survival, moving from one place to the next and searching for life possibilities or at least running from the forces of death. Luke has already shown us a God in Jesus who was comfortable with roads, whose feet touched the good earth, never searching for home or despising itinerancy, because his life redefined both home and away (Luke 9:57–58). This is a God who wills to be found on the road in order to transform it, collapsing near and far, domestic and foreign onto the body of the Son. There on the road that leads from Jerusalem to Gaza, from the near and known to the distant and unknown, Philip will again witness a God whose love expands over every road and transgresses every bordered identity. The Spirit is Lord of the road.

The scene that now unfolds is astonishing and a little comedic. A fine chariot moves by, and on it at least one driver and his chauffeured rider, an Ethiopian eunuch. Before we turn to the specifics of this exalted rider we must hear the Spirit's instruction to Philip. "Catch him!" Running, Philip comes next to the moving chariot, and he hears the eunuch reading Isaiah, and then he asks the question, "Do you understand what you are reading?" (v. 30) The question and the position from which it is being asked are both crucial, because together they show us more of God's lowliness and boundary-transgressing love.

God is chasing after this eunuch. We can say this because Philip has been brought exactly to this point by the Holy Spirit. He must run behind the horses, because God will not leave this traveler alone with the text. No one should be left alone with the text, any text. God is watching over the word to perform it, and in this scene that performance will involve Philip and the Ethiopian. Now at the command of the Spirit, the reading and the interpretation of holy word must always bend toward the communal, and it must ultimately issue in a joining. "I need a guide," he says in effect. The response of the eunuch to the question opens up the moment that God has been hoping and waiting for—Philip is invited to join the Ethiopian in his chariot, as he reads Isaiah, on his way home. We could call this private space, and here in it, God will be revealed, intersecting and intercepting the identity of this rider. The text in question is the Septuagint Isaiah 53:7–8, which captured a body in disgrace and pain:

> And he, because of his affliction, opens not his mouth: he was led as a sheep to the slaughter, and as a lamb before the shearer is dumb, so he opens not his mouth. In *his* humiliation his judgment was taken away: who shall declare his generation? for his life is taken away from the earth: because of the iniquities of my people he was led to death.[10]

Luke gives us God's exquisite timing—divine disclosure with this particular text read at this particular time by this particular traveler. This is what Gloria Anzaldúa would call a borderland moment where people of profound difference enter a new possibility of life together in a shared intimate space and a new shared identity.[11] Here we must pinpoint the site of difference, because the Ethiopian eunuch is of Israel and of diaspora. Even on this road he is still within Jerusalem's spiritual jurisdiction. His difference is marked by his origin in Ethiopia, the outer limits of the known world, and is even signified by his blackness.[12] His difference is also marked by his sexuality, neither unambiguously male nor female. His difference is marked by his possible position as what Orlando Patterson termed the ultimate slave, one who has tremendous power and is close to royalty yet is not a man in the ancient sense of having phallic authority to penetrate rather than being penetrated.[13] As an ultimate

10. Lancelot C. L. Brenton, *The Septuagint LXX: Greek and English* (London: Samuel Bagster & Sons, Ltd., 1851), www.ccel.org/bible/brenton/Isaiah/index.html, emphasis added.
11. Manuel Villalobos, "Bodies *Del Otro Lado* Finding Life and Hope in the Borderland: Gloria Anzaldúa, the Ethiopian Eunuch of Acts 8:26–40, *y Yo*," in *Bible Trouble: Queer Reading at the Boundaries of Biblical Scholarship*, ed. Teresa Hornsby and Ken Stone, Society for Biblical Literature Semeia Studies 67 (Boston: Brill Academic Pub., 2011), 191–221. Also see Gloria Anzaldúa and Cherríe Moraga, eds., *This Bridge Called My Back: Writings by Radical Women of Color* (New York: Kitchen Table: Women of Color Press, 1983).
12. D. K. Williams, "Acts," in *True to our Native Land: An African American New Testament Commentary*, ed. Brian K. Blount (Minneapolis: Fortress Press, 2007), 225–28.
13. Orlando Patterson, *Slavery and Social Death: A Comparative Study* (Cambridge: Harvard University Press, 1982), 299–333.

slave, he would be simply a body in use.[14] This Ethiopian eunuch is the outer boundary of the possibility of Jewish existence, and there at that border God will bring that difference near, very near, to hearth of home in the Spirit.

Who is this person in pain and suffering, humiliation and shame? (v. 34). This is the third question of the story. The first question drew attention to the mystery of the text, the second question showed the limitations of the reader, and now this question will draw them forward from possible captivity between these two questions. That captivity is not only possible but for so much of the history of the church it has been a constant occurrence. It has been too easy for us to be captured between textual inscrutability and reader shortcomings and never come to the third question. Everything pivots on the third question. The third question turns the closed circle of the first two questions into a spiral that leads to the threshold of the new order. This is not simply a third question provoked by this text within the text. It is a question that shadows every biblical text and every fledging interpreter, inviting us to see the One who would bind together exegesis of text to exegesis of life to illumination of new life in the midst of sorrow. The eunuch asked the right question, one that is like a prayer that God will answer. Now the body of God will be seen where no one would have imagined or dared to look, at the place of humiliation and pain and on a eunuch's chariot.

Philip preached to him an intimate sermon for one. This is a lavish act of divine self-giving that should not be explained by utility. Too often the eunuch has been interpreted simply as an instrument, as a necessary linchpin for evangelization and mission into the unknown parts of the world. Such ways of reading this story miss the joy that fills this scene and reflect a vision of humanity as nothing more than tools and a vision of God that has forgotten the extravagance of divine love. God has come for the eunuch precisely in his difference and exactly in the complexities of his life. He matters, not because he is close to worldly power and thus a more appealing pawn. He simply matters, and he is being brought close. He will no longer be far from home. Philip while interpreting a text is performing another text, Isaiah 56:3–5:

14. Jennifer A. Glancey, *Slavery in Early Christianity* (Oxford: Oxford University Press, 2002).

> Let not the stranger who attaches himself to the Lord, say,
> Surely the Lord will separate me from his people: and let not
> the eunuch say, I am a dry tree. Thus saith the Lord to the
> eunuchs, as many as shall keep my sabbaths, and choose the
> things which I take pleasure in, and take hold of my covenant;
> I will give to them in my house and within my walls an hon-
> ourable place, better than sons and daughters: I will give them
> an everlasting name, and it shall not fail.[15]

The eunuch is being brought into a future promised especially for him, one in which he will not be in the shadows or at the margins of the people of God, but at a center held together with strong cords that capture our differences, never despising them but bringing them to glorious light and life. Philip pressed by the Spirit is gesturing what Gloria Anzaldúa would call a *mestiza* consciousness: "the conscious-ness of the *mestiza* is one of ambivalence and contradiction, ready to embrace change and create new paradigms of family and society. The *mestiza* by her very nature is willing to travel into the unknown, allowing mystery to be revealed in each step."[16] Philip and the eunuch are in that strange new unknown that surrounds divine presence. Where God comes a surprising new follows, such that no one in Israel had ever seen (Luke 5:26). The strange and the new wrought by God will now bind together Philip and the eunuch in a new para-digm of belonging. They will now forever travel the same road.

"What prevents me from being baptized?" This fourth and final question of the story follows from the third question. It is the only real question that makes any sense once the "who" question has been answered, heard, and seen. This Ethiopian has found his body in Jesus. He is in Christ and Christ is in him, and now the water waits for the joining. All that remains in reply to his question is his own confession. "I believe that Jesus Christ is the Son of God" (v. 37).[17]

Between his question and his confession, Philip stated less a condition necessary for baptism and more a recognition that faith has already arrived. Faith found the water. Faith will always find the water. The immediacy of this blessed event is beautiful. It sets no

15. Brenton, *The Septuagint LXX.*
16. Manuel Villalobos, "Bodies *Del Otro Lado*," 195.
17. This verse may have been added later in the textual tradition, but it yet represents a text present in the reading and teaching traditions of the church.

precedent for catechetical procedure; rather it establishes the necessary hunger for the water and Spirit. The eunuch wants God as much as God wants him. They will wait no longer for each other. We must not run past the powerful and even erotic gestures of Luke in this story. The chariot pulls to the side of the road, the journey stops, they descend from the chariot into the water, and Philip baptizes the Ethiopian. A new journey begins. There is an abruptness to baptism and an eagerness to the water that cannot be weakened even with long preparation and deliberation. It is the slicing into a life's control center and its redirection toward life in God that makes every baptism a lightning bolt.

Bodies have been joined in holy travel, down into the water and now up out of the water. The eunuch is new and so too, in a sense, is Philip, who will now join a select few prophets who have been snatched away by the Spirit of the Lord (1 Kgs. 18:12; 2 Kgs. 2:16). Philip is gone "and the eunuch saw him no more" (v. 39). The Spirit has intervened, and that intervention was also redemptive. The eunuch is not left alone. He is left free in his joy. Disciples do need direction and guides, but first disciples must know their freedom in Jesus Christ. The church has often been too impatient and sometimes downright fearful of that freedom, choosing instead to quickly impose an image of the true, the good, and the beautiful example on those who have been made free by the Spirit. God would have none of this for the Ethiopian. There will be no correct or proper image of a disciple, no bodily model by which to pattern himself, and no one to begin a process of erasure or eradication of his differences. Philip will not be allowed to stay to tell him who to be or how to be, how to see himself or receive a preloaded life script in Christ.

"He . . . went on his way rejoicing" (v. 39). The Ethiopian eunuch is free as an Ethiopian eunuch, and he may move forward in joy. His future is open-ended now, and God has broken the connection between identity and destiny, between definition and determination, and inserted a new trajectory for his life. He is moving forward toward God through the Son and in the Spirit.

The complexities of his identity no longer prescribe a way of life, because he has been found in Christ, and his flesh is now bound to the Spirit through baptism. His body belongs to God. His story ends with an implicit question that follows from the other questions. What will become of the Ethiopian eunuch? This is not a question about his connection to the historical origins of Christian heterodox or orthodox movements or the churches in North Africa, or about his relation to or influence on other figures of Christian antiquity. The question concerns his future and the future of the church. Can one who has lived at the margins of community or in its liminal spaces because of their identity live free in Christ, or will social forces constrict that freedom and strangle redemptive joy? Equally important, will we see in him our freedom in Christ, in our differences, and in the ambiguities of our existence? His journey into the unknown is our journey. He moves forward into the future of the church, and he will be for the church a question that is yet to be answered.

FURTHER REFLECTIONS
Evangelization and Loving Difference

The appearance of the Ethiopian eunuch has occasioned questions about his origin and his place in the unfolding of Christian history and the spread of the Christian mission. In more recent years, the eunuch has become a focal point for seeing sexual and racial difference. Both forms of consideration are appropriate and highlight a crucial question that the church has struggled to answer—What does it mean to embrace those different from us for the sake of the gospel? The story of the Ethiopian eunuch is a story of divine compulsion. The Spirit is driving a disciple where the disciple would not have ordinarily gone and creating a meeting that without divine desire would not have happened. This holy intentionality sets the stage for a new possibility of interaction and relationship. Christians have lived inside this dynamic from the beginning of our faith and have often not been able to master its intricacies. We have more often than not sought to eradicate the differences we perceive in those new and strange to us through soul killing and life draining forms of assimilation. Or we have locked people in a vision of their difference that they themselves would not have created or ascribed to if they had been given the freedom to speak for themselves.

Faith in Jesus of Nazareth does draw us to a new way of life, a shared life that disrupts old patterns of living and breaks open cultural, familial, and tribal alliances and allegiances. This requires a new negotiation within ourselves and with our peoples regarding the shape our lives will take as Christian disciples. The Ethiopian eunuch was already exploring such possibilities as suggested by his examination of the Hebrew text. He was already considering the shape and contour of another people's story. Philip's presence is not only a catalyst for that consideration but also a witness to its normalcy. A disciple of Jesus is someone who not only enters the story of another people, Israel, but also someone ready to enter the stories of those to whom she is sent by God. Christians have often failed to see difference as an invitation to change, transform, and expand our identities into the ways of life of other peoples. So our embrace of other cultures and ways of life have most often in our long history not pressed toward the depth and intensity of the divine embrace of their lives. We have therefore undermined their freedom in Christ to be themselves and yet more. Too often Christianity has bequeathed to many peoples a derogatory gaze of their own cultural ways and their own peoples and turned the life of faith toward being little more than cultivation projects aimed at western civilization, western styled development, education, and so forth.

The history of modern colonialism is inside this history of modern Christianity, and we cannot escape its legacies; but we can end its trajectories by asking ourselves, Who are the people nearest me that the Spirit is pressing me to get to know, come to appreciate, and ultimately join? Such a question presses us beyond the still common way of embracing different people, either through assimilation or segregated toleration. These options make impossible an evangelism that follows the movement of the Spirit. The Spirit convinces through love, reveals God's life through our lives joined to others, and exposes the divine touch by how we touch with joy and pleasure the ways of life of others. This truth has been covered over by a history of forced conversion, evangelism at the tip of a sword or the barrel of a rifle, and a faith formed to worship whiteness. Indeed for some, evangelical acts of any kind are deeply problematic, especially if we wish to honor other faiths that are themselves ways of life.

Evangelism, offering witness to the gospel, is quite unavoidable if one seeks to yield to the Spirit of God. The gospel exposes a life captured by God's love, a love that overflows, constantly pulling us more deeply into God's own desire for other people and for all of creation. Too often Christians are unable to see the boundary-crossing reality of God's love. This means it is possible for Christians to enter the ways of life of other people, even religious ways of life, and in and through those ways of life perform love of the triune God revealed in Jesus. It is possible, but not easy, or not easily accepted by those who demand religious purity or who see the clear cultural and/or theological betrayal being enacted by such a lover of Jesus. Christian faith does announce disruption and redirection of worship to the one true God of Israel found in Jesus Christ, and for some people the price of that disruption and redirection has been severe, costing them their families, their closest friends, their social standing, and even their life. The potential for cultural, familial, or religious betrayal resides in every Christian as they announce by their life their love of Jesus; yet the greater untapped potential that resides in every Christian is showing God's love for a people's cultural and even religious ways. By their life that disciple may illumine a reality of acceptance that is not merely tolerance but embrace.

There are Christians all over the world in quiet spaces and places who are doing precisely this kind of loving, showing their love for a people not their own, or not Christian by and through their love for the Christian God, entering or remaining inside a way of life that they have turned toward the Way. There is, however, a position between tolerance and embrace and that is celebration, celebration of difference. There are some ways of life that are beyond our embrace not through prohibition but through our constitution and orientation. Yet we can and must celebrate the difference that speaks to the majesty and mystery of creation. Just as the church has an underdeveloped practice of embrace so too is our ability to celebrate difference. This is especially the case for those whose sexual orientation moves beyond heterosexuality. God's love presses us beyond quiet toleration (and certainly beyond lightly concealed revulsion) and toward extravagant appreciation of our creatureliness woven in difference and destined for communion with the divine life. Our life with God does entail an all-encompassing reality of change toward the life of the Son in the Spirit; however, too many churches have prematurely and obsessively pressed the question of change on those whose bodies mark difference and variety. Change is not a compass, but it needs a compass. Only an *ecclesial practice of celebration of difference* can make visible that compass and make intelligible and redemptive any reflection on and process of change that would draw us ever deeper into God's love and God's power. The witness of the gospel, enabled by the Spirit, exposes us to the triune God's feverish desire for the creature and all of creation. It is a desire that cannot be abated, will never relent, because it is a consuming fire.

9:1–19a

Disrupting Life

There is no rationale for killing that remains intact in the presence of God.

9:1–9

The scene shifts but the Spirit's action remains the same. God disrupts the old order by interrupting lives. Luke has removed every temporal wall that might separate in our thinking the God who moved in ancient Israel from the God present in the world in Jesus from this God of untamable love. This is that same Holy One, and Saul too will fall into the hands of this desiring God. Saul is a killer. We must never forget this fact. He kills in the name of righteousness, and now he wants legal permission to do so. This is the person who travels the road to Damascus, one who has the authority to take life either through imprisonment or execution. No one is more dangerous than one with the power to take life and who already has mind and sight set on those who are a threat to a safe future. Such a person is a closed circle relying on the inner coherence of their logic. Their authority confirms their argument and their argument justifies their actions and their actions reinforce the appropriateness of their authority. Violence, in order to be smooth, elegant, and seemingly natural, needs people who are closed circles. The disciples of the Lord, the women and men of the Way, have no chance against Saul. They have no argument and certainly no authority to thwart his zeal. They are diaspora betrayers of the faith who are a clear and present danger to Israel. This is how Saul sees them. His rationality demands his vision of justice. But what Saul does not yet know is that the road to Damascus has changed. It is space now inhabited by the wayfaring Spirit of the Lord. Saul pursues, but he is being pursued.

"*Suddenly a light from heaven flashed around him*" (v. 3b). The long history of the church has turned the Damascus road into shorthand for a life-changing experience, and rightly so, because Saul, the closed circle, is broken open by God. Yes, a killer was confronted and stopped in his tracks, but equally powerful, the rationality for his murderous actions was shattered. There is no rationale for killing that remains intact in the presence of God. The power of this event almost overwhelms its textual witness. Luke is handling holy fire now. The question comes directly to Saul. This is a question too massive for him to handle because it is an intimate one. "Why are you hurting me?" (*Saoul Saoul, ti me diōkeis;* v. 4). In our world, this genre of question flows most often out of the mouths of the poor and women and children. The question casts light on the currencies of death that we incessantly traffic in, and it has no good answer. The only good answer is to stop. But now this is God's question. It belongs to God. It belongs with God. Hurt and pain and suffering have reached their final destination, the body of Jesus. Now the divine presence will be revealed to Saul, not simply divine revelation, but a new revelation.

Saul knows he is on a road that has been made holy ground, and he asks the right question of God, "Who are you, Lord?" The mustard seed that was planted now grows strong, and what was hidden to the wise will be revealed. The Lord has a name (*egō eimi Iēsous,* v. 5).

> May all who suffer oppression in this world reject the self-defeating method of retaliatory violence and choose the method that seeks to redeem.
>
> Martin Luther King Jr., "Nonviolence and Racial Justice," *The Christian Century* 74 (February 6, 1957): 165–67.

This is the bridge that has been crossed in Israel. The Lord and Jesus are one. This is the revelation that now penetrates Saul's being and will transform his identity. He turns from the abstract Lord to the concrete Jesus. A future beckons in the pivot from holy faith to holy flesh. The abstraction in this regard is not found in the faith of Israel or the theologies of Judaism. Saul moves from an abstract obedience to a concrete one, from the Lord he aims to please to the One who will direct him according to divine pleasure. Discipleship is principled direction taken flight by the Holy Spirit. It is the "you have heard it said, but I say to you"—the continued speaking of God bound up in disruption and redirection.

Saul turns from defending the name of the Lord to serving Jesus, and for this he will soon suffer. He has crossed that line that separates this faith from all others. He has heard the voice of a crucified God. There is a stark truth here in this conversion so poignant that we sometimes ignore its abiding effect on us. Saul *experienced* the Lord Jesus. He encountered him, and this made Saul vulnerable. Experiencing the Lord Jesus makes us vulnerable. It is impossible to sufficiently explain an experience of the Lord, to make it a winning argument, or to present it as irrefutable justification for one's life choices. We must not run from this vulnerability supposing that we can overcome it by denying experience its place in witness or juxtaposing something called reason as over against it as a separate way of giving testimony. Soon Saul will present arguments, cogent ones that draw on all his knowledge and rhetorical skill and make a powerful case for faith in Jesus. His accounts, however, will draw as much heat and fire as light, because he has crossed a bridge that others must yet cross. The Lord and Jesus have been connected in Saul's body, and they can never be separated again.

"I am Jesus, whom you are persecuting" (v. 5). The revelation of God in Jesus, the joining of the identity of the Lord to the identity of Jesus is not the only joining revealed to Saul. Indeed the second joining is as great as the first and forms the great consolation that will unfold in his life. Jesus is one with the bodies of those who have called on his name and followed in his way by the Spirit. Their pain and suffering is his very own. This too is scandal. This too is a crossed line. The mystery of God is found in human flesh, moving in and with the disciples who are a communion of suffering and a witness to life. Saul is meeting a God in Jesus who is no alien to time, but one who lives the everyday with us. The shared life of Jesus continues with his disciples as he takes hold of their horrors and they participate in his hopes. Yet just as he confronted Saul, this God is no passive participant in the suffering of the faithful, but one who has reconciled the world and will bring all of us to the day of Jesus Christ. Saul has entered that new day.

Saul will now be on a journey with God that is both public and private, because this is the nature of divine revelation. Those with Saul also heard a voice, but they saw no one. The revealing God yet remains hidden in revelation. This hiddenness is not because God hides, but because, as Karl Barth says, God controls God's own self-revealing, we do not.[18] God comes to us one at a time, specifically, uniquely in the singularity that is our life. God comes to you and to me, as only God can come to you and me, as God, our God. The coming is a calling, a drawing, an awakening of our life to its giver and lover. The others with Saul were in the presence of the speaking God, but God was not speaking to them. Indeed they were speechless (*eneoi*), their words not to be confused with divine word and their sight offering them no pre-approved visual access to the divine life. They were helpless in this moment watching a powerful Saul prostrate on the ground. They witnessed a body under divine influence. Helplessly watching God deal with someone else is in fact an aspect of divine revelation that teaches us not only that God is Lord of the unveiling, but also shows us a God who never loses sight of us, who knows us by name and is coming just for us. Look, an awesome God is speaking. Who this God speaks to and where this God will appear we cannot control. All we can do is watch and wait for God to speak to us.

"*And though his eyes were open, he could see nothing*" (v. 8). The time of Saul's blindness is purposeful time. Luke will use this time to show us a Saul who now exists in the sudden need for another and the tension of waiting for help. José Saramago, in his powerful novel *Blindness*, explored a time of blindness when an epidemic of white blindness strikes a population beginning with a single individual

18. Karl Barth, *Church Dogmatics*, I/1, 315.

driving his car home from work. Mysteriously struck blind, the man emerges from his car pleading, "Please, will someone take me home."[19] In Saramago's novel, this man's need for help will soon cast light on the human struggle to show mercy and compassion when the unexpected transforms life for everyone. In Luke's account, Saul is now in the unexpected, far from home, but he will be joined in the unexpected by another, Ananias.

9:10–19a

Ananias, this Damascus disciple, appears in Luke's story quite unassumingly. He is in the story simply because he is now like all disciples of Jesus inside the ongoing history of God. God gives vision within vision, weaving together two strangers in a shared destiny. The Lord speaks to Ananias in a vision that there is a man named Saul who sees in a vision this very Ananias coming to him. There is nebulousness and fluidity to visions. They seem to be auditory, visual, and cinematic all at once. Figures are sometimes clear and sometimes offstage, clearly heard but just beyond the visual register. The visions that God gives are less about what we can capture in sight and sound and more about being captured, being drawn into the guiding hand of the Holy Spirit. This is what Ananias is facing—God gives dream and vision in order to take hold of our lives for wonderful purposes. Ananias, however, has some concerns, which often come with divine vision.

"Lord, I have heard . . . about this man" (v. 13). The Lord has commanded, and Ananias has heard. Saul waits in blindness, praying and fasting, hoping for a future, and Ananias the disciple must go to him in order that Saul may see again. Ananias, however, knows a truth about Saul, an indisputable truth. Saul is a killer of disciples. So now a disciple must face a decision. Do I act on a truth about someone, a truth that may put me in danger, or do I follow the word of the Lord and touch this dangerous person? Luke does not tell us whether Ananias was afraid of Saul but only that he was honest with God. We must not run past his honesty with God. He reminds God that Saul is a killer, and God in turn calls Saul his vessel who will carry the name of Jesus. God sees us differently no doubt, but the question always for disciples is, Can we see with God? Can we see those who

19. José Saramago, *Blindness* (Orlando, FL: Harvest Book, 1997), 2.

are in rumor or truth dangerous as God sees them—with a future drenched in divine desire? Ananias in this regard is given sight of another person's future. God has shown him the road Saul will travel, to Gentiles, to kings, to the people of Israel, and to suffering. So Ananias goes to Saul armed with Saul's future and not his own. For him the dangerous unknown is real and the future uncertain. The scales of knowledge are never balanced for disciples who have heard God say, "Go to *that* person." They often have a better sense of another's future in God than their own immediate future. Yet this is where discipleship, truly being a follower of Jesus, presses us to reorder our knowledge. The truth we know of a person or people must move to the background, and what we know of God's desire for them must move to the foreground. The danger we imagine inscribed on their bodies must be read against the delight we know God takes in their life. That same divine delight covers us.

Ananias must go for the sake of Jesus, the one deemed most dangerous and worthy of death. The meeting with Saul is beautifully rendered by Luke. Ananias touches him, saying, "Brother Saul." He acts inside a conclusion—God has already claimed this man and made him one with the other disciples. We cannot say that Ananias no longer sees Saul as dangerous or a killer. We must say that he indeed acts in faith, touching and believing in the power of God to heal and transform. Something falls from Saul's eyes, and he can see again. But Ananias now disappears from the story, his work done. Ananias is now enfolded inside the actions of Saul. Saul is baptized, he breaks his fast, and he regains his strength. Yet Ananias was there for the crucial time of blindness when someone could not see their way and did not know their future. Luke makes sure we see the courageous actions of this disciple, even if Saul does not. Such actions add another distinguishing mark to discipleship as those who will go even or especially to killers.

9:19b–30

The Diaspora in Faith and Fear

And so it begins. We have already spoken of beginnings (in Acts 2), and here is another beginning at the very heart of diaspora life and at the very heart of following Jesus. Unlike the savior he follows, Saul embodies a great inexplicable reversal. His life is now a question. A life turned into a question will repeatedly be the result of life with Jesus. But to whom is the question addressed? First and foremost, the question is addressed to Israel, to the people of God, but secondly the question will address any and every people who will have one of their own become a follower of Jesus. Saul became a question the moment he rose from the waters of baptism, just as all followers of Jesus become permanent questions after their watery resurrection. The question is many-layered, but it starts simply with, What happened? What happened to Saul, the Saul we thought we knew and understood? The question then moves to its second layer: What is he saying, and what does that mean for us? Then we meet a third layer: What should we do with him? This dense question is unbelievably serious because it exposes the direct implication of someone who interrupts the given social order of a world—they now stand in the position of a betrayer.

Saul now emerges as the great betrayer. He is that which is most feared by diaspora, someone who is poised to destroy our fragile and tender existence in foreign land and space by undermining our common life. Saul, who had been trusted with the story of Israel and trusted to uphold the narrative that shaped its political and social actions, is now doing something different with the words of God and the liturgy of the people. Saul has become a storyteller in league with Stephen and with the apostles and with all the disciples who sing a new song of Israel in diaspora places. He is weaving Israel's story through the body of Jesus and drawing all hopes and aspirations of his people to this man's life. This is stunning improvisation that Luke declares is powerful and confounds those diaspora Jews who heard it (v. 22), but we should recognize the political urgency and social poignancy of Saul's new faith and newfound performance.

He may not see this as betrayal but as simply taking the hopes of Jewish life and making a tight turn into their long sought after destination, turning his people's story more intensely into God's own life. His listeners, however, see and hear a betrayer. This is what begins with Saul—faith in Jesus will clearly look like betrayal of one's own people, their story and destiny. Make no mistake, faith in Jesus must make us potential traitors to our peoples because we will turn their story toward Jesus, draw their destiny into his life, and say he alone is the answer they seek. This turning of our people's stories is not eradication but redirection toward the God who we believed created them. But for many of them they

> **Make no mistake, faith in Jesus must make us potential traitors to our peoples because we will turn their story toward Jesus, draw their destiny into his life, and say he alone is the answer they seek.**

will see no difference, only loss, only confusion, and someone who was once with us but now is no longer of us. They are wrong in being right. They are right that the story is being told differently, but they are wrong in seeing this as loss. It is gain. It is a joining.

Jesus is the Christ (v. 22). We must not run past the absolute shock of these words coming out of the mouth of Saul for his listeners. It was as though they were being knocked to the ground by him. His listeners and observers are the crucial matter here because they must figure out how to take him. The scandal of the message about Jesus has now become the scandal of Saul's own life. Saul in proclaiming Jesus is moving quickly toward what Orlando Patterson has defined as a slave's lot, that is, one who is natally alienated, dishonored, and subject to violence.[20] Saul will in fact later see himself as a slave, but most immediately he will be hated. As someone hated by the faithful, he will join Jesus as the object of assassination. It seems absurd to tie faithful adherers of ancient faith to would-be assassins, but how would they not see Saul as Saul himself saw the disciples as dangerous threats that must be eliminated? Saul, who was once a closed circle of violence, is now encircled in hatred. He escapes in the solitude of a basket, a person dangling in the air between life and death, between his people's hope and his people's hatred. In this regard, there is a loneliness slowly appearing now that will accompany Saul. He is moving toward a liminal space where he will always need help, always need friends, and always look for community. He is moving toward church.

"The disciples . . . were all afraid of him, for they did not believe that

---

20. Patterson, *Slavery and Social Death*, 3.

he was a disciple" (v. 26). These folks are not Ananias. They have no vision of Saul's future and no urging of the Spirit to touch him. Like Ananias they know his truth, which for them is yet to become his past truth.

Though he is out of the basket, Saul is still dangling in the air. Barnabas returns to the story. Luke brilliantly prepared us for him by introducing him earlier with the apostles and with strong diaspora credentials and even stronger commitment to Jesus (4:36–37). Barnabas will be the go-between, bringing the apostles and Saul together in true sight of each other, but first Barnabas is the one who takes Saul at his word and binds Saul's testimony to his own. There is no fanfare to Barnabas's action. It is not signaled by divine intervention, but it is an action of marvelous faith and thereby totally and completely guided by the Spirit. It is faith in God in another, belief in the workings of Jesus in the life of someone others will not trust. Barnabas became his advocate, proclaiming the mighty acts of God in and through Saul. Saul is freed to be trusted, freed to do his work among the disciples because two testimonies have been joined in unison to declare his new truth—he has been changed. This is quiet redemption found in a simple act of taking hold of someone who stands alone waiting for help. This too is the way of disciples shown to us in Barnabas, who is skilled in quiet redemption. Saul will need such help because he has become a traveling storm cloud, gathering to himself swirls of angry winds everywhere he speaks. He is now deeply mired in a diaspora politic, the intensity of which will soon spill over, touching the lives of every believer in Jesus. This is the way it should be.

9:31–43

The Repetition of Jesus

It seems that for a moment Saul has collapsed the animus against believers in Jesus onto himself. His great reversal pulled back the terrorism he was inflicting on the church. The church had a moment of peace, but that peace was not everywhere. The church in Judea, Galilee, and Samaria enjoyed the benefits of Saul's transformation.

Once again we see the unevenness of persecution and suffering—one site of faith knows peace and increase while other sites hope for it. Indeed Luke in this part of the story is keenly attuned to geography and movement. Peter returns to center stage and engages in a bit of wayfaring life, echoing again his history of following Jesus and doing as his savior had done. He is on the road and comes to Lydda to be among the living saints. Luke slips in this strange word, "saints" (*hagious*, v. 32), here in this chapter, first in the mouth of Ananias and now in his own voice as the hidden narrator. This word, "saints," meaning holy or sacred ones, will multiply in use as the speech acts of Christians expand, but we would do well to remember its marvelous signifying power.

Israel knows a holy God whose holiness is untouchable by fallen human flesh. All those bound to Israel's ancient faith knew the line that cannot be crossed except from God's side. Only God can make something or someone holy. Only God separates or singles out vessels for hospitality of the divine presence, and in Jesus, God's holiness is intensified, because he is not simply a site of holiness. He is the Holy One in fallen human flesh. What seemed to be a contradiction, holy and human, is in fact the home of God's generosity, mercy, and sovereignty. Jesus is God drawing the everyday into holiness, into God's own life. Everyday people are made holy in Christ. Everyday people are made holy by Christ, and this is a holiness that will last, not be episodic, and constitute a new space for living life and knowing ourselves. "Saints" are those marked by the new gestures of belief in Jesus. They worship a crucified Lord in the Spirit, and in the Spirit they live the everyday, knowing that each moment has been made sacred by God's faithful presence. Peter travels from the saints to the saints inside the inescapability of a God who is making people new.

Peter repeats Jesus. The short appearance of the man Aeneas is not a minor matter. No one of sick body is a minor matter, and Luke in bringing Peter to Aeneas brings Jesus to Aeneas. This is the continuity that must be made clear to his readers. Peter is not moving by happenstance. He is not traveling by accident. He is with Jesus, following where his savior wants to go. Once again a marvelous act, a touchable miracle, will turn people to the Lord (v. 35). This is repetition that illumines the inexhaustible riches of God's love for the fragile creature and God's desire to constantly touch us, hold us, and announce the victory over death. There is yet more for Peter in this journey as he is approached by two disciples from another city (Joppa) for the sake of one disciple who has died.

Tabitha, the disciple of Jesus—Luke opens her story inside of Peter's journey and in so doing makes a point more powerful for us in our time than probably for him in his time. Tabitha, a woman, is a disciple of Jesus. Whether this vignette is evidence of Luke's positive view of women or not, he has certainly given us a plateau from which to view a new future in which men and women in Christ have a different way of seeing themselves—as disciples. We come to the story of Tabitha with Peter at the very end. There is glory and grief at the end. The glory is a life lived well, lived in service to others. Tabitha's life, even in the fragments we gain in this story, hangs together beautifully as someone devoted to helping people, especially widows. Widows, that group of people vulnerable in ancient and current times, made vulnerable by death's sting, have always been a special concern for God and here for Tabitha as well. We know from this story that Tabitha's life was woven in good works and acts of charity ("she was devoted to good works and acts of charity" v. 36). So the widows weep. They weep for her and maybe for themselves. We do not know if Tabitha was in fact one of them, but we do know that they claimed her as one who cared for them. Here glory joins strong grief because to lose someone who cares for the weak and vulnerable, whose life is turned toward making a difference in the world and who is making a difference, is a bitter loss. The widows have lost Tabitha and a disciple is gone. This is what Peter steps into in Joppa.

Peter's presence declares an unmistakable truth: women matter. This woman matters, and the work she does for widows matters to God. It matters so much that God will not allow death the last word. Others had been raised from the dead in the Gospels and in Luke's Gospel (8:49–56), but this is different. This is not a little girl or the brother of a friend of Jesus; this is a disciple raised from the dead. Tabitha is not finished in life or service. "Tabitha, get up." Peter repeats Jesus. Tabitha is an activist who lives again in resurrection power. Her body has been quickened by the Spirit, and her eyes are opened again to see a new day. She has work to do and joy to give to the widows: you have not been abandoned, dear widows, God has heard your weeping and returned her to you. More importantly, *she* is alive. We know that death imagines a special claim to the bodies of women. Their deaths are normalized and naturalized in social orders that value men's body far above all others. It will not be so among the disciples. They will find Peter standing next to Tabitha, a gift of God who has been given again the gift of life. It is no accident that the first disciple to have this little taste of the resurrection is a woman, because it was a woman who gave birth to the resurrection. And Peter is there once again to see a miraculous sign point to faith's direction—many who found out about this believed in the Lord (v. 42).

The story, however, does not end there with Tabitha, because Peter stays in Joppa, and who he stays with points to an earth-shattering future. He stays with Simon, a tanner. Tanners worked with death flesh—the skin of animals and tanners were, theologically speaking, unclean. Few if any pious Jews would normally or easily stay with a tanner, but here was Peter with Simon the tanner. Peter is indeed moving from saints to saints, and soon he will find out just how far the generosity and mercy of a holy God reaches. Soon he will see just how far God will extend holy place and holy people. Peter is with a man who touches the unclean, and soon he will see God do the same.

10:1–15:41

The Desire of God Exposed

10:1–23a

The Revolution Comes to Us

God's desire placed in us makes us holy, and it will be the foundation on which God creates the new. Prayer and hunger, hunger and prayer— these will be the pillars on which God will build the future of the creature.

10:1–8

We have noted two beginnings, one that took place in a room and another on a road, and now a third beginning involves two places: the room of a soldier and the rooftop of a tanner. This third beginning is inconceivable without the first two. In fact it is yet inconceivable. It yet escapes our full comprehension. Here now the revolution of the intimate enters its full force. Now the acceptable day of the Lord will explode across space and time reaching to us and beyond us into a future we cannot see. Luke at this point in the story inscribes the door through which we, Gentiles, enter in and, in so doing, performs what Karl Barth called the strange new world within the Bible. Once we see, really see, into the world of the Bible, then in an instant we really see our world, there and here, our world in all its intensity.[1] That intensity shines through because we see that our world is actually God's world. God is moving, living, fully and freely acting in the world, beloved and cherished. This world matters

---

1. Karl Barth, "The Strange New World within the Bible," in *The Word of God and the Word of Man* (Cleveland: Pilgrim Press, 1928), 28–50.

to God. We matter to God far more than we matter to each other. Luke's narrative from this point forward will strain under the weight of the obsessive love of God. This chapter is the pivot, the turn that makes intelligible everything before it and after it.

Here for the first time we, Gentiles, fully appear, no longer hinted or suggested or glanced or insinuated. Here and now, like a Bertolt Brecht play, the stage opens to include the audience.[2] We readers and hearers are surrounded by the scene, tumbling helplessly into the script, already anticipated and addressed. Cornelius is us, but not typically so. He is a man of war, bound to the Roman state. He is a master, an owner of slaves. He is a ruler, a leader of men. He is what so many men *and* women in this world aspire to be and what so many peoples want to be defined as—a strong self-sufficient people who look to the world like one unified, strong, self-sufficient man. Cornelius is an aspiration, but he is also an anomaly. He is a God-fearer. He is one who stands at the door of Israel and knocks, praying the prayers of God's people as though he is one, following the gestures of worship and life of God's people as though he is one, embodying the hopes of God's people without them knowing it. Cornelius is thusly a living contradiction. He is in the old order, but his actions are preparing him for the new order.

Cornelius does not know it, but God knows him by name. Again divinely given vision captures and will soon compel—Cornelius's prayers were not wasted speech. His life of giving was present to the divine life, noted and remembered. Cornelius will learn what all those outside of Israel who come after him will learn, that God hears and answers prayers. God pays attention to us, even when and if we forget that we glanced toward heaven by our actions or our plea. This however does not suggest a casual or contractual relation between God and the pious, and it certainly does not imply a righteousness acknowledged by God through the sheer consistency and generosity of this man. Such a reading would miss this moment in which God will wait no longer for love's sake. God has found the appropriate excuse to give the gifts designated for us from the foundation of

---

2. Bertolt Brecht, *Brecht on Theatre: The Development of an Aesthetic,* ed. and trans. John Willett (New York: Hill and Wang, 1964).

the world. Cornelius, the citizen-solider who is also the God-fearer, is the occasion for God's touching, holding, and having.

"Send . . . for a certain Simon who is called Peter" (v. 5). This is an extraordinary act through which God will usher in a new ordinary. God's guiding hand is not the new thing here, but now God reveals the immeasurable size of those hands. They reach out to capture the lives of Gentiles, and they reach deeply into our hopes and prayers. These are times being made strange by the fulfillment of divine promise, and at the heart of that strangeness will be a meeting orchestrated by the Holy Spirit. Cornelius must search for and find Peter. The powerful self-sufficient man must find the disciple. This is strange. Too often Christian commentators on this text have rushed past this searching to get to the meeting, but the event of searching is within the significance of the meeting event. The searching is already a breaking open. Ironically there is an awkward and problematic similarity between what God does and what the centurion does. God dispatches an angel to do the divine bidding, and the centurion dispatches two house slaves and a solider to carry his inquiry. This is analogous power, the power of God mimicked in the power of the Roman state, and the ways of God imitated in the ways of the world. A world order is searching for Peter just as a world order searches for us today. That ancient world order signified by a domestic regime necessary for stabilizing the Roman state is approaching Peter.

These two slaves and the soldier represent Cornelius. They exist in a relation to him that allows his body to gesture through their bodies, his words to move through their words. They belong to him. His obedience to the vision is now their obedience to the vision. An ancient way is being presented here by Luke. It is the way of the powerful in this world who have others to walk, talk, and inquire for them. Yet as they move toward Peter they are moving toward the overturning of that way. Soon the powerful and the powerless, the superiors and their surrogates will be confronted with a new way of being in the world, a way that crumbles these identities of the old social order from within. Soon they will meet a disciple of Jesus. The urgent question is whether Peter or any disciple will recognize the confrontation of the old with the new and the unraveling of the fabric of social hierarchies that clothe us.

10:9–10

"He became hungry and wanted something to eat; and while it was being prepared, he fell into a trance" (v. 10). Now God comes. Peter will be the site of the in-breaking. God's timing is purposeful, like a musician with perfect rhythm and pitch, whose entrance defines the song. The old order approaches on foot, and the new order drops from the sky. God comes to Peter inside of Israel's first and deepest gesture—in the moment of prayer. God comes to Peter inside the creature's deepest truth—in the moment of his hunger. Prayer and hunger, hunger and prayer—these will be the pillars on which God will build the future of the creature. These are the pillars on which God will constitute the new order. Hunger and prayer go together, completing each other in God. God wills the creature to pray, and God wills the creature to hunger. God wills Israel to pray, and God wills Israel to know itself in its hunger. Painfully, tragically, the church has too often turned prayer against hunger, imagining prayer as the antidote to hunger, as medicine to a bad condition. This is not so. Hunger needs prayer, but prayer needs hunger. Hunger sets the stage for prayer, and prayer sets the table for hunger. God works through prayer, but God works on the site of hunger. God glories in our hungers and speaks to us in the precisely ordained reality of it. Indeed nothing that God will now say to Peter makes sense unless we remember that the divine word came to a hungry creature. Prayer and hunger are the inner realities of a disciple of Jesus.

> An all-embracing and intense longing for God binds those who experience it both to God and to one another.
>
> St. Thalassios the Libyan, *The Philokalia*, vol. 2 (London: Faber and Faber, 1981), 307.

10:11–12

The revolution descends on a sheet. The sheet is everything. The sheet is radical. The sheet shatters and destroys. Its four corners are harbinger of its range and its reach across a planet and a universe. Peter in his hunger beholds his horror. The sheet contained the

known (culinary) world and unknown tastes. It contained animals,
clean and unclean, appropriate and inappropriate, appealing and
repulsive, desired and despised. The sheet from heaven contained
the common. And then the word of God comes to Peter. "Arise Peter,
kill and eat!" (v. 13) These words stand over against all other words
of God, forever recasting them and turning them to new purposes.
Again this is the "you have heard it said, but I say to you." This is the
living *Dabarim* (words) of the living God. These words echo across
the church's history, but they have rarely, if ever—maybe never—
really been heard in all their redemptive density.

We have not deeply sensed the creative power of these words, first
because we have not sufficiently reckoned with how God works in
and with our hunger. If you are hungry, you are vulnerable. It is a
vulnerability of the creature usually submerged with a full belly but
unleashed in the space and time of real hunger. In real hunger, the
kind that brushes against starvation, one is within sight of the abyss
of desperation, fear, and madness. Peter is not in real hunger, but
God brushes up against Peter's vulnerability and draws him toward
a new kind of bread from heaven. The second reason that many of
us have not heard this creative word in its freeing power is because
we have not reckoned with animals. We who live on the other side
of the colonial moment live within the absolute commodification
of animals. For so many of us, animals are for the most part utility,
natural resources, and sites of consumption. There was, however, a
time that revealed a different way of viewing animals, and there are
yet people in this world that hold to these old ways. The old way
of viewing animals bound them to us as extensions of family, faith,
memory, and body. We and our animals were one, our identities
encircling and being encircled by them. Whether people of the black
bear or the salmon or the raven or the horse, we lived not simply
viewing the animals but, as John Berger said, being viewed by them.[3]
We lived knowing that we lived with them, in relationships that we
saw as mutual, reciprocal, and joined.

To see animals was to see peoples. To touch and eat an animal
was no thoughtless act. For many peoples, their elders would have
to seek permission from the animals to eat them in due season, and

---

3. John Berger, *Why Look at Animals* (New York: Penguin Book, 2009), 15.

with the eating, something would have to be returned to the earth to balance what was taken and who was taken.[4] Gaining permission to eat was gaining permission to live. The space of eating was also the space of living that wove together the bodies of earth creatures in shared recognition of one another in ways ignored only by the very foolish. Thus to eat the animals that were associated with a people was to move into their space of living, a space of people and animals. To take hold of their animals was to join them and imagine the flourishing of life through participating in the community of creatures that surrounded their bodies. A sheet of animals descended from heaven, and the Creator of the world granted to Peter permission to eat. In so doing, God placed Peter in the midst of the world and said to him, "Join it, join them."

This word from God, "Get up, Peter; kill and eat" (v. 13) must be read first communally before it may be read consumptively. For us this word of God is a dangerous word because we are conditioned to read it inside an unrelenting chauvinism and the victory of capitalism that constantly turns the world of animals and peoples and the very earth itself into nothing but natural resources. We are the inheritors of histories that have imagined the entire world through scenes that mock this moment in Acts, imagining God to be actually saying to a man, "Look here on the unknown world and take all you want." These are the histories most immediately of whiteness and white male supremacy. But this is not at all the direction of this text. Peter is not being asked to possess as much as he is being asked to enter in, become through eating a part of something that he did not imagine himself a part of before the eating. This new eating grows out of another invitation to eat, one offered by his savior and friend: "This is my body, which is given for you" (Luke 22:19).

10:13–16

Peter resists the divine command. This too is extraordinary, and this too requires we slow down to capture sight of the birth pangs of the new order. Peter is not being disobedient. Indeed in Peter we have

4. Clara Sue Kidwell, Homer Noley, and George E. Tinker, "Creation: Balancing the World for Seven Generations," in *A Native American Theology* (Maryknoll, NY: Orbis, 2001), 32–51.

a servant who lives on the other side of betrayal, denial, repentance, and forgiveness. His obedience was refined through suffering and trial, beatings and death threats. Peter obeys, but now that obedience must take flight with the Holy Spirit into an uncharted world where the distinctions between holy and unholy, clean and unclean have been fundamentally upended. Yes, this is a moment when old word of God connects to new word of God, a moment where purity is expanded to cover what had been conceived as impure, but more crucially this is a moment of struggle for Peter to allow his vision of faithfulness to God and the covenant with Israel to expand. Is it possible to be faithful to the God of Israel in a new way? God has brought Peter inside this question and presses him toward its positive answer. This is a risky time, second only to Good Friday and Holy Saturday, in which God risks with Peter and Peter risks with God. Will Peter hear this *new word* from God, and will Peter believe that this is a new word *from God?* This is the condition of risk in which Christianity comes to exist and without which authentic Christianity does not exist. This is the risk of faith that comes to each of us, but none of us carries it alone. The risk here is found not in believing in new revelations but in new relationships. The new word that God continues to speak to us is to accept new people, different people that we had not imagined that God would send across our paths and into our lives.

10:17–23a

The interpretation of the vision will not be private for Peter. He has company. There at the door of Simon the Tanner is the future God desires. The God that Luke presents here is an extravagant busybody, pressing the actors to move wholly inside the divine will. God's word to Peter is direct and stunning: don't analyze, critique, or think too long or hard about it, just go with these men, because I have sent them (v. 20). This is aggressive community organizing by God in which the divine hands are quite heavy in a meeting that would not have happened without them. The Spirit of God is on both sides, outside the door with the seekers and inside the door with the perplexed Peter. God, however, is no puppet master in this scene. God is simply, beautifully interrupting conventional and normal structures of relating by mapping God's own relational logic across their bodies. Peter is now in the strange position of listening where he would have normally been speaking of the directing of the Lord. Rather than reciting the words of angels given to him, Peter hears of divine visitation with another, a Gentile no less. The world is turning over, and Peter turns with it. He invites Gentiles into the house that is not his own; the house belongs to Simon the Tanner. Both Peter and these sent from Cornelius are guests in the house of the unclean, and together they are inside the story of God. Together they sojourn into the depths of divine longing. Peter will now enter more fully into the richness of being a witness found in the sharing of space, food, and drink.

10:23b–48

This Is What Intimacy Sounds Like

10:23b–27

God, Peter, and Cornelius—this is the unexpected. God brings Peter to Cornelius—this will be the new thing. Luke slows down the common gestures of meeting so we might see and feel the unprecedented. Peter enters the home of Cornelius. Cornelius falls at his feet in worship of him. Peter picks him up and says, "Stand up; I am only a mortal." (v. 26). Together they talked and moved toward a room where Cornelius's family and close friends were waiting. The stage is set. How do you change the world? How do you turn it right side up if not by turning it upside down? Now God will transgress border and boundary in the best place for such transgression. It will be done in the intimate spaces of family and close friends and in a clandestine illicit meeting of those who should not be together. Peter and Cornelius should not be together. The disciples who came with Peter should not be in the same room with Cornelius's family and close friends, his household, but there they are together. The cultural codes and social rules and theology that normally apply are being suspended in this encounter, and no one knows what will happen next.

10:28–34

God works in and from tight spaces, intimate settings of family and close friends, to change wide open spaces of peoples and nations. Peter is now caught up in the revolution of the intimate. God has pushed him over the line that separated Jewish bodies from Gentile bodies, holy bodies from unholy ones and pressed Peter to change his speech acts by never again calling anyone unholy or unclean. It is not at all clear that Peter sees into the depths of what he is saying, but that does not really matter. What matters is that he has been driven to this place by sheer divine desire and not his own desire. What matters is God's transgressive longings and the divine refusal to allow bodies to be separate even for theological reasons.

This moment schools us in divine transgression. God brings Peter to one outside of the covenant, transgressing God's own established boundary and border. We must not weaken the radical implications of this epic meeting. This meeting has yet to gain its proper place in the historical consciousness of the church because the actions of God here are taken for granted. God's actions here have been imagined by so many Christians through a mangled vision of providence that conceals the real God behind a strange universal god. That universal god in this line of thinking has always been poised to render Israel inconsequential and now was moving on past covenant with Israel and finally overcoming their religious ethnocentrism. The universal god was fulfilling a hidden wish to make Israel a doorstop put in place to grant the world access to salvation. This line of thinking imagines God's life with Israel as simply a dress rehearsal for the real play. The universal god of this distorted providence had all of us, the Gentiles, the rest of the world in mind all along, even as Israel was turned inward toward its own struggles with covenant faithfulness. This sick providence falsely reads Israel's history as their many failures to get beyond themselves and their petty religious or nationalist interests. That false history interprets God's actions toward Israel as so many attempts to break out beyond them. It therefore ultimately suggests a clear division of operations: Boundaries and borders were human doing, not God's doing. God is on the side of universal concern, and particular interests are always and everywhere a sign of the fall, an example of human undoing of the divine will.

Luke's narrative, however, should not be read through such a bad vision of providence, as though this encounter was expected. It was not. Divine touch is always unexpected and usually unconventional. Israel is the sine qua non for God's serious touch. In Israel God is schooling the creature in the ways of the divine life. Luke had already shown us from the very beginning of his narrative that in Israel God intensified touch, reaching to its uttermost limits, from birth to death, and drew the creature from its uttermost limits, from death to life (Luke 1–2). Jesus was God transgressing, and now in the Spirit and in a private room made public, that transgression will take its full form. Jesus will draw Jew and Gentile together, not moving past the one to get to the other, not choosing one and rejecting the other, but precisely bringing together, drawing close what was far apart. The meeting is the new order—Jew and Gentile will share in one Spirit. This is the will of God, made known in the Son and realized in the Spirit, and this new order requires new listening.

10:35–43

Peter has been on a journey of listening, and in the intimate space of Cornelius's home that journey continues. Cornelius reveals to Peter the extension of the divine hand reaching out and down into the life of this citizen-soldier. Peter listens and hears the word of God in new and unanticipated places. Before Peter will offer his truth he must listen. This is the key currency of the new order. This is the engine that will operationalize holy joining. Listening for the word of God in others who are not imagined with God, not imagined as involved with God, but whom God has sought out and is bringing near to the divine life and to our lives. Peter speaks, and now his earlier conclusion—that he should no longer call anyone unholy or unclean—joins an additional insight: God shows no partiality (*prosōpolēmptēs*, v. 34). God's tastes are much wider than Peter had imagined until this moment. Peter is at the threshold of revelation. That revelation is not of God's wider palette for people, but that Peter's range of whom to love and desire must expand until it stretches beyond his own limits into God's life. God is pressing Peter's aesthetic toward death and resurrection—the dying and rising to new desires is now the call emerging for him.

This revelation, however, is beyond Peter. God at this moment is pressing him to his limits. Peter can only locate in these historic unprecedented actions an ethic of divine acceptance: "but in every nation anyone who fears him and does what is right is acceptable to him" (v. 35). Peter is saying that if any Gentile does what is right and fears the Holy One, they will be acceptable to God. But there is much more going on here. Peter has been taken up in an event of listening that is nothing less than sacramental, through which he will hold up the body and blood of Jesus to hungry people. Cornelius and his family and friends are listening. There is great power in the quiet of their listening because they are angled toward the new, ready and poised for it. They already know and sense the divine hand guiding and leading them to this messenger. So Peter preaches. His words summarize the story, but Luke allows his words to do more. Peter now claims even more of the power of the storyteller to re-narrate the world and life itself.

The Jesus of recent history becomes the defining moment of all history. Here is the deliverance of the world and its restoration toward health and life. Luke presses the cosmic through the words of Peter, pulling back the curtain to reveal the hand of God in Jesus. The unbelievable has happened: Jesus was killed and rose from the dead. Death has been overcome in and through him. Yet this was no singular miracle but rather the great announcement of the new order—Jesus is the judge of the living and the dead. He is the Lord of all. All living creatures are now bound to him. In him and through him, there will be forgiveness of sins. In him and through him, prophetic word finds its final and definitive home. Peter is speaking about nothing less than the incarnation of God in flesh. The content of the gospel comes home in this sermon to its sharpest truth. This is God. Peter's words echo the divine presence and will now become the stage on which God continues to take hold of wayward creation.

While Peter speaks, God moves. Once again feverish divine love cannot wait. We could imagine that Peter's listeners jumped ahead of his words, connected the dots, joined belief to his speech, and turned in supplicating plea to God. The story, however, does not give us all those mechanics, because this is not about their actions but God's outrageous act. The Spirit takes hold of them, just as happened with the disciples of Jesus, bringing them into the desire of God witnessed through language. Peter and his band looked in shock and awe (*exestēsan*, v. 45). Nothing prepared them for this witness. Nothing suggested that this was coming. They certainly imagined their witness to the world of the diaspora, maybe even to a world beyond that diaspora, but never a witness *from the Gentiles to them*. The Gentiles speak in tongues, and Israel hears. This is a speaking back to Israel and through Israel to the world. Gentiles give witness, and that witness is always first to Israel, first angled toward Israel and then to other peoples and other places. This will be the way the Son of David will reign over all flesh as judge and lover. Jesus will be worshiped in Israel and outside of Israel, and that worship of God will go forward from Israel and be echoed back to Israel.

How could it be otherwise? Jesus binds Jew and Gentile together, and that binding has direction. The Holy Spirit has come on the Gentiles, and they speak in tongues toward Israel. The tongues are always toward Israel. Even if those tongues are aimed at heaven or at and with other Gentile peoples, Israel is the first stop so that they may overhear, just as the Gentiles overheard the words of Jesus. That overhearing is purposeful witness. This is what the church is yet to grasp of its own beginnings in its multitude and in its multicultural plenitude. The first reader and hearer of our witness are Jewish people, past, present, and future. Each song we sing, every testimony of faith we give, every action of life-service we render speaks to Israel of the victory of Israel's God. Of course, we yet live in the shattered remains of our grotesquely distorted witness to Jews, having inherited the legacy of hatred of Jewish people and the refusal to live faithfully in the obligation of our witness toward them. That obligation is precisely the site where we, in the words of Judith Butler, give an account of ourselves in such a way as to make intelligible to ourselves our own identity and agency in the world.[5] We are people joined to another people and in this way born of and nurtured through the joining.

5. Judith Butler, *Giving an Account of Oneself* (New York: Fordham University Press, 2005), 84–101.

The languages of others have come on the Gentiles also, not by their choice, or their wish, but by divine imposition. This will be the message in Gentile flesh—God is calling you too to join others, enter into their language and their life, become one with them, become lovers of those outside yourself, beginning in Israel and with Israel. Israel then is the *unrepeatable* exception that no other people or nation may claim in time or space or place. Through Israel God announces desire for the creature and embodies that desire through concrete relationships. We might call this an inverted exceptionalism. Unlike American or other forms of nationalistic exceptionalism, this form of exceptionalism turns people outward not inward. God has brought Peter to Cornelius, Israel to the *goyim*, unfolding that Jewish exceptionalism into a new focus on other people that will shape Gentile lives. Gentiles may now see the world as God desires Israel to see the world—as specific and particular sites of love— where the Spirit would send us to go, announcing in and through life together with people God's desire for joining and communion.

10:44–48

The waters of baptism signify the joining of Jew and Gentile, not simply the acceptance of the gospel message. Yet both are miracle. Both are grace in the raw. The Spirit confronts the disciples of Jesus with an irrepressible truth: God overcomes boundary and border. God touches first. God does not wait to be touched by us. This is the boundary not of our failure but of our truth. We cannot reach up to God and bring God down to our embrace. We are creatures. Yet God takes touch seriously and initiates the embrace. This is the border not of God's desire but of our need. Our senses are dull and our attention weak. We are easily distracted by other things, drawn so deeply into obsession with these things that we will worship them and make them our gods. We must have the space and time in which to have our senses trained to understand authentic divine touch. We must have the time and space to learn the way of Spirit caressing flesh, holding it, moving it, directing it toward life and light. We are the boundary and border God has transgressed, and that transgression is real. Here at the site of miracle, space and time are being given for Jew and Gentile together to press in deeply to the caressing of God through the flows of water on the body and the joining of our bodies together and to the body of Jesus.

Peter's final question asked among Cornelius's household (Surely, no one can refuse to give water if the Spirit has been given, can they? [v. 47, paraphr.]) answers his first question (Why am I here?). Both these questions will haunt the apostles and the church built on their witness. Yet the greatest event of this story comes after the miracle of baptism. It is the beginning of life together, "Then they invited him to stay on for several days" (v. 49). The reading habits of the church tend to run past these slender words, but they capture divine design. This is what God wants, Jews with Gentiles, Gentiles wanting to be with Jews, and together they eat and live in peace. This is surely not the eschaton, not heaven on earth. It is simply a brief time before the chaos and questioning descend on Peter and the other disciples who will follow the Spirit, before the returning to the old regime, and before the lust for the normal returns. But in a quiet corner of the Roman Empire, in the home of a centurion, a rip in the fabric of space and time has occurred. All those who would worship Jesus may enter a new vision of intimate space and a new time that will open up endless new possibilities of life with others. Peter, however, must soon do a strange thing—he must give witness to the witnesses of Jesus and try to convince them that God transgresses.

11:1–18

The Transgressing God

Only bodies formerly imagined as properly separated but now bound together by the Spirit can become bridges from the old to the new.

11:1–3

Peter is caught up in the strangeness. He is back in Jerusalem where he must give an account of his actions. The good news had reached Judea that the unexpected happened: Gentiles received the word of God from a Jew. It was, however, not yet received as good news by the Jewish followers of Jesus in Jerusalem. Questions had to be answered that would determine whether Peter had betrayed sacred covenant and covenantal identity by communing with Gentiles in the intimate space of food and fellowship, eating and desiring, speaking and disclosing. Such a serious matter always haunted diaspora. Would the journey to distant lands, surrounded by *goyim* (Gentiles), weaken the commitment of the faithful to the story of God's promise? Would a people be lost from the inside out? These questions were now angled toward Peter and his disturbing actions.

This is the trouble that comes with transgressing cultural and theological boundaries, especially if those boundaries had been divinely ordered. Luke captures the gravity of the situation. Peter steps into thick criticism, growing out of one massive question: Why did you share intimate space with the uncircumcised? The line between the circumcised and uncircumcised is no false binary fabricated through religious ethnocentrism. That line is the difference between existence and nonexistence, between the story of a people that lives on and a story that has come to an end. Peter's sisters and brothers in the new faith are quite serious about that faith's sure foundation in Israel, and now this traveling apostle must give a justification for his actions. This is an impossible assignment for Peter because he must explain the inexplicable. He must suture together a known faithfulness with an unknown faithfulness and bring together obedience to ancient Word and Spirit with obedience to Spirit and present Word. Indeed nothing has changed, but everything has changed. Peter must lay his body across the line between circumcised and uncircumcised and give witness to its transformation into a bridge. How can bodies become bridges? Only through the Spirit and in the body of the Son may we become those who force a question from the mouths of others—why are you where you are not supposed to be? Why are you in intimate settings (with all that it suggests) with those not of your people and not of your story?

11:4–18

Peter has only one option: He must give voice to his experience. Commentators on this text tend to read past its most surprising reality. Here powerful word is present in weakness. Peter stands before his redeemed kin in utter vulnerability. He has no textual witness to fall back on, no prophetic utterances to conjure from the collective memory of his people. The prophets of old did not prepare him for this Gentile emergency. He is speaking to those who know him and know the faith. This is always the most difficult site to speak from for any servant of Jesus, one drenched in the familiar. This was also the case for Jesus. He too spoke on well-worn paths of hearing and seeing, knowing and doing to those who resisted his embodied newness. The only argument Peter could give with kinship eyes bearing down on him was no argument at all, simply an experience. The idea of experience has gotten a bad reputation in Christian thought in recent years, and for good reason. Claiming an experience of God, of faith and truth, has served as an ideological tool for every will to religious power. The claim to an experience has graced greed, violence, and oppression with halos of righteousness. Yet Peter shows us its proper use, to confront the cult of the familiar—of family, faith, nation, and story.

His hearers know him, so he brings them more deeply inside himself, stretching their knowledge of him to its breaking point. This is how experience thwarts the power of the familial gaze. Step by step (*kathexēs*; v. 4), Peter will explain himself, but it will not simply be an explanation of himself but also of God pressing in on him. It will be, in the words of Friedrich Schleiermacher, an experience of absolute dependence on God.[6] His experience reveals God. Why does Luke need to repeat in detail the events of chapter ten? For emphasis of course, but more importantly he does it to show the breaking open of a life, Peter's life, and to show the breaking open of a people's life, Israel's life. The drama must be told in detail so the hearers can begin to see their lives in it. God spoke to Peter, and now through Peter God is speaking to the saints gathered there to hear. The power of God is present in weakness, in the voice of one disciple of Jesus who simply tells the truth of what has happened to him and what God did through him. He remembered a promised baptism for the Jewish body and saw with his own eyes that baptismal promise stretched over Gentile bodies. "Gentiles have been touched by God, just as we have," Peter states, giving witness to the itinerant longing of the Holy Spirit. This is a miracle, this is earth-shattering, world-altering

6. Friedrich Schleiermacher, *The Christian Faith*, trans. and ed. H. R. Mackintosh and J. S. Stewart (Edinburgh: T. & T. Clark, 1986), 577–78.

truth, and it can only be carried through testimony, only through story told by one dangling between the past and the future with no ground to stand on except the ground created by the Spirit of God. Peter speaks and his own people are reduced to silence.

This silence is a break in space, and time, and sound that God has orchestrated. This break does not silence Israel's past, but it is a break in the musical sense, in the sense of jazz improvisation. As Wynton Marsalis reminds us, in the break the band stops playing and leaves space for a soloist to play. In the break the soloist is alone for a moment *carrying* the time, suspended in air and holding everything together in a singular performance: "It is a pressure-packed moment, because you have to maintain the time flow of the whole band by yourself: Our time becomes your time—yours and yours alone."[7]

Peter brings them to the break, but the Spirit of God carries the time, holding it in the silence. The moment of silence after the testimony reveals a God who has been keeping time beautifully and faithfully with Israel and now expects the hearers to feel the beat, remember the rhythm, and know the time. These listeners follow the break and join back into the ongoing song and praise of Israel. God has again done a marvelous thing beyond our anticipations: even Gentiles receive the repentance that leads to life (v. 18). This is a new song sung for those outside of the household faith. It is a word of celebration that a lover and their beloved have been brought together, the God of Israel and the Gentiles. We must not lose sight and feel of the strangeness of all this. The restoration of Israel will involve divine love for the Gentiles. After the silence God's love has modulated into a new key, but the rhythm and song of Israel continues. The beat goes on.

FURTHER REFLECTIONS
Word of God against Word of God

"You have heard that it was said, . . . but I say to you . . ." (Matt. 5). These often repeated words of Jesus set the stage for our interaction

---

7. Wynton Marsalis, *Moving to Higher Ground: How Jazz Can Change Your Life* (New York: Random House, 2008), 29.

with the living God, whose words to us are living, because they are bound up with the source and giver of life itself. Acts 11 is a moment of reorientation where the Spirit is teaching us a crucial lesson that the church must constantly remember: God yet speaks and word of God always presses against word of God. What God has said in the past is pressed against by what God is saying now. Israel shows us that the human creature is always positioned between these two words and destined for yet more hearing from a God ever extended in grace toward us. This in-between position has often been painful for us as we try to grasp clarity of thought and action on a walk of obedience to God on a well-lit path, albeit with multiple twists and turns. (Ps. 119:105) In this regard, the struggle of the church has been twofold: we struggle to hear the new word that God is constantly speaking, and we struggle to see the link between the new word and the word previously spoken.

The church from its beginning has rightly grounded its thinking in historical continuity with the word of God registered in, for example, the canon of Scripture, liturgical tradition, testimony, and dogma. Yet such historical grounding has been fraught with problems, because invoking the past (in terms of what Christians have thought, said, practiced, decided, affirmed, and denounced) has often been used in destructive ways in the present. For Christians, the past is extremely important, but what is far more important is how we deploy the past in order to prescribe present and future actions. To declare what God has said is tantamount to declaring what ought to be the case now, much like a lawyer or judge invoking legal precedent to revoke or establish current laws. Such declaration presents incredible power and the potential to order a world. It also creates the temptation to fall into theological nostalgia for past forms of Christian life and practice that never really existed in the way we imagine them.

There is also the problem of living oblivious to the past and functioning without any historical consciousness. The church exists only because God has spoken in the past, and without a sense of that history we lack clarity about our current path and journey. Yet the history we must remember includes more than ecclesial discourse and deliberation: it also includes the shaping of the world and the formation of its most devastating operations and regimes that we Christians have sometimes collaborated with and helped create. This kind of full bodied memory work requires disciplined remembering that wants to learn from the past but does not fantasize or demonize it, but looks to discern the word of God in and through the past.

The past, though important, is never the point for the life of faith. The point is the present moment with the living God who is with us, beckoning us to communion. The God who speaks to us now calls us into the risk of hearing a new word, a word that orients us toward the unanticipated and the unprecedented where the reconciling God is active. Peter found himself in the midst of such a word in Acts 11, where what God was doing in and through him among the Gentiles pressed him body and soul up against the word God had spoken to his own people, Israel. The key for us, seen in this moment for Peter, is to refuse the binary of naming the past word false and the present word true or the present word false and the past word true, and to discern through the Spirit the line of continuity between past and present. We may do this because such discernment is not a burden but is the joy we have in participation with the ongoing life of Jesus, who has claimed this space between past and present word as his own and invites us to join him in it. "You have heard that it was said, . . . but I say to you"—Jesus' words—point to the present and intimate speaking of the living God made flesh and one with us in the challenging task of hearing God's new words pressed against the old ones.

What does a new word look like? We will know it by its fruit. That which builds life together, life abundant, and deepening life in God is truly a new word from God. That which speaks the community of Christ and echoes a desire for shared life, shared hope, and redemption from death and all its agents is always a new word from God. Indeed an old word registered in the canon of Scripture, liturgical tradition, testimony, and dogma can become a new word to us through the Spirit and a new word found in bodies and through experience, in places strange and alien to us, among peoples not our own, can also become a new word of God to us. Yet these words should never be understood to live antagonistically. They are bound

together in the life of a speaking God who wills to bind us together
through space and time, through borders and boundaries, from life
through death and to the life anew and eternal found in Jesus Christ.

11:19–30
The World according to Antioch

11:19–21

The scene shifts in this chapter, but the situation remains the same.
The story continues from chapter 8 with those who were scattered.
They follow the logics of diaspora even in their being scattered. They
offer the word of God exclusively to the Jews (*monon Ioudaiois*, v. 19).

That logic is not evil or immoral. Indeed their actions resemble
Jesus' words to seek after the lost sheep of Israel (Luke 19:1–10).
The words and actions of Jesus, however, always carried an eros that
spread beyond Jewish bodies, touching a Gentile here or there. But
now the far off places and distant peoples are coming ever closer as
the Spirit draws more disciples in this work of revolutionary intimacy. Among the scattered were those of diaspora who shared in the
language and culture of Antioch, for whom the space was familiar
space. They were of Israel, but they were also of Antioch, being both
Jew and Greek. They too would now by the work of the Spirit spread
their bodies across a holy divide of circumcised/uncircumcised for
a holy purpose. Luke does not give us a dramatic vignette as he did
with Peter, yet there is just as much risk in the actions of these disciples of Jesus.

These disciples already exist at the site of the bicultural and the
biracial (of Jewish and Hellenistic). It is, no doubt, a bit anachronistic to speak of bicultural and biracial reality here, but it helps us see
what is at stake in this insurgent act of speaking (*euangelizomenoi*,
v. 20) across a boundary and drawing the reign of Jesus to a new
territory and into new bodies. These disciples are already in the in-
between spaces of cultures and life, and it is precisely from that in-
between space that the Spirit creates new life. Peter was pressed into
the in-between, and these disciples, seemingly by choice and not

by force, moved effortlessly into this place of divine presence. The actions of the Jerusalem-bound apostles are echoed in these mulatto disciples in Antioch—the Lord was with them and great numbers turned to the Lord (v. 21). Here a pattern of pleasure seems to be emerging. God enjoys the liminal space and from the in-between draws creatures to the divine life through the Son. Could this be so? Dare we think such a thing? We must always follow the repetitions of God in this drama of the Spirit. What God repeatedly does says something of the divine will. In this case, God repeats desire and repeatedly reveals the desire to drive Jew and Gentile into each other's lives and enfold us all in divine desire.

With characters and plot lines rivaling those of the most imaginative fiction, the saga of the Freedom Rides is an improbable, almost unbelievable story. In 1961 . . . more than four hundred Americans participated in a dangerous experiment designed to awaken the conscience of a complacent nation. Inspired by visions of social revolution and moral regeneration, these self-proclaimed "Freedom Riders" challenged the mores of a racially segregated society by performing a disarmingly simple act. Traveling together in small interracial groups, they sat where they pleased on buses and trains and demanded unrestricted access to terminal restaurants and waiting rooms, even in areas of the Deep South where such behavior was forbidden by law and custom.

Raymond Arsenault, *Freedom Riders: 1961 and the Struggle for Racial Justice* (New York: Oxford University Press, 2006), 2.

11:22–24

Word reached home, surprising words joined surprising words. Peter's testimony is now joined by news of more Gentile conversions. We are still within diaspora concerns, diaspora anxieties, and breathtaking surprises born of the news of faith in strange places. So Barnabas appears again in Luke's story in what Phyllis Trible would call narrative power.[8] Barnabas carries the story of newness in his body. He is a site of the in-between. He is like these disciples who crossed boundaries in Antioch. He is a Levite of Cyprian birth

---

8. Phyllis Trible, *God and the Rhetoric of Sexuality* (Philadelphia: Fortress Press, 1978).

(4:36). He speaks their language, which is also his language *and* the mother tongue of Jewish faith, which is also his faith. Barnabas goes to Antioch fully cognizant of the anxieties of Jerusalem and the power of the gospel. Not everyone who believes in Jesus is ready for newness. Not everyone who follows the savior can come into the unanticipated places of the Spirit's work. Some saints don't like surprises. Barnabas is not one of them. His eyes are ready for the new. He has seen the grace of God before, and he knows what it looks like in new places and on new bodies. So in Antioch he repeats the sound of those in Jerusalem who heard Peter's words—Barnabas rejoices. There is yet work to be done, people to be taught to live in the way of Jesus, and there will be many questions about ways of life, of merging and mixing, of adding and taking away aspects of culture and practice. But the first response must be joy, the joy of joining, and the happiness of new life together. Here in Antioch, Barnabas gets it just right.

Much hangs in the balance with Barnabas. This is another pivotal moment in Luke's literary work. If Barnabas questions the strength of this conversion of his non-Jewish people, then the reach of the gospel falters beyond Jewish bodies. If he concludes that the deliverance of Israel has indeed found a Gentile home, then what of his Levite heritage? Barnabas thankfully is not stymied by this extraordinary situation; he simply yields to the Spirit. He follows the movement of grace and presses these people he knows so well to press into the Lord. This is the model of faith for these new strange times— go with the flow of God and follow what the Spirit is doing in the world. Barnabas came to Antioch to assess (and possibly to help) and found himself deep in the midst of the divine gathering of lives into life in the Messiah. As Luke would have it, Barnabas connects Jerusalem and Antioch in his own body and by his own joy, not two communities but one, not two peoples but one Spirit. Luke has rendered Barnabas's body supremely a bridge to Peter and soon to Saul. This is in fact what the Spirit does. The holy work of drawing communities into shared life only happens through those willing to bare the space of the in-between in their bodies. Only those who hold inside themselves an awesome concourse of difference can channel this new reality, much like a child carried by a virgin.

11:25–30

Barnabas and Saul, their names together mean more than we often realize. Their collaboration will remake the world. We know Barnabas as a radical friend. We saw his friendship with God at the feet of the apostles (4:35). We witnessed his risk of friendship with Saul, a killer of disciples (9:27), and now he again charts new terrain by reaching out to Saul for help. Barnabas brings Saul to Antioch. We must never forget the order here. Barnabas invites Paul into the newness of this moment. Together Barnabas and Saul will spend a year teaching what they did not yet fully understand. Together in this cosmopolitan city far removed from the theological universe of Jerusalem, they will hammer out a song, a sound of their own that would become our own song and sound. Antioch is mixture and blessing—it is that place that God sometimes gives where cloaked in the theologically inconsequential and ignored site, the Spirit builds a future. This place of multitude will be a place of newness and a site of creativity. Away from Jerusalem, this diaspora community will give birth to a different community, a Christ-different community. This is not the first time such a gathered group was called church (5:11; 8:1, 3; etc.), but this is the first time that newness found its way to a name, *Christianoi*. Such a name, however, was not a badge of honor but of ridicule that registered the strangeness of their song and of their sound. But like a new song that announces a new time in present time, it may often seem and sound strange. Christian in its plural form always equals a strange new future.

Why have Gentile Christians forgotten their radical beginnings? Because it was too much for us to take in—not only are we those outside of Israel who were never fully imagined to be brought in, but we grew in the cosmopolitan places of diaspora through the in-between pedagogy of an in-between Barnabas and an ex-killer Paul. Luke saw this tension between a church of home and a church of the mixture, and he narrated our joining. Yet the complexities of our beginnings do not stop there. The Spirit speaks to us of what afflicts the world. This too is our birthmark. This too is our inheritance. We are those who from the very beginning are always caught up in what destroys life and threatens the world. A prophet named Agabus does what a prophet is supposed to do—speak by the Spirit of where the church must be active, and in what the church must be involved, in this case, famine relief and care for the suffering. We cannot escape these beginnings and what they mean for us now. The Spirit always brings to the church specific knowledge of the world and the specific sites of divine concern. A church that knows not the particular needs of its time and place is a church that has not heard the Spirit speaking. The church is marked by the Spirit with an inescapable action and an irrefutable demand—we must do what we can to address the particular needs the Holy One confronts us with. So the Antioch church sends relief to the Judean church by the two most appropriate to speak for them, the two that spoke their difference into existence: Saul and Barnabas.

12:1–25

The Prison Returns

The problem with prisons is that they remain an addiction for those who wish to silence voices, destroy bodies, and maintain hegemonies of all kind—political, social, sexual, economic, and religious.

12:1–11

Just as we never leave the presence of the Spirit in Luke's narrative, we never leave sight of the prison. It is always with us, always offering the antithesis to the good news. The prison always announces worldly power and reveals those intoxicated with the lust for violence, but not primarily from the site of the cell but from the place of the warden, the guards, and those benefiting financially and politically from the mechanisms of incarceration. The church cannot and must not ever seek to hide itself from the prison. Confrontation with it is fundamental to our ordination, our way of following Jesus. What would the state be without prison? Would it cease to be a state if it did not have this power to hold captive, to incarcerate? Indeed to challenge the prison is to challenge the state's very existence. Surely, the state would yet exist without prisons, and without the mechanisms of arrest, arraignment, trial, verdict, and sentencing, but it would be a different kind of state—one whose power over bodies has been checked, reduced in size and scope because the prison (and the mechanisms of incarceration) was no longer an attractive tool for the powerful and the keepers of the status quo. The problem with prisons is that they remain an addiction for those who wish to silence voices, destroy bodies, and maintain hegemonies of all kind, political, social, sexual, economic, and religious. Another King Herod appears in Luke's story, and he is much like the other King Herod who was acquainted with Jesus. This King Herod deploys the same anti-messianic weapons of statecraft, but now used against Jesus' followers. James the brother of John is executed by the state.

What was the charge? Does it matter? It rarely matters. All that matters is the illicit power to take what the state cannot give, life. This action brought pleasure to both political and religious leaders. Here is a sign of human sinfulness—pleasure at the death of one's enemies and satisfaction at the silencing of opposition. So in hopes of more pleasure, the king arrested Peter. Back in prison again—if the church is formed around the life of the apostles, like Peter, it is also formed inside the problem of recidivism. We are fated to repeat the behavior that brings incarceration. We speak truth to power, which will put us again and again inside locked doors, and braced by chains. Christians, like no one else, should understand how easy it is to return to prison, not because of human failing but because of failed systems that are calibrated against the powerless, the weak, and the poor and work best against insurgent voices pressing for systemic change.

> One has a greater chance of going to jail or prison if one is a young black man than if one is actually a law-breaker.
>
> Angela Y. Davis, "Racialized Punishment and Prison Abolition," in *The Angela Y. Davis Reader* (Malden, MA: Blackwell, 1998), 105.

Peter's arrest mocks his savior. Like Jesus, Peter's ordeal comes at the time of Passover. Like the Son of Man, Peter will be taken like a lamb for the slaughter. Yet unlike the time of Jesus, this captivity of Peter exists on the other side of the Son's torture and death. It exists on the other side of resurrection. So this incarceration exists in the midst of a praying church that knows it must earnestly pray to God for the power to intervene in these killing actions of the state. Those killing actions are acutely realized on Peter's body. He will be placed in maximum security—an inhuman place for anyone. There is no possible justification for maximum confinement, no human reason for an isolation that drives the broken to madness. This is not maximum security as we know it now, yet it still counts as a "malign conjunction of prison and madness . . . [which is] the experience of 'being locked in a small space with intractable mental discomfort.'"[9]

Peter's body is covered in chains and guards. This is the insanity of maximum security. He sleeps in a cell bound between two guards, his body not his own, ritualizing a kind of rape. How is it possible to think or breathe in such a frozen state? As Angela Davis notes, our prison system is born of slavery. It is kin and kind of the absolute absurdity of turning black bodies into commodities.[10] Here Peter is placed in the midst of a turning that is immersed in violence and aiming at death. Lorna Rhodes, in her book *Total Confinement*, tells us that for prisoners in such strangled states the only weapon they have to fight against the absurdity is their body waste. Only their fluids and their feces can push against the chains and the guards.[11] Luke once again slows the action down long enough for us to see a church in total captivity. This is a knowledge that not enough Western Christians know or understand. Not enough of us know what it is like to be trapped in space and wrapped in prison guards. Indeed the pedagogy of this lesson is yet to penetrate our collective ecclesial consciousness.

Peter's only hope of escape is intervention. It is predicable to read the fantastic in this portion of the story. If such a prison break would feel like a fantasy for us, it is one that the Spirit wants us to have and hold and make real in people's lives. The angel comes and piece by piece removes Peter's captivity and restores his humanity. Both actions are tied together and both are within the liturgy of this holy

9. Lorna A. Rhodes, *Total Confinement: Madness and Reason in the Maximum Security Prison* (Berkeley: University of California Press, 2004), 110.

10. Angela Y. Davis, "Racialized Punishment and Prison Abolition," in *The Angela Y. Davis Reader* (Malden, MA: Blackwell, 1998), 96–110.

11. Rhodes, *Total Confinement*, 43–49.

deliverance. First, *"a light shone in the cell"* (v. 7). The angel brings light to the cell, exposing the horrors of this captivity. What is happening to Peter will no longer be concealed in darkness. Second, *"He tapped Peter on the side and woke him, saying, 'Get up quickly.' And the chains fell off his wrists"* (v. 7). Peter must be awakened to life and his freedom. One of the horrors of incarceration is the way it strangles the senses and drains the joy of being alive to the world. It seeks to turn those confined into the walking dead. Yet Peter's freedom is connected with his becoming alert. He awoke and the chains fell off immediately. This twofold action of the Spirit brings clarity to what must be our work in participation with the divine life and will for those in captivity. We must work for the freedom that awakens and frees people as quickly as possible. The possibilities of freedom for the incarcerated move slowly, more slowly than should ever be accepted by the servants of God.

Then third, the angel tells Peter to *"'Fasten your belt and put on your sandals.' [And] 'Wrap your cloak around you and follow me'"* (v. 8). The angel attends to Peter's body. This bit of the scene may seem trivial, leaning toward the silly, but it is neither trite nor a joke. Nothing speaks of dehumanization more than the stripping away of familiar clothing, the exposing of the body to nakedness and shame, and the donning of garments that remind the prisoner of a suspended identity and a loss of story. But here the angel demands Peter dress himself for the journey and prepare himself for freedom. The angel tells Peter to put back on his clothing and take back his life. These clothes not only return his actual life, recapturing an identity that is greater than prisoner, felon, ex-convict (to use our nomenclature), but these signal his readiness for the journey ahead. Again God frees and God prepares Peter for freedom. We must do the same with those we seek to liberate.

Luke marks the steps toward freedom as though each one was precious in God's sight. Peter is dreaming but not dreaming. Luke's words echo the testimonies of so many formerly incarcerated women and men. They dreamed so long of freedom that they struggle to see the difference between the dream and the reality. But the Spirit is pressing Peter on, and the angel of the Lord is guiding him up out of the cell, past the layers of guards, through the iron bars, and into the city. The angel departs and Peter comes to himself. What is this "coming to himself" (*en heautō genomenos*, v. 11)? He awakens from the hope to the reality and clearly identifies the political and religious forces that were working against him to do him this injustice. Should Peter have considered his own culpability in his incarceration? We recognize the absurdity of the question, because Luke tells us that those in power are behind and underneath this prison sentence. Why has the church too often forgotten this angle of perception in its life and work? Of course, people do horrible things worthy of prison and tied to capital punishment.

But Christians are given a wider lens than media fictions of crime and punishment. We have an inheritance born of life inside the cell, and the intimate knowledge of power misused through the facile foolishness of equating crime and punishment with wickedness and righteousness. The state wants us to forget what we know and see only singular bodies, dangerous and detached, kept from us and our possessions only by the iron power of kings and rulers. But the church is formed in a pedagogy of prison that we must never forget, lest we forget ourselves and forsake our mission.

12:12–19

Peter's return home exposes two kinds of presence. Peter is present in memory and hope bound up in prayer and petition. But he is also now present in person, released from captivity and waiting to come in. Luke allows us a slight comedic relief in this moment. He is a narrator with a sense of rhythm who knows how to balance the intensity. This release is a complicated celebration. We can sense this too in Luke's telling as the disciples of Jesus are not quite sure what to do with their newly released brother. First they do not believe he is free even as he stands at the door and waits. And then when this truth is present in front of them, they are amazed, but we hear no shouts of praise to God, no rejoicing in the Lord. Surely such rejoicing could be implied, but all we have is the silent listening to Peter's testimony. Yet Peter does advise them in the right direction, letting the church leadership (James and the believers) know that he was free by the hand of the Lord (v. 17). But then the strangeness continues: Peter leaves. This leaving could mean nothing more than he goes some-where else, but it follows the complicated nature of this deliverance. Did he leave because he needed to hide himself for fear of recap-ture and re-incarceration? Did he leave because there was fear mixed with their amazement, fear that they may be implicated in his unau-thorized release? These are projections for sure, moving from the complicated celebrations of released former inmates that mark our time back toward Peter and his friends. The church often fails to find the amazement, the joy, and the celebration for and with those who have been set free. Uneasiness often greets them in the church, and a reluctance to let them fully into our shared life even if we knew them before and know them now. Peter leaves for unknown reasons, but we often know the reasons that former inmates leave churches: they waited too long at the door hoping to come in.

Great tragedy ends this story beginning with the fate of the guards. To be a guard is to be bound to violence and death. It is work, but not good work. Anybody who claims its goodness is lying to themselves. The best that might be claimed is its necessity in a system that wants us all to confess its necessity. Yet this moment in the story strips away even that necessity. These guards were there to maintain the captivity of other human beings, and once Peter escaped, the obvi-ous question pressed on the guards was one of allegiance: Are you working for the opposition? This is what hides beneath the surface for every guard, the conflict between those with power and those who live against that power, between a social order that advantages some and disadvantages many more others. The guard stands at the line, her or his feet close to the edge, and an escaped prisoner or an out of control prisoner suggests that their feet have slipped over the line. So they interrogated these guards, which might suggest a cross examination with torture. Whether they were actually tortured with their interrogation is not the point, rather their captivity to a system of violence and death is the point, because in the end the guards *are* put to death.

We would do well to remember this slender verse (v. 19) as more and more people are being invited to participate in the ever-expanding prison industrial complex as a robust site for the expansion of capi-tal and the growth of new markets. Could it be that the church must now seek the deliverance of not just the prisoner but also the guards? Could it be that we must intervene between two captivities, those in prison and those who would run the prison? We are all ripe to be made prison guards whether we work in prisons or not, because we are slowly being desensitized to prison horrors, slowly being baptized in capitalist logic as the natural order of things, and slowly being brainwashed into believing that Christianity goes hand in glove with the pseudo-morality of our judicial and penal systems. Every increase of the guard population is an increase in the power of death, every new hire who draws a paycheck from prison work draws more death into society, and every church that sits silently at this expansion denies the power of deliverance given them by our risen savior.

12:20–25

This tragedy continues with King Herod. It seems every King Herod in Scripture is tragic. Luke performs the majesty of biblical narrative by once again reminding us that we should never be intimidated by those in power, no matter what power they wield. To us they are all too human even if they imagine they have the power of death in their hands. Luke shows us a world at the fingertips of a king and people trapped in the royal game of courting political favor. This is a story about a cancerous relationship between rulers and dependent people. It is a relationship that has turned sick because people are petitioning the ruler for what they should have by right and justice—food and protection from threat of death. The relationship is sick because the king claims what only God may claim—the power over life and death. Such sickness seems to always attend this relationship, whether it is ancient kings or modern governments or our current multinational financial institutions. All imagine they have the right to make us dependent subjects.

Herod drew on ritual to expose his power. But it revealed his sickness. In royal robes and public presentation he spoke definitively, as one who imagines he has the last word. This too comes with this malady. Rulers imagine they have the last word when it can only ever be a penultimate word, and sometimes not even that. Yet the people join in the sickness. "A god's voice, not a man," they shout (v. 22). They are mistaken. It is a common mistake, but a serious one. People trapped in fear and dependency, moved by spectacular sight and sound, and caught up in the illusion of political games often find themselves repeating idolatrous refrains. They push rulers where they desire to go—to the heights of heaven and the eternality of power. Yet God interrupts this degrading hookup, breaking up and opening a relationship by ending its misdirection toward the creature. As John Calvin suggests, such misdirection shows human beings imagining themselves giants able to pluck God out of the seat of power.[12] God's judgment on Herod is the ironic reversal of Herod's judgment on James. Herod took a life that he did not give. God took back the life God had given. God withdrew life from Herod and revealed the truth of who we are: decaying dust. The worms wait for all of us, only Herod found his way to them sooner. Here a system, all systems of reciprocal power show their truth. They are all dying from the inside out, but the word of God is forever. We who follow the Spirit are inside the word of God before we are inside any system. We are to be guided by our relation to the Word before we are guided by our relation to worldly power. King Herod's time came to an end, as will the endeavors of all rulers, but the mission of those who follow the Spirit continues.

13:1–12

The Unambiguous Spirit

Wherever women and men give themselves to the disciplines that attune the body to its hunger for the Spirit they will find themselves receptive to the voice of God.

Luke has stripped away any ambiguity about who is driving this story. This is the Spirit's doing, the Spirit's work. By this chapter we find the Spirit speaking clearly through and to the disciples. The

---

12. John Calvin, *Commentary on the Acts of the Apostle*, vol. 1 (Grand Rapids: Christian Classics Ethereal Library, 2009), https://www.ccel.org/ccel/calvin/calcom36.i.html.

voice of the Spirit and the voices of the disciples are together but not confused. The agency of the one does not negate the action of the other. At Antioch, we find people who know how to listen to the Spirit. This kind of cooperation may in fact be rare for us, but it never had to be. Wherever women and men give themselves to the disciplines that attune the body to its hunger for the Spirit they will find themselves receptive to the voice of God, and they will hear the Spirit speaking and offering guidance. Luke destroys the bad image, the sick fantasy of a silent Spirit who only occasionally whispers to a still heart. Rather we have a communion-bearing, community-forming God who speaks in the midst of the multitude and makes known where we must go to follow the Spirit's movement.

Barnabas and Saul, along with John Mark, are driven by the Spirit. Luke is clear about the Jesus pattern he is inscribing again. He repeats the truth he registered with Peter and with Stephen, and now with Barnabas and especially Saul: to follow the Spirit is to follow Jesus, in his way, in his ministry, and in his body, and as with Jesus, the struggle will be in the house of God and with the household of faith. They reach their destination only to find exactly what Jesus found: demonic opposition. This conflict is ancient, but not of good versus evil, but of a creature who resist the will of the creator. Elymas (Bar-Jesus) has positioned himself between his own people and the gift of God for them. The irony of this should not escape us. How can there be those in the household of faith, among the people of God, who in fact, in word, and in deed become barriers to the flourishing of their own people in God? How can there be those who traffic in spirituality while seeking to block the Spirit? Saul, now become Paul, names the problem: here is one who has made himself a child of the evil one, an enemy of righteousness, and an obstacle to grace.

Paul follows Jesus in calling out his opposition and, by the power of the Spirit, collapses the operations of this man back on himself. Just as he would conceal the gospel from others, he will be made blind for a season and will need someone to lead him. Observing all of this is the proconsul, a servant of the State who is also a human being and also in need of the gospel. In all this we must not make too much of the conflict and too little of the proconsul. Unfortunately,

Christians have often read this text with skewed focus, seeing this primarily as a contestation of religions or a battle between religious worldviews when in fact an overcoming has been revealed. The Spirit yet overcomes false prophets and the Spirit can reach even servants of the State. Elymas is Jewish, yet of the people of God even in his allegiance to the devil and thusly he cannot stand in for other religions as a symbol of an imagined inherent opposition. There will be opposition (religious and otherwise), but we have already found its crucial sites, from within the household of faith and from the political and economic elites. It would be good for Christians to remember these primary sites of Spirit resistance and the Spirit's power to triumph even over them.

13:13–52

Between Diaspora and Antioch: The Christian Cosmopolitan

13:13–45

From the cosmopolitan church in Antioch to the diaspora synagogue, this journey is everything. Indeed Luke never gets beyond this movement. Even if the names of the churches change and the locales of the synagogues are different, this journey marks the rest of his narrative. The gospel that came for the Jews and found its way to the Gentiles is always of the Jews, and the gospel that came for the Gentiles and marked the way of the Jews always echoes back to the Jews their life in and with the Gentiles. Jew and Gentile together— this is the will of the Spirit, and it is also the story of Israel and the desiring God who seeks after them. Luke's narrative now takes on the unrelenting tensive character of a lover pensively speaking to her or his beloved. The lover here is not Luke, but God, and the desired love is Israel. Paul takes center stage and his voice, sometimes brutish, sometimes elegiac, sometimes eloquent, becomes the habitation for the Spirit's longings. Again Luke reveals the power as the storyteller as he refreshes the history of Israel. He moves from their beginning toward their telos in Jesus of Nazareth, and on the way he draws their attention not first to patriarchs or prophets but to the actions of everyday people who watched, and listened to Jesus, and participated in his murder.

It is the common people, formerly spectators, whom God is intensely watching and now addressing by the Spirit. For Luke, history turns directly in toward the bodies of those listening to Paul, who invites them into the freedom of Jesus. The story of Israel being told now enfolds its listeners by the Spirit, drawing them into the reality of the living God, who is the alpha and omega. It has always been about the crowd, the multitude, those in and outside of Israel. Paul and Barnabas are here speaking to the whole city, and the opposition is again present. This is the tension from which Luke can never find release, nor should he, because this is a tension of love. This is a call and a quarrel within Israel being overheard by those outside of Israel. Jewish leaders opposing Jewish followers of Jesus constitute a dilemma connected to an ancient struggle that reaches back to Moses and his desert wanderers and forward to the burden of Jesus. The dilemma intensifies that burden: if a resurrected Jesus and the presence of the Spirit are not enough to convince you, then what will? Luke does not have an answer, only another step forward—the Gentiles.

13:46–52

". . . we are now turning to the Gentiles," Paul and Barnabas say. This turning is cosmic and inclusive. God has already made clear the divine longing for the creation, so this is a turning toward Gentiles and not away from Jews. Gentiles are included in divine desire for Israel. The joy of Gentile inclusion is matched only by the pain of Paul and Barnabas' expulsion. So they do as disciples were commanded to do by Jesus: they shake the dust off their feet in protest. This should not be. There is pain in this passage, and we who read it now no longer sense the anguish of this story and the sorrow of its telling. That pain stands in stark contrast to the joy of those who were already and those who had now become disciples of Jesus. This is a contradiction at home in Luke's two-volume gospel. We have never handled this contradiction well in the church. Rather we have imagined God turning away from Israel in the face of

Jewish opposition, but such was never the case. Joy and sorrow are found at the site of this resistance. This is contradiction embedded in love, and to understand it requires the ability to enter the longings of the Spirit and share divine joy when anyone comes to the savior.

14:1–18

The Threat of Loss and the Promise of New Life

We who follow Jesus announce the corralling of violence, the drawing down of its range of influence, and the shrinking of its power, not by our ability to handle violence in its "proper use" but by our refusal to live subject to its power, or persuaded by its effectiveness.

We are now entering the serious struggles of diaspora. Lest we too quickly read Paul and Barnabas's enemies as pure reprobates, we must remember the anxieties of diaspora, the loss of identity and the confusion of peoples. Paul and Barnabas announce mixture and a theological cosmopolitanism that brings the bodies of Jews next to the bodies of Gentiles precisely in intimate holy space, the space where God is to be known and worshiped. They are, from the perspective of many faithful Jews, frightening insurgents who are drawing the people of God into sinking sand. These disciples were like an invading force. They dug in, stayed for a long time, and with word and incredible deeds gained strategic ground. Now the city is divided between them and us. This is the logic of those trapped in the fear of loss, of identity, of story, even of faith. Much is being threatened by Paul and Barnabas, and the only answer to this threat is extreme— by any means necessary. Nothing is off the table: deception, lying, manipulation, and violence. Ironically, Jews will call on Gentiles to help thwart this joining of Jews and Gentiles in Jesus. These apostles will know what so many disciples have known and continue to know—you will be threatened with death for the sake of the gospel. A disciple's life is often bound to death threats, and Luke does not portray their response as some kind of heroic ignoring of the danger. Such threats burden the soul. These disciples, because they can, flee the threat and thwart the planned assassination. We see here again a tragedy rooted in vision-distorting fear and resistance to the Spirit: the enemies of Barnabas and Paul would bring death to those who wish only to announce life.

There is, however, a disclosure of magnificent graciousness in this tumultuous situation. Paul and Barnabas enter Lystra, a strongly Gentile space, and offer the word of God. Luke again covers Paul in the mantle of apostolic authority. Paul heals a man unable to walk since birth. The choreography of the scene of healing that Luke gives us is beautiful. Paul was speaking and looking intensely at this disabled person. This man looks and hears Paul in faith. Paul can see faith in this man and then speaks loudly, "Stand to your feet" (v. 10). The man, as if joined to the strength of Paul's voice, gains strength in his limbs and leaps to his feet (*hēlato*) and begins to walk (*hēlato kai periepatei*, v.10). This is a dance of mutual recognition: Paul sees this man and the man sees Paul, and between them is a faith that heals. Together they are flowing in the currents of divine presence. Others sense that presence but misname it inside a Lycaonian cultural logic. They would mistake Barnabas and Paul for Zeus and Hermes.

Such mistakes are common without those who can clarify divine presence. These disciples begin that clarification by resisting any attempt to be equated with the divine. They tear their clothes, expose their flesh, and announce their share in the human condition. This is always the first work of clarification, the separating of the messengers of God from the presence of God. The church born of Gentiles always needs this clarification. We too often confuse our presence with the presence of God. We have indeed been joined but from God's side and not our own. These disciples, echoing the wisdom of Israel's life with God, know their difference pivots on the turning away from idols, especially human idols, and toward the living God. It is a turn they proclaim is possible for all. Again we see the graciousness of God embodied in these disciples. The God who has created all things allowed all peoples to follow their own ways and even in their waywardness offered to them the good gifts of a good creation. This is also the work of clarification. Divine presence is gracious presence, calling wayward creatures back to the creator and making clear a path toward life. This is a word from Israel for those outside of Israel, and only this word separates life with the living God from life with idols. Barnabas and Paul in this moment are at the frontier of faith and the threshold of God's love for those who sense divine presence but do not know God's name.

14:19–28

The Victory over Violence

Saul, who had found the use of violence an effective tool for promoting the cause of Israel's God, now finds himself subject to violence for the sake of that same God. There is of course a world of difference between the Saul who saw stones hit the body of Stephen (chap. 7) and this Paul whose body received stone blows. It is the difference of a world turned upside down by a God who always surprises us with a new word that can change us. Yet the connection of violence to a religious imagination seems to be unavoidable. Is it actually the case that the disciples of Jesus will always need to negotiate the realities of violence? Will violence always circulate around our bodies and near our words? The life of Jesus and now the life of Paul seem to suggest that this is so. Violence is in the world that God never ceases to love, and the disciples are placed between that violence and those subject to its pull. We who follow Jesus announce the corralling of violence, the drawing down of its range of influence, and the shrinking of its power, not by our ability to handle violence in its "proper use" but by our refusal to live subject to its power, or persuaded by its effectiveness. We remember: "When those who were around him saw what was coming, they asked, 'Lord, should we strike with the sword?' Then one of them struck the slave of the high priest and cut off his right ear. But Jesus said, 'No more of this!' And he touched his ear and healed him" (Luke 22:49–51).

Those who stoned Paul used violence's power to ensure their victory. They removed him from the scene of their crime and the attention of those who saw it. Concealment also seems to go with violence; the deed done is a deed to be hidden. Paul is left for dead, and here we meet more holy work. The disciples are those who surround people left for dead. We have no indication of a prayer, a word, or medical intervention made on behalf of Paul, only a group of disciples surrounding his body. None of these things (prayer, word, or medical intervention) is demanded by the text, but all of it could be implied by it. What *is* clear is the encircling of a wounded body and soul by those who would care for him. Could it be that what allows Paul to rise from a deathlike state is precisely the strength that flows through those who have yielded to the strength of the Spirit? Paul gets up and returns to the city. He returns to the work, and this is astounding and will be paradigmatic. What does it mean to offer good news to those who tried to kill you? What does it mean to offer the word of life to those angling for your demise, and after they had almost accomplished your death?

Disciples get hurt. Disciples carry wounds and before we make them metaphysical, drawing them into a spiritual alchemy, we must keep them real. We who follow Jesus are working in wounds, working with wounds, and working through wounds. The "we" is crucial here. Paul returns to Barnabas and together they go forward. No one should work with their wounds alone, indeed the words that follow Paul's rising from the stones is a word put in the plural. *They* strengthened the souls of the disciples, *they* encouraged them to continue in the faith, and *they* said in seeming chorus, "It is through many persecutions that we must enter the kingdom of God" (v. 22). The shared work of disciples in strengthening and encouraging others can make the pain productive, not because we ignore the wounds but rather we come to see them in their true light. These are the wounds of Christ that we share for his sake. These are the marks of rejections and shame carried for the sake of this world. So these disciples continued to establish the church, moving forward by the Spirit, because it is the Spirit who heals us and calls us ever more deeply into the divine longing, ever more deeply into the divine desire for the world. These travelers returned home to Antioch after a journey filled with pain and joy and most importantly filled with the presence of a God of indefatigable love. There in Antioch they tell their story with its new chapters, and it is a story that confirms the truth of Antioch: We are church together, Jew and Gentile.

15:1–33
The Antiochene Body and the Jewish Body

*We struggle over what faithful bodies must look like and
over their alignment—their conformity to dominant culture,
normative orientation, aesthetic form, or intellectual
temperament. We, like the Judean disciples, are tempted
to control the unknown and domesticate difference.*

15:1–6

Judean believers came to Antioch with what they took to be a clarifying word. They entered Antioch in clarity, clear that they knew Gentiles and their idolatrous ways. These Jewish disciples knew where Gentiles would lead them if left unchecked. So they came seeking to establish alignment—in order to enter the way of salvation you must follow the way of Moses. At one level we should understand this as cultural and theological alignment, but at another level it was an alignment of identity and story for the purpose of control. If Gentiles were now within the story of Israel, then their bodies must be brought into conformity. Circumcision was at the center of a world of signifiers that announced a body changed—gone the Gentile and now appears the Jew. Others who worshipped the God of Israel and found the Torah a source of light had already found such alignment. It was a proper step, and a necessary step. It would reestablish the line between Jew and Gentile, yet within the saving sphere of Jesus.

The Judean disciples did not know, however, that Antiochene bodies, that is, Christian bodies, were spread across the line dividing Jew/Gentile, forming a bridge that would never be destroyed. Much like the people who stretched their bodies across roads and bridges, highways and city halls, during the civil rights movement, forming a bridge from the hateful South to new possibilities of justice, the saints at Antioch were what Katya Gibel Azoulay calls an interruption. These Antiochene bodies "represent[ed] a contestation, and [they] undermine[d] the authority of classification."[13] The smooth flow from Gentile to Jew, from other to an assimilated other,

13. Katya Gibel Azoulay, *Black, Jewish, and Interracial* (Durham: Duke University Press, 1997), 41.

was being challenged not by Jews and Gentiles who resisted the life of Israel but who were inside its expansion. This is the struggle of faith that is about the faithful, who they may be and *how* they may be. We yet struggle over faithful bodies and over their necessary alignment—their conformity to dominant culture, normative orientation, aesthetic form, or intellectual temperament. We, like the Judean disciples, are tempted to control the unknown and domesticate difference. Paul and Barnabas, however, said no.

Sometimes the new requires we say "no." "No, we will not conform to what you imagine as the will of God. No, we will not become what you imagine we must be." Paul and Barnabas embodied the Antiochene "no." Luke clearly has his hands on an irrupting volcano scarcely below the easy surface of the narrative. Here is great dissension (*stasis*) and debate (*zetesis*) that led Antioch back to Jerusalem and the joining of spaces that would mean the joining of worlds. How do you capture in words the dynamic of life together, not just life together but a holy joining of life, the life of the Spirit of God within our lives? How do you capture not simply a new movement but a movement that always renews and makes new? Luke has from the very beginning of his narrative set about the task of ascribing a creative process of obedience to the Spirit that draws us into God's desire to commune with creation. The goal is love and the place is us. This chapter pivots into our present moment, weaving together our crucial beginnings and our present endeavors. Luke made sure we understood that this was coming. From the stunning beginnings of the assertive Spirit who overshadows the disciples and draws them into the lives of others, to the intense pressing of other disciples to go where they would prefer not to go, to the binding together of Jewish and Gentile bodies in the life of the Son, Luke performed through writing the new thing God was performing. God is always ahead of us, calling to us to keep up and not turn back. We sometimes forget how strong the pull back is for us. This is not a matter of sin or our sinful condition. Nor is this a matter of faithlessness. It is fundamentally the struggle with the new and the unknown even if it is perceived by us as neither new nor unknown.

They were all there—Luke's protagonists, Peter, and James, Paul, and Barnabas—and so was the debate. Luke holds up this debate and the obvious pain and struggle that must have been part of it as a reality of the Spirit working the divine will. Yet no one was cast as evil, a child of the devil and thereby relegated to blindness or death by worms. We could call this debate, this struggle, the necessary birth pangs of the new, but that would border on the trite. No woman in the misery of childbirth finds it ordained. No couple captured in the turmoil of life's beginnings in labor would call it right and good.

15:7–33

This debate is a river that must be crossed. It is a mountain that must be climbed as they follow the Spirit. The fact that they could even have a debate might be interpreted as a sign of salvation and a sure mark of a shared story, a shared way of reasoning that could bring them light. But that would be too simplistic a way of grasping the salvation in their midst. The debate itself brought no light, only the need for light. Only when Peter recalled where the Spirit of God had led him, into the lives of those he did not want to know, did this group see the way forward. That way forward was found in testimony, in truth embodied in flesh. Yet it was the Spirit's testimony, the Spirit's experience of indwelling the Gentiles, that Peter had heard and seen. It was the work of the Spirit in cleansing hearts (v. 9) that brought to Peter the radical truth that the line between Jew and Gentile has been crossed.

Peter is thinking out loud, moving on new terrain created by the Spirit. He is yet speaking in Israel and to Israel, but the ground has shifted, cracked open to expose another layer beneath the layer they and their ancestors had been moving and living on. This under layer had been there all the time, giving life to the people, and now that grace was being exposed not by the cunning of reason, but by grace's embodiment, Jesus Christ. God's hand on Gentile flesh was just as full and free as it was on Jewish flesh. Luke has brought us inside a paradigm shift as it is taking place in Israel. What God is doing now will become the way in which the faithful must discern what they should be doing and how they should interpret God's actions in the past. This is risky work. It is as though Peter is suspended on a tightrope high in the air, and those watching him are reduced to wonder and silence.

We have already suggested that silence might fruitfully be seen in these Lukan passages like musical breaks, where a space is created for someone to solo, carrying the rhythm and the sense of time. So Barnabas and Paul step into the silence and continue in the power of testimony, recounting like Peter the signs and wonders (*sēmeia kai terata*, v. 12) God was doing among the Gentiles. This is word of God exploding in front of them, and what must now happen is nothing less than quilting work. James, in a beautiful moment of pure theological interpretation, performs this quilting work. James pulls fragments from the prophets and weaves their words to this word of God revealed in the Spirit's workings on flesh. This will be the way forward—interpreters of biblical texts that yield to the Spirit recognizing the grace of working with the fragments. As Luke Timothy Johnson suggests, "the text of Scripture does not dictate how God should act. Rather, God's actions dictate how we should understand the text of Scripture."[14] Quilting Scripture is of the new order. Such interpretive work takes seriously a living God who lives in and with the human creature and who invites us to weave together word of God spoken (in the past) with word of God being spoken into lives (in the present) by the Spirit.

Luke's James weaves a tapestry that strains at its seams as it tries to cover Gentile flesh. This is not a failure of his quilting technique, nor is he resistant to the work of the Spirit. James is groping to conceive the new possibilities of relationship with Gentiles. His decision, while aimed by Gentiles, is in fact for Jews. His recommendations would make table-fellowship with Gentiles possible for Jews. Indeed such table-fellowship does open the door to the possibilities of life together precisely in the most intimate reality of communal existence, the sharing of food. Yet James's powerful recommendation is at a distance. We must never forget this distance.

Unfortunately, it has often gone unnoticed by too many readers and commentators on this scene in Acts. The Gentiles are there, but not there, spoken *about* but not spoken *with*. This is a scene of

14. Luke Timothy Johnson, *The Acts of the Apostles* (Collegeville: The Liturgical Press, 1992), 271.

the Gentile-in-theory, not the Gentile-in-reality in conversation, in reciprocal and mutual interaction. How could there have been mutual interaction and reciprocity at this early stage? Would that not have been premature, problematic, or even impossible? The danger with thinking pragmatically at this moment is to normalize this absence.

The church has been guilty of just such normalization. We have too often imagined ecclesial deliberations about others in abstraction, even if they have been bodily present. Even if the words spoken are good and accepting words as long as those words turn bodies into objects, they have not yet reached their intended goal. What is the goal of James's words? They seem to be aimed at removing impediments for communion. What should be the goal of our words? The goal must be communion and joining. The church in many instances and in many places is yet caught in the moment of objectification of others—the other-in-theory. We have normalized this privileged position and failed to see it for what it is—a step in the right direction that yet lacks the full humanity that must be realized in Christ. So a delegation is sent to the Gentiles with James's words, and the Antiochene saints rejoice at this word of inclusion. But the real joy is what comes after at the place where humanity appears in communion. There is time together: Judas and Silas and Barnabas and Paul are there together with the Christians in Antioch, the church of Jerusalem with the church in Antioch, Jew and Gentile. Recommended life gives way to real life.

The only body capable of taking us *all* in as we are with all our different body marks . . . is the body of Christ. This taking us in, this in-corporation, is akin to sublation, not erasure, not uniformity: the *basileia* praxis of Jesus draws us up to him. Our humble engagement in his praxis revalues our identities and differences, even as it preserves the integrity and significance of our body marks. At the same time, those very particular body marks are relativized, reoriented, and re-appropriated under his sign, the sign of the cross. Thus in solidarity and in love of others and the Other, we are (re)made and (re)marked as the flesh of Christ, as the flesh of his church.

M. Shawn Copeland, *Enfleshing Freedom: Body, Race, and Being* (Minneapolis: Fortress Press, 2010), 83.

FURTHER REFLECTIONS
The Seduction of Segregation

Acts 15 confronts us with the difference between Jew and Gentile, and between the people of God and Gentile peoples. This difference is crucial because it illumines a God who creates all peoples and through the Spirit issues an invitation to life together. The difference between Israel and the Gentiles and the differences among Gentile peoples does not occasion God's anger but God's delight, because the creation's multiplicity and variety signal the mystery of the creature that God embraces as its creator. Israel's life reveals that their God is also the God of the Gentiles, but the point of this revelation is not merely shared knowledge of God but a shared life with God (Isa. 2:1–4). The differences among peoples in this regard is not an inevitable impediment for relationship but the very stage on which God will create a deeper and richer reality of communion with the divine life.

Acts 15 brings us to the interface of creaturely difference and divine desire where God exposes both bound toward each other in ways never before seen in Israel and among the Gentiles. God draws us without destroying us, without eradicating the differences among the creatures. Jews with Gentiles and Gentile peoples with each other, all borne on the wings of God's desire toward life together in the Spirit of God. The single greatest challenge for disciples of Jesus is to imagine and then enact actual together life, life that interpenetrates, weaves together, and joins to the bone. We have been unable to imagine and enact a together life that flows inside the subtleties and intricacies of peoples' differences, of such things as language, story, land, and animals. It has been easier to imagine either loss or resistance—loss of difference through assimilation or its control through conquest, or resistance to its loss through active segregation. *How can peoples be joined together, truly joined together without loss, without the death of one (people's ways) for the sake of the other?* This question's strength lay in our centuries-long inability to answer it.

The dominant way of imaging people together has been forms of cultural and social parallelism (peoples living parallel lives) that underwrite segregationist mentalities. Segregation is an ancient strategy for constructing a world, and we could categorize it in three forms that often enfold and inform each other.

There is *spatial segregation* that creates distinct geographic spheres of life and activity that maintain and control populations and guide the flows of commerce. Spatial segregation easily works itself down into our collective subconscious and teaches us to see peoples as naturally and normally separated for their own good and according to their own desire for separation. Spatial segregation gets woven into the material reality of habitation in the design of buildings, streets, neighborhoods, and cities, and can help perpetuate inequalities, xenophobia, racism, and violence simply by how it has arranged our daily movements and activities.

There is *cultural segregation* whereby people maintain subtle or obvious boundaries to their language, stories, practices, indigenous knowledge, or even history. They may live and interact with other peoples but they maintain a psychic distance and a clear and palpable sense of the other as outsider.

Then there is *desperate segregation* characterized by its fragmentary and episodic character. Here people seek to separate for the sake of survival. They are inundated with the forces of assimilation that constantly seek to render their peoples, their bodies, their ways of thinking, speaking, and being in the world as negative realities—deficient, unworthy of respect, ugly, dangerous, primitive, backward, shameful, or hopeless. They seek solace in the company of their own people for whatever time they need to gather the fragments of their cultural life to clothe themselves afresh for their troubled journey into a hostile world.

We are the inheritors of the legacy of segregation that has powerfully and successfully reduced the way we imagine church life. We have settled for what was gestured at in Acts 15, a form of segregation that allowed Gentile believers to go their own way and for Jewish believers to leave them alone (Acts 15:29). We have followed a segregationist trajectory and settled for a unity in the Spirit that denies that the creaturely body is destined for communion not only with God but with others. Churches are woven in difference, different cultures, languages, forms of life, histories, stories, hopes, and dreams. This difference is never static but always moving, breathing, living, changing and adapting, filled with continuities and disconti- nuities, augmentations and transformations, some to be celebrated and some to be mourned. This is the way of the creature that God has created and intensely loves. Yet the fallacy too many people have accepted is that difference can only be maintained by some form of segregation.

Difference is best maintained, maintained in its life-giving reali- ties, through communion with others. Only in life, shared, joined, and exchanged in desire of being made permanent, can differences emerge in their deepest beauty—as invitations to the expansion of life and love. The Gentiles learn of Israel's story, enter its prayer life, learn its songs and in turn bring into Israel a world of difference that expands the contours of its life with God, and all of this through Jesus Christ, the giver of life. Of course, we live in the aftermath of modern colonialism and its intercourse with Christianity, which has robbed the church of the imaginative habit and the strong cour- age to embrace difference knowing that, through the process of embrace, its own creaturely life will expand, drawing it into more intense awareness of God, its creator. For too many peoples their sense of safety, comfort, and normalcy only comes in and through forms of segregation, because they have never seen or felt anything otherwise. Segregated spaces are for them the places where they see and know themselves.

This is especially the case for too many Christians. The seduction of segregation, however, hides the fact that such self-knowledge is facile and conceals our true calling—to be joined to another and then another. Self-knowledge and the knowledge of a people are quilt-like. They are designed to be broken open and woven with other knowledges, patterned in and with peoples so that sight of each can be seen together with others in ways that illumine each in its majesty. Here in such shared self-knowledge, fragmentation works life not death, indeed it overcomes death and isolation. What are these fragments, and what does it mean to be broken open in this way? Is this a matter of violence, conquest, and brutality? The breaking open is not an external action but an intimate one, like the breaking of a loaf of bread and the sharing of a meal. The breaking open is when someone chooses to offer what is in them to another. These are the fragments of life, of memory, story, hope, dream, touch, laughter, tears, friendship, family, and so forth.

Admittedly, the breaking open and the fragments now exist for us under the melancholic conditions of the aftermath of colonialism, where too many peoples in this world have had and are yet having their cultural realities shattered by nations and multinational corporations who relentlessly commodify their remains—their foods, their animals, their land, their stories, their rituals, and even their body parts. Yet the way forward is not through re-segregation but through the breaking open of the lives of those who benefit greatly from the soul-killing operations of nation-states and multinational corporations, and through joining with those whose bodies and stories have been marked by an unanticipated and unwanted shattering that yet haunts them. A quilting of lives together is always possible, no matter how profound the tearing. This is what those who have released their social imaginations to segregationist ways of thinking must come to see. Segregation, then, is not simply a political or ethical problem. It undermines our doctrine of creation, and it constantly robs us of sensing together the full reality of our creatureliness and the embrace of God our creator.

Segregation is powerfully seductive because it joins the aspirations of the rich and powerful to the aspirations of those of diaspora and exile. Segregation gives to both groups the illusion of a self-determination that will run from the present moment into the future. Yet segregation also promises a space of relief, rest, and safety where the secrets of a people may be spoken without shame or fear of retaliation. Life in cultural, economic, and social silos, performed in multiple parallel lines, is the inner logic of too many communities, and such configurations accepted by Christians confront the church with its deepest sin: it denies the power of the living Spirit.

Indeed too many pastors and church leaders have made themselves the high priest of segregationist practices. They have settled for the love of their own people instead of a love that creates a people. They have, out of the sheer need to be accepted, embraced, and celebrated, refused the holy work of the people of God to accept, embrace, and celebrate others different from themselves. Too many pastors believe that a pastoral ministry that upholds the dignity and cultural integrity of their own people must come first in some strange hierarchy of ministerial tasks that would later (at some point in time) open toward embracing other peoples. Of course, the time for fully embracing others never comes, because it cannot emerge in this distorted vision of pastoral ministry. These pastors and church leaders have forgotten the basic truth of their faith and their calling— they serve the God of another people, a Jewish God bound to the people of Israel. Indeed they eat this Jewish God's body and blood with great joy. They belong to the multitude that includes their own people as well. They belong to a God who has filled them with the Spirit and who has opened their lives toward that growing, swelling multitude.

God sees better that they do the urgent needs of their own people. God understands more intimately and deeply than they do the need for advocacy and support for their own people. Yet God asks of us in our hearing and feeling and doing to sense a wider urgency that binds us together in shared hurt and pain, need and longing. God seeks to join the vulnerable together across boundaries that have taught them to see their vulnerability in isolation, in separation from the others who cry out in need and live in hope. To be a disciple of Jesus is to be a bridge between the cries of my people and the cries of other peoples that can be heard in the distance. Every word we speak belongs to the multitude, before it belongs to our people. Every holy utterance aimed at our own people moves to them and through them to others waiting and willing and eager to hear that word. All that is necessary is for all of us to yield to the eager Spirit who waits for us to see beyond a segregationist mind into the mind of Christ and hear a calling that cannot be contained but only obeyed.

15:35–41

The Risk of Trust

It is a small scene in Luke's panoramic vision, but it deserves our attention because it gives witness to a struggle the disciples of Jesus know so well. Whom can one depend on and trust? Paul and Barnabas now know the cost of discipleship and the perils of following the Spirit. Their lives have been and will continue to be on the line, and they need those who will share in the risk of ministry with them. There is an inescapable vulnerability that shapes the lives of disciples, and it cannot be borne alone. Companions are needed and friendship is required, the kind that carries the same realities of covenantal loyalty to the God of Israel and faithfulness to the gospel. This is companionship and friendship in a different key, a different, more intense register. It carries the emotional density of life in the Spirit. Yet disappointment and betrayal also mark human relationships, even for those joined in the gospel.

Mark had failed Paul and Barnabas. We do not know the details, but we know enough to know this familiar terrain. It is the jagged edges of working with people who are uneven in their temperament, capacities, or consistency precisely in the moments that we cannot afford that unevenness. Mark had abandoned the mission. This was an act of apostasy (*ton apostanta*, v. 38). For Paul, this was a nonnegotiable, a line that could not be crossed. If discipleship is a choice then companionship is as well. If discipleship is not a choice for those who have been chosen by God, then companionship may also not be a choice. One may be forced to work with those whom God has given. Trust, however, will always be a choice. Paul did not trust Mark, but Barnabas was willing to move forward with him. We are not sure why Barnabas was willing. It could be that he was related to Mark and imagined him inside of kinship care. It could also be due to another reason that we now know so well, a reason that draws us close to the character of Barnabas in Luke's narrative.

Barnabas's voice has always been complicated in the narrative because it is seemingly always bound to Paul's voice, inseparable from his actions. Barnabas is, however, more than co-traveler with Paul. Barnabas always seems to be ahead of Paul, drawing Paul to where he should be. It was Barnabas who was there at the Apostle's feet (Acts 4:36–37), giving his possessions and thereby showing us how it should be done. It was Barnabas who took a dangling Saul up to Jerusalem so he might be accepted by the apostles (Acts 9:27). It was Barnabas who set Paul's hands to the right plow in Antioch, making him a co-laborer in the new work among Gentiles (Acts 11:25). Barnabas was a bridge for Paul from the old to the new. If the apostles had named him the "son of encouragement," then Luke's narrative names him risk-taker, because Barnabas seemed to always make heavy wager on people.

Now was no different. Mark should come with them. This is Barnabas's wager. As is the case in the other appearances of Barnabas in the text, we do not have his own words. We never have Barnabas's words. It is as though Barnabas's actions speak for him, and now Mark stands between Barnabas and Paul, each reading Mark from a different and completely true angle. These perspectives on Mark could not be reconciled and neither could Paul and Barnabas. There is no tragedy here, simply the truth that the risks of ministry are inseparable from the risks of relationship. Yet it seems that Barnabas was still ahead of Paul, trying to bring him where he needed to be in that inescapable struggle of trusting those who have or might or will fail us. Barnabas took Mark and disappeared from Luke's narrative, but he entered our future marking the path for those who would be the disciples of Jesus. That path requires trust—sometimes, often times, almost every time—of those who are marked by failure in relationship.

16:1–21:40

The Spirit and the End of Segregation

16:1–8

The In-between Disciple

The power of in-between existence (Christian existence) is love without contradiction, and such love is always possible. It is possible for Timothy to love the Gentiles of his father and the Jews of his mother and with both and through both and in both to perform his commitment to Jesus. This is the inner logic of a Christian—to perform multiple loves in loving Jesus.

16:1–2

Timothy appears, the mulatto child. He was destined to appear, because they are always present in diaspora where Jew and Gentile meet in the spaces of exile and longing. Luke notes the mixed marriage that gave life to him: his mother was Jewish, and his father was Greek. His mother was a believer, his father seemingly not. There somewhere between Derbe and Lystra was someone who enfolded interracial space in his body. We must again acknowledge the anachronism of suggesting interraciality at this moment in history. Yet it captures the depth of diaspora concern that flows through these few verses. Commentators tend to run much too quickly past Timothy to come to Paul and the complications of his mission. The mission, however, should in truth be read through the prism of Timothy's body. The mulatto body is always the individual body and the social body at the same time. It is simultaneously the body of hope and the body of fear, the body of revulsion and the body of desire.

What every people find most unsettling is a body formed between two peoples, their people and that of another people, especially an enemy. That body already suggests betrayal and undisciplined desire and maybe even loss, the death of identity and story. Who are you? What a strange question. Yet this is the thorn-infested question that many interracial children have pressed back on them as though they can answer a question that only a people can answer. Such a question is and will always be an unfair burden for any one person whose mother and father flow from different and sometimes antagonistic streams of culture, language, land, or story. The question becomes even more acute in diaspora space, where the cultic identity and story of a people must be guarded against destruction and decay.

We stand on a history of such destruction rooted in the hyper-acidic effects of colonialism and Western imperialism on so many of the world's peoples. So many are now awash in whiteness, trying to swim against the tide of an abiding Euro-centered aesthetic regime that seeks to define the true, the good, and the beautiful in and through and around white bodies. So many imagine themselves (whether at home or abroad) in diaspora space with all the fears and anxieties of cultic erasure and cultural loss at the hands of those with the power to impose their formidable preferences as the true universals. But what about the disciples of Jesus, and what about this disciple of Jesus, Timothy? Timothy constitutes the in-between. His life presents the shifting plates of identity on which we all stand. Ironically, the mixed child should not answer the question of identity but *is* a question simultaneously pressed back toward at least two peoples—do *you* know who you are? Timothy is the truth that no people are closed off and completely sealed unto themselves. No people group is beyond the embrace of God, which is not a hypothetical or ephemeral embrace, but an enfleshed embrace. Timothy is Jew-Gentile-Christian. He is dangerous power born of the Spirit and desire.

16:3–8

Timothy is not a wanderer or homeless. He is at home in the worlds of Jew and Gentile precisely because he is a Christian. He is already

what the Christian must be—a question to everyone and every people—and he is also an answer. Commentators argue endlessly over
Paul's actions with Timothy here, but what if we read this text from
the sight lines of Timothy? He is circumcised, his body made acceptable to Jews. It was indeed Paul's design, but it was also Timothy's
choice. It was the choice of a disciple of Jesus who, with Paul, was
following the Spirit. This is the way of in-between flesh, of mulatto
existence. Timothy, through his flesh, pressed deeply into Jewish
flesh not as an evangelistic ploy or as acquiescence to assimilation,
but out of his commitment to his people, that is, one of his peoples.
The others were there too with him in the cutting of his flesh. Their
flesh was cut as well.

It would be confusing at this point to separate the cultic from the
theological, to see in Timothy's discipleship a cultural act devoid of
theological content or a reversal of commitment to Jesus in order
to reclaim faithfulness to Torah. Such ways of reading this have not
followed the way of the Spirit registered by Luke. Through the Spirit
nothing is lost, but other things are added. Timothy is registering his
love for the people to whom God is sending him, and he does so in
the way that discipleship demands, through his flesh, and so must
we. This is the way of the Spirit. The power of in-between existence
(Christian existence) is love without contradiction, and such love
is always possible. It is possible for Timothy to love the Gentiles of
his father and the Jews of his mother and with both and through
both and in both to perform his commitment to Jesus. This is the
inner logic of the Christian. We can inhabit new cultural sites of love,
different languages, different holy gestures, different customs and
rituals of life, and perform through the Spirit deepening love for the
world and for Jesus the Christ, the savior of the world. Such loves
presents no competition and no conflicted loyalties. It only gestures
overwhelming addition. This is a work of the Spirit for those led by
the Spirit.

Timothy is an embodied word that matches the word of Paul and
Silas. How can this be? How can newly circumcised flesh present
the new order? By drawing the story of Israel forward through the
body of one whose body is also of the Goyim—Timothy is born of

transgressing love, and his circumcision confirms and transgresses. He is of Israel, but now Israel's promise is enfolded in Gentile flesh. But does Timothy need this enfleshed conformity to be acceptable and safe from persecution, maybe even violence? There is no doubt that this is the case. He moves with Paul and Silas in a dangerous world of diaspora anxiety. That world, however, while new to Paul and Silas, is not new to him. Yet Timothy will draw circumcision into the improvisation that has always been his life. Now through the Spirit of God that improvisation has been taken up into the Spirit and drawn inside the Spirit's own creative work. Old (circumcision) will gesture the new body. Circumcision will not be necessary, but it will be made beautifully useful for faith and in faith.

FURTHER REFLECTIONS
Intercultural and Interracial Life

What does it mean to be born of two peoples? This is not a question of genealogy, or of genetic testing or of ancestry. It is a question of boundary, and of being both inside and outside simultaneously, and how to negotiate a life that interrupts the smooth flow of cultural alliance and racial reasoning. Timothy's appearance in the book of Acts raises these kinds of questions. Throughout history there have been those born between peoples, sometimes warring peoples. In other times there have been those born between peoples simply foreign to each other. The modern period wove together two kinds of in-between existence, racial existence between white and nonwhite (between peoples of European descent and peoples of non-European descent), and existence between people of different cultures, tribes, or nations. However complicated it may be to conceive of two within the strange muddy waters of racial reasoning and cultural difference, the crucial dynamic remains the same—two peoples are within one body. Something new, unpredictable, and, even for some, terribly threatening presents itself in the life of a person who presents such unions.

They represent less a loss of purity (although there have been those obsessed with such a notion) and much more a question of allegiance. Timothy faced a question of allegiance that did not draw from his actions but simply by his in-between existence. Allegiance tests are ancient, and today they exists among us in their most insidious and destructive forms—at the intersection of racial reasoning and cultural difference. They exempt no one. They are presented to us at every stage in life. They are presented to kids who look, talk, act, or respond too much like kids from the other group. They are presented to adults who appear too comfortable or too friendly with cultural rivals or racial enemies. They move effortlessly through political parties, theological positions, social, and class tastes, working their way down to the choices we make in food, dress, entertainment, and pleasure. Who we love and how we love must negotiate allegiance tests, and no one ever moves beyond the possibility of an examination. People who embody the in-between often expose more intensely than any others the relentless pressure of allegiance tests.

Inter-existence, bicultural or biracial, could be held softly or strongly, be acknowledge or denied, be actively resisted or passionately affirmed. It does not necessarily dictate a melancholia or existential turmoil and a hapless longing for the calm waters of homogeneity. To live in between presents a possibility of turning a question on peoples that has rarely been asked: Could you imagine a new way of seeing and being yourself? For us captured in the cross currents of racial and cultural forms of belonging, such a question must be asked. Too much of Western life and all those sites touched by the legacies of colonialism are dogged by forms of belonging that narrow the possibilities of life lived in its fullness. It remains a horrible fact that racial and cultural belonging are most often far more powerful and compelling than Christian belonging. The form of belonging that Christians witness should in fact be a profound question to everyone who encounters us: Could you imagine a new way of seeing and being yourself, a way that weaves together the ways of many peoples?

So many churches have never understood their in-between reality, their Timothy-like existence. Indeed the church is formed precisely inside the very body of Jesus Christ, fully human and fully

God. Jesus presents to us a question: Could we imagine a new way of seeing both God and human existence? Would we enter a new way of being in and through him? The church worried over how to uphold the integrity and dignity of both human existence and the divine life in how it articulated the life and reality of Jesus. Even while the language churches have used over the centuries has struggled to adequately speak the beauty of Jesus' life, one insight remained clear—humanity and divinity are not ideas that we must find ways to fit Jesus into, rather Jesus defines for us both humanity and divinity. His life does not simply hold them together; his life shows us what they are, and who we are in God. Jesus turns the question we might bring to him regarding how he is the God-human into a question for us: Will we join him on a life journey woven in God and bound to eternity?

The church should be the place that suspends the worry of how multiple peoples may coinhere together, not by avoiding such complexity but through showing a collective body moving, living, and struggling to form a space of life and love. Indeed the joining of multiple peoples is born of the desire of the Spirit and enabled only as we yield to the Spirit and turn in relentless embrace of one another. Too few churches have been able to live the in-between because it requires entering the humility formed in the crucible of Jesus' body, where we see God's own desire to touch the creature from within the realities of creatureliness and in the midst of our hostilities and hatred of God (Rom. 5:6–10). To give way to that divine desire means to attune our minds and bodies to the joy of learning and living with other peoples precisely within the contexts of histories and social matrices that have made and yet press us to be enemies. Such in-between existence is not an unattainable goal. It is the reality that surrounds the Christian. Our goal must be to embrace to it.

16:9–19

A Tale of Two Women

Through dream and vision, the Spirit leads the disciples. Paul and Silas are flowing in the liminal space between spaces where they are present to others through the Spirit and where their senses are tuned to wider frequencies of communication. Dream and vision are not counter to the concrete realities of this world, but rather they present this world in its fullness. Dream and vision are from God but also bound to our bodies, and they constitute a concourse for the activity of the Holy Spirit. Luke draws us inside his geographic imagination, which moves us through Troas, Samothrace, Neapolis, to the Roman colony Philippi, and to following the disciples outside its city gate and down to the river to a place of prayer. There, in approximation to this place of prayer, the disciples enter the lives of two very different women, Lydia, the businesswoman, and another woman, a slave girl.

So much of the concrete work of discipleship can be located between these two women. Together they illumine the space in which the living Christ will further enact the new order. Lydia's heart has been opened by the Spirit, and she will follow a pattern similar to Cornelius: she and her household will be baptized, and she will draw the disciples into her home. Equally powerful, she draws the new order of discipleship into the economic order that has established her life as a wealthy woman. Again possessions are placed in service to the reign of God, and Lydia is at the center of this reordering of economies, both civic and domestic. She makes her home a site of the new intimacy of the Spirit and forms it into what will become a cell of the church. Luke leaves ambiguous whether she is Jewish or Gentile, only that she was in the space of listening Israel, and from that space she hears the words embodied in these disciples.

Like Cornelius, Lydia is a person of power and prestige. She is a wealthy businesswoman and finds herself a harbinger of the new—a wealthy woman whose center of operation has been given over to the Spirit of God. Surely, we can see and sense in this story a giving up and a giving over in Lydia's actions similar to those who laid their possessions at the apostles' feet. Here is power put to good use. This exact dynamic has been at the foundations of so many social movements in the world where women of wealth have turned the full power of their resources toward insurgent endeavors that would facilitate a day of liberation. Lydia the rich woman is also a disciple of Jesus. This is a template that promises to redefine the identity-constituting forces of money and gender. Lydia is now living *contra mundi*, against the world, even as she is yet marked by the worldly trappings of domestic dominance. The Spirit is leading her to act out of the social order and into the new order. Yet to see the full potential of this template we must also see its deep connection to the other woman in this story, the slave girl.

Again the place of prayer looms in the backdrop of the disciples' encounter with this other woman. As the disciples journeyed toward prayer they gained a co-traveler who haunted their prayer walk. Such haunting is necessary and of the Spirit, as the tormented cries of the enslaved must always encumber the pious actions of the faithful. This young woman spoke a tangled word, one that wove together the old order with confused sight of the new order. She was a slave girl and nameless. These realities went together, because in the ancient world to be a slave was to be only a commodity, only a body in use, and a site of penetration. Yet she followed these disciples of Jesus, announcing their mission. But here the entanglements are severe and expose the often mutual indwelling of religion and slavery, and of religious discourse and captivity to an economic order. It is no accident that she is drawn to these disciples, because the enslaved are often drawn to those who are religious, either as an echoing sign of their own enslavement, deepening further the power of that captivity, or as a hopeful possibility of their emancipation.

> We do not . . . always find women in the Bible who provide answers for the problems of today. But we do find women who inspire *us* to devise the answers.
>
> Mercy Amba Oduyoye, *Daughters of Anowa: African Women and Patriarchy* (Maryknoll, NY: Orbis Books, 2000), 192.

This woman seems to see herself in the disciples. They are slaves as she is a slave, her religious proclamation somehow matching their word. This, however, is a sick optic. The slaveries are not the same, yet they exist in the same world and can be and have been historically easily confused. One great danger for the disciples here is precisely such confusion. Repeatedly the church has confused its obedience with the obedience of those enslaved, imagining the ordered and organized life of a Christian or a community to be a similitude to a slave body or a slave plantation. There is great pleasure in imagining someone or some people doing exactly what we want, especially if we fantasize that what we want of them is also what God wants of them.

This danger is bound to another great danger for disciples and that is to see the words of the slave girl, such affirming proclamation of their ministry, as part of the good news. It is not. It is the tortured speech of the enslaved masquerading as gospel word. These enslaved and enslaving words can become intoxicating to the disciples of Jesus, because they come to those who journey into new or foreign places, carrying all the intense realities of missionary vulnerability where you hope to be accepted and heard. Disciples can become addicted to such praise and affirmation and indeed can reinforce the exploitation of the enslaved by keeping them close only for their use-value. The slave girl performs her captivity precisely in her religious speech, and disciples can get high on and become addicted to such talk. Disciples can ever turn the ministry of the gospel into the feverish activity of an addict. There is a deep connection between her god-talk and her fortune telling: both are inside the logic of exchange of spiritual power and material wealth. However, her agency in all this is quite complex, as agency is always complex. A demonic spirit is making use of her body just as her owners are making use of her. Indeed the demonic and economic are bound together here, and Paul touches their connection.

> Disciples must never turn the ministry of the gospel into the feverish activity of an addict.

"I order you in the name of Jesus Christ to come out of her" (v. 18). Paul's words slice between structure and agency, between a network of oppression and a fragile vulnerable life. He speaks to her and to the spirit at work in her that binds her body to her owners. This is what the disciples of Jesus must do. They must see beyond pious talk, religious god-talk into the oppression of people. Paul is moved by no great spiritual discernment, and no righteous indignation, but simply and beautifully by annoyance. Paul was annoyed, and this suggests a level of frustration through repetition. Enough of the religious noise! Enough of the mindless praise of God and God's servants that mask demonic activity! The point was not to silence

her voice but to release it from its networked captivity. Ministry in the name of Jesus Christ releases people to speak, especially poor women, by challenging the voices of their own oppression that constantly wish to speak through them. The text does not give us the freed voice of the slave girl. Luke has, however, set us up to hear it freshly, newly, and without its chains. Churches should long to hear freed voices and follow the Spirit in increasing their number. Yet to free someone is never without cost, as Paul and Silas will soon discover.

16:19–24

Ownership and Discipleship

The prison returns in all its horror. Luke never allows us to wander too far away from its reach and its many signatures. Torture and violence are signs of the prison. Lies, deceptions, and falsehoods that lead people to be incarcerated are signs of the prison. Exploitation, racism, and bigotry also encircle the prison and its judicial system. Our break in the text does not follow the natural break in the story. Our break is for emphasis. We must slow down again and see the operations of incarceration in their intimate relation to the forces of death. The disciples of Jesus cannot escape our necessary confrontation with prisons. Arrest, incarceration, and imprisonment have never been and never are neutral processes, functioning according to basic rules of justice and human utility. Incarceration is a process at the disposal of the rich and powerful, and here we see it unleashed against the servants of Jesus.

We are yet within the story of the slave girl and the wealthy woman Lydia. Commentators tend to forget the reality that bookends this story. It is because of the slave girl's release that Paul and Silas will be seized. Had they left her in her pious slavery at its conjuncture between religious speech, fortune telling, and commerce, they would have been able to flow freely through the city. They would have experienced no trouble had they not disturbed the smooth interplay of religious and economic practice. But they freed her from her use-value, broke her out of a spiritual and material system that made her visible only as flesh to her owners. Now the disciples must face the awesome power of the owners. Who are the owners? Owners are the high priests of the economic world. They announce what blesses and what transgresses economic life. Owners fear no religion, no faith or its adherents. They only fear interruptions to the smooth flow of capital. These owners unleash an imperial power that is always at their disposal, one drenched in the seductions of money and influence. They take Paul and Silas against their will and bring them into the marketplace in front of the authorities, and from the site of commerce and control, they say the words that will bring exactly the desired effect: "These men are disturbing our city; they are Jews" (v. 20).

One sentence, this sentence, captures history. Contained in it we find Gentile hatred and Jewish diaspora fear. The owners perform through their words the great demonic juxtaposition—the stability of a city, a social world, and a people on one side and the "problem" of the Jews on the other side. This is an ancient juxtaposition deeply familiar in Israel, reaching back to their wilderness wanderings between Egypt and Canaan and exposing a trajectory foreboding the horrific future that we now know too well. This sentence exposes Jewish difference, the difference of the people of God and those who are willing to exploit that difference for political and economic gain. Here ownership is no blessing, only curse, only a sign of hatred of God's people. These owners have given into the great temptation of ownership and have become protectors of capital at all cost, by manipulating peoples' fears and activating their xenophobia and bigotry. So they invoke Roman identity against Jewish identity, suggesting the freedom (religious, economic, and social) guaranteed by the state is at stake in the ways of the Jews.

Ownership and discipleship are never easily aligned. Luke has made this clear from early in the Acts narrative. Ownership aligned with discipleship is possible, but only under the conditions witnessed by Lydia and not the owners of this slave girl. It is possible only under the conditions of a life being drawn irrevocably by the Spirit into the new reality of intimacy and community. Only those willing to open their lives, their homes, and their possessions to use for the sake of the gospel can escape the seduction of ownership.

Only those whose ownership tips the economic balance away from enslavement might inhabit a form of ownership that follows Jesus. The church has always struggled against the identity-constituting powers of ownership and has often been overcome by its seductions. We are yet to grasp fully the struggle of discipleship precisely at the site of ownership where the voice of the Spirit must be heard over against those voices that wish to weave together in us possession with social control, the concern for maintaining our things with the willingness to kill others to do it. These owners enact the same logic of violence that was pressed on the body of Jesus. They have the disciples stripped and beaten. Again disciples will wear their familiar clothing—humiliation and torture and chains—and in this way perform the body of the slave that is also the body of the prisoner and that is ultimately the body of Jesus.

16:25–40

Shaking the Prison Foundations

We would do well to remember the details Luke gives us here, the repetition of the familiar suffering. Why tell us again about this process of imprisonment? By so doing he brings our discipleship to one of its crucial centering realities from which we gain clear sight. Disciples care about how bodies are treated and mistreated. Such matters are never minor matters for us. Paul and Silas from the place of vigorous oppression (lies told, whipping inflicted, locked in the depths of maximum security) shows us why prayer and worship matter for bodies. This scene of their worshiping God is startling and surreal only if we forget that this scene is the originating scene, the place from which all prayer to and through Jesus finds its beginning point and then moves toward heaven. The christological center of prayer is revealed at the site of suffering and rejection. There is an organic connection between Jesus praying in the garden before his torture and Paul and Silas praying in the prison after their torture. This is for the sake of Jesus and the humanity he saves. Worship in churches can be obfuscating and unintentionally quite misleading if we fail to remember this original format. Praying and singing join us to tortured and chained bodies, both past and present, and to the real pressure placed on disciples' bodies as they look toward God. Praying and singing are acts of joining that weave our voices and words with the desperate of this world who cry out to God day and night. Each time we gather in the name of Jesus and lift our voices, this point of reference should shape our reverence and drive us to see and learn and know and change the situations of those who suffer especially in that holy name. Each time we pray and sing we are also joined to the shouts of joy and praise to a God who saves and delivers and invites us to take hold of divine power by faith.

"*The foundations of the prison were shaken*" (v. 26). This is no small word, and no simple report. These disciples are numbered among the prisoners. They have been joined to them. Such joining is clearly indicated in this text, because the miraculous deliverance is not simply for Paul and Silas but for all the prisoners. Now a world is overturned. For those of us in the prison-drenched West conditioned to believe our safety is directly tied to bodies locked behind doors and prisoners chained, the sheer idea of prison doors wide open and chains loosened strike many people with stark terror. In this regard, we have become one with the jailer, one whose sense of well-being is shattered if people are set free. We are yet to see this God-given earthquake as the desire of God marked by this moment. The prison guard moves to the center of the story now, and with good reason. This moment of jail breaking will also be his salvation.

The jailer sits in darkness and fear. We don't know if he fears death at the hands of escaped prisoners or because he will be punished by the magistrates for allowing the prisoners to escape. Paul's words to him separate light from darkness, life from death, and clarify for this man charged with maintaining the imprisonment of others a way out of death. His question, "*What must I do to be saved?*" (v. 30), we have heard before in Acts, but now it is asked from the site of the prison and the position of the guard, and from that unique space, salvation will come to his household. This deliverance of the captives must include the jailer because redemption must come to him if the prisoners are to be set free. Those who are aligned to the technology of the prison must be shown the new order of life in the Spirit if they would imagine life beyond cell and chain. Certainly not every prisoner is awarded the freedom enacted by the Spirit at this moment. Indeed this is an event that issues in help only for Paul and Silas, but a template is forming and a trajectory is captured here. Yet another household has become a place of God's reign and is poised to become a cell of the church, and a jailer witnesses the actions of the Spirit against the injustice of the prison and unjust imprisonment and torture. The Spirit breaks the prison, crushes its technologies, and saves the jailer who treats the wounds of the tortured. This is the will of God.

Paul will not keep silent. An injustice has been done against him and Silas, and they will not go quietly into freedom, relieved that their ordeal is over. More is at stake than their freedom. This is a matter of justice. Paul and Silas are acting as disciples precisely in this moment of invoking their Roman citizenship and precisely in claiming their rights as citizens. Disciples are positioned against this political power of the secret. That power seeks to isolate and individuate injustices done, turning them into singular, episodic events that do not point to systemic, structural, and serial realities of oppression and the misuse of power. These disciples call out such operations, and they will use whatever resources of the nation state to do so. Roman citizenship will be used for the sake of another identity—a disciple of Jesus. We could also see reflexes of ancient honor systems at work here—the public humiliation and shame of these citizens demand public apology. No doubt this is a deeply masculine performance not easily accessible (if actually inaccessible) to women imprisoned or tortured. Paul and Silas demand the restored honor of a Roman citizen which is the restored honor of a man, and in this regard they utilize the weapons of the world against this world. We must not, however, baptize into Christ this use of citizenship and its honor system, in this case that of being Roman (v. 38). Nor should we see in this strategic use the approval of aspirations toward citizenship as the necessary path to freedom.

The church has always been tempted to confuse citizenship with discipleship. The citizen who is a disciple can no longer be a citizen in the abstract, no longer a citizen in theory but only in the concrete practice of a disciple. The disciple is a citizen who has had their citizenship tightly bound to the body of Jesus and ordered by the Spirit of God toward one purpose—to expose the concealed architecture of oppression and violence and to set the captives free. Of course, the citizen may do other things to promote the well-being of the republic. Yet the disciple must never forget the site from which they are obligated to think citizenship: the prison. Luke has already shown us the truth of the owner's operation, and now we see the magistrates' collusion with the owner's deception. The disciples demand that those who imprisoned them step out into the light and into the open. This is the beginning of the exegesis of corruption and the exposition of evil.

They will also leave the prison on their own terms and not the terms of those that locked them away. The magistrates (*stratēgois*, v. 38) want this incident and the disciples with it to go away. This too is the way of the secret in which people are removed from the scenes of injustice in the hopes that no dangerous memories of what has happened will be lodged in particular spaces. So an apology was mixed with a political operation—a request to leave the city. This episode is similar to the story of the release of the great South African leader and (later president) Nelson Mandela. As Mandela tells the story, F. W. de Klerk, then president of South Africa, informed him quite abruptly and without warning that he was going to be released from prison the next day. De Klerk told Mandela that he would be flown to Johannesburg and released there. His quick release after decades of unjust imprisonment would be for the expediency of the government. Mandela had a different vision for his release:

> I told him that I strongly objected to that. I wanted to walk out
> of the gates of Victor Verster and be able to thank those who
> looked after me and greet the people of Cape Town. Though
> I was from Johannesburg, Cape Town had been my home for
> nearly three decades. I would make my way back to Johannes-
> burg, but when I chose to, not when the government wanted
> me to. "Once I am free," I said, "I will look after myself."[1]

Mandela's refusal echoes back to the disciples' refusal to go quietly. The disciples return to Lydia's home and a fresh calibration of the mission. Again we meet here the emerging characteristics of this fellowship of servants. They are a mixture of rich and poor, with those

---

1. Nelson Mandela, *Long Walk to Freedom: The Autobiography of Nelson Mandela* (Boston: Little, Brown, and Company, 1994), 485.

who had been beaten and tortured and imprisoned, and who are struggling against economic and political forces aligned to do them harm and who want them to disappear. Lydia's home now houses ex-offenders and is also the place where the Holy Spirit dwells. From this place of encouragement (*parekalesan*,. v. 40) and edification the Spirit will guide the servants of Jesus on their journey.

FURTHER REFLECTIONS
Christian Witness against the Prison

The prison has never been about criminals but about societies. As this story of Paul and Silas indicate, the prison is a tool for control and containment. The question we must continually ask is, Who desires to use this tool? This question turns a searchlight toward finding who, how, and why the prison gets used. The prison is in fact an enticing power, because it shares with violence its powerful attraction. Violence and the prison issue the false promise that they can recreate the ground upon which life may be built freshly, by removing the impediments to flourishing life. This has always been an arrogant promise because it pretends to exist at the same level as God. Only God can bring life out of death. Only God can transform life at the sites of destruction and despair. Just as no nation-state can resist the lure of violence, so too can none resist the pull of the prison as a technology necessary for its well-being. The prison however has always had a strange ally—morality and moral language.

Incarceration and prisons have constantly been placed right in the middle of moral discourse about right and wrong, good and evil, innocence and guilt, and crime and punishment. People do bad or horrible things. This is an irrefutable fact. And people go to prison. This too is irrefutable. But there is no direct connection between these two facts. Indeed when we collapse these two statements into each other in our thinking, we lose sight of the horror that is prison, and we also forget that horrible things are being done every day for which no one is being held accountable. The point here is not that we need more surveillance and more incarceration. The point is that there is a space between the truth that people do wrong and horrible things and the truth that people go to prison. The disciples of Jesus live in that space, because it is the space where the incarnate God has chosen to be seen and known. Jesus from that space shows us what to do with both truths.

We serve a God who was arrested, convicted, and sentenced. We must reflect deeply on this fact. Jesus was found guilty of both sedition and heresy, as both a threat to the Roman state and to Jewish faith. We may from our vantage point claim his innocence, but such a view was absent at his incarceration and trial and in the shouts of the crowd that demanded his punishment, just as such a vantage point is often absent from the judicial proceedings that have placed and continue to place innocent people in jail and prison today. Yet the innocence of Jesus was not illumined by his ordeal, by the horror of an incarceration system, the brutality of the Roman state at the local level, and the ease with which popular opinion can be manipulated to evil ends. He shows us how people come to be seen as criminals in the making in the contexts of oppression and intense surveillance.

Jesus was not simply someone who got caught up in a judicial system but the one who shattered its connection to morality and righteousness, because the righteous child of God was imprisoned. As Paul and Silas show us, Jesus' disciples too are caught in this holy work of shattering the false connection of morality to prison, but also of the connection between imprisonment and the people who are incarcerated. The prison is used to teach us how to see people both in prison and those outside its walls and gates. Its way of instruction views those in prison as spoiled bodies, unfit for life in community and those outside its walls as victims in potential, needing to be shielded from these menacing humans. Such bad anthropology often binds itself to those released from prison so that they forever carry the social effects of being seen as spoiled bodies. But the Christian life is a witness against such bad anthropology, and the disciples of Jesus are forever poised to oppose this sick pedagogy.

We have been brought into the space between people and prison systems through the Spirit who guides us into God's liberating work (Luke 4:18–19). The disciples of Jesus cut through the quick and easy alignments of crime and punishment, knowing that what constitutes a crime is a complex reality created at the intersection of public policies, government actions or inactions, and concealed private interests. Who gets arrested, charged, tried, and convicted is very often a matter of who has access to resources or who enters judicial processes already profoundly disadvantaged. This means that we resist the collapsing of our moral vision into the moral language that surrounds judicial systems and imprisonment. The question is not can a judicial or prison system be moral, but rather how must a disciple of Jesus give witness to its end and the beginning of a new way of life together?

We must ask this question because the Christian finds herself in the midst of God's transforming power, a power rooted in God's reconciling life (2 Cor. 5:17–21). We are those already convinced by the love of God that no one is beyond change, no one deserving of death's reign either through execution or abandonment to solitary confinement. This is why we are told to visit those in prison as though we ourselves were imprisoned with them (Heb. 13:3). We must be present in the prison to destroy its anthropology and challenge its false morality and to witness to all those incarcerated a God familiar with confinement and torture, disrespect and abuse. Yet we must also be present in all the places where laws are made and modified to advantage some and disadvantage others, and to challenge social policies that align those already suffering under poverty on a pathway to prison by strangling off the resources and social services they need in order to build a flourishing life. Some consider the prison a natural and normal aspect of society, necessary for maintaining order. But now we live on the other side of a crucified God and a risen savior, and a band of followers that stretch from that motley group imprisoned for Jesus' namesake to those now in prison and tortured. We know too much to ever be fooled into believing that prisons are natural or normal.

17:1–15

The Struggle between Text and Life

The good news of God is a troubling word. This is the irony that greets those who become disciples. They now carry a life-giving word that brings hostile opposition. We understand that this opposition does not spring from pure evil or hatred of God, but for diaspora people it is rooted in perceived theological insult, disrespect, and fear. For Gentiles this opposition grows from the perception that a new god competes with the old gods and a new order is challenging the established order. As C. Kavin Rowe notes, Caesar now emerges as a counterfeit, "a rival to the Lordship of God in the person of Jesus Christ."[2] Readers of this text must always remember to humanize this opposition, not in order to soften its tensions but to see into its depth so that we might more clearly grasp its historical trajectory that reaches to us at this moment. This section of Luke's narrative brings us deep inside diaspora politics and the inner struggle for control of the master story of Israel's past, present, and future.

17:1–5

Paul and Silas have invaded sacred space and taken up camp. Their entrance into the synagogue for so many is a harbinger of chaos. Three Sabbath days is no insignificant amount of time, and with each new Sabbath these disciples further overturn the world. Evangelical time is accumulating around these disciples, and the Spirit is making visible messianic hope and more. The more is precisely the problem because Jesus is being presented as the embodiment of that hope, a hope realized. Jesus is being announced as the reality of the resurrection, and the end of the power of death and equally stunning, the beginning of the new age. Textual struggle at this point is also a struggle with embodiment. Text and body are joined at the site of the Spirit's working, and now every

> We must never glorify argument as the engine that moves the thinking of a community forward. Such a way of thinking reflects a profoundly chivalric and masculine vision of progress where truth wins out through combat and violence, and in the end power begets more power.

---

2. C. Kavin Rowe, *World Upside Down: Reading Acts in the Graeco-Roman Age* (New York: Oxford University Press, 2009), 112.

word is serious business. The house of God is a place of struggle fully immersed in the cultic anxiety of identity loss and the theological fear of being unfaithful to God.

We must be careful in how we understand that struggle of text and body and the arguments that constantly encircle it. Argument must always be kept on a historical plain, grounded in an historical materialism. If we fail to attend to the real histories of concrete and particular struggles then we will baptize argument, debate, and conflict as simply part of community life and ecclesial life, or even worse as part of the good and healthy gifts of God. We must never ontologize argument as the engine that moves the thinking of a community forward. That is pure foolishness and a denial of real history. Such a way of thinking reflects a profoundly chivalric and masculine vision of progress and success where truth wins out through combat and violence, and in the end power begets more power. Luke shows us his susceptibility to such a vision and the high cost for our shared humanity when we are lost in the heat of theological argument. Here we must read this text in its terror and not simply as a report on the mission. Luke is caught up in the struggle of diaspora and registers his side of it. We now know the tragic history of the seeds planted by New Testament texts like this one that became fuel for a virulent anti-Jewish apologetic. Yet in its dynamic setting this small story exposes how a gospel vision of humanity might be eclipsed by the desire to overcome opposition.

Luke sharpens a distinction here that he has operated with from the beginning of his narrative in Acts. We could call this a class distinction. That distinction is now doing strange twisted work. Jewish opposition to the gospel is being presented here as a lowering of the collective cultured self, a denial of the best sensibilities of an uplifted people, and moving away from diaspora hope of social ascendency. Luke is not only unleashing cultural insult inside cultural code, but he is also deploying a dangerous optic—the perception of status and the status of perception. So Luke wishes us to note that many devout Greeks (*sebo Hellen*) and a significant number of leading women (*protos gune*), women of a stature similar to Lydia (chap. 16), became followers of Jesus. This way of perceiving status is being mixed with perceiving conversion. This has always been an intoxicating and horrific mixture of perception. The high and mighty become followers of Jesus—what disciple of Jesus would not want this and not become absolutely thrilled with this turn of events? The church is yet to comprehend fully the trouble with this mixture. Luke illumines a trajectory that will move toward the conversion of Emperor Constantine and that reaches to us today. This perception turns us away from the creature loved by God, from specific people known by name by God, and toward what they represent with their money, and/or their power and their status.

The problem here is not that the powerful become Christians. The problem is that Luke does not *perceive them* as a disciple of Jesus ought to perceive them. We know this only because he exposes the other aspect of this troublesome optic when he tells us of "Jewish jealousy" that led to the enlisting of wicked men from the marketplace (v. 5) to help form a mob. These low-lifes, or more precisely "ruffians" as he calls them, have disappeared as human beings sought by the Spirit and emerged as nothing more than problematic and dangerous bodies that wander in a city.[3] Luke at this moment has lost the gospel even as he tells us of its opposition. To be fair to Luke, he is captured in narrating to us the willingness of these men to operate as violent quasi-mercenaries, so their wickedness is not in question. Yet others have incited mobs, participated in mobs, and escaped such labeling. Here Luke's class distinctions participate in the very wickedness that he is describing to us. This is no small matter because from such a social optic grows the impatience to see people in their complexities and the justification to treat them like trash. That optic grows inside Christianity, threatening the gospel from within and distorting Christianity's power of discernment.

17:5–9

Jason is not a bystander. Nor is he collateral damage in a struggle he did not initiate. This is the cost of association with the Holy Spirit. The mob was looking for Paul and Silas and they found Jason. Good

---

3. Luke Timothy Johnson, *The Acts of the Apostles* (Collegeville, MN: The Liturgical Press, 1992), 306.

enough. This is the manifestation of a holy calling. Any disciple of Jesus can stand in proxy of Paul and Silas. Any disciple of that man from Nazareth could share his fate. So Jason (not Paul) along with some others are violently grabbed by a mob and dragged in front of the leaders of the city (*politarchas*, v. 6). Jason (not Silas) with other disciples faced the outrageous claim of associating with world over-turners, revolutionaries in the absolute sense of destroying the established order and presenting a new one. The irony Luke wishes to underscore here is that the exact same jingoistic ideology that the owners in Philippi deployed against the Jews is being used by these Jews against the converts. Jason's actual crime was hospitality. This of course is the dangerous hospitality of a believer in Jesus where their home becomes a revolutionary cell of the Spirit's working. The voices from the mob are exactly right—in Jason's home resides one whose words are more decisive than the decrees of the emperor and who is acknowledged as the one true king.

Homeownership and discipleship appear again as a primary site of struggle. To be a homeowner in the ancient world already aligned you with the social order, already suggested you were embedded in the social fabric of Roman rule. Yet discipleship meant a rip in that fabric and misalignment with the order of things suggested by owning a home. Could this be why the Spirit always invades homes, sets up camp and station in the material structures of life? By divine decree, not the emperor's, the house must become the church, and this is what the church today seems to have forgotten. Homes must be invaded by the Spirit in order to reorder the world. This is the revolution of intimate spaces in order to overturn all social spaces. It is not by happenstance that the mob attacked Jason's house, because they knew it was occupied by revolutionaries. Of course, we know that homeownership is not a given. As in the ancient world, in much of the world today it represents the dividing line between the haves and have-nots and in many cases the dividing line between those who resist the economic order and those who have declared by word and deed their allegiance to it. Yet by the Spirit, homes may become sites of holy contestation between ways of living that affirm the emperor and ways of life that announce a new reign and a new leader.

17:10–15

Luke prefers the Jews of Beroea to those of Thessalonica. What is their difference? It is their receptivity to the gospel. Yet there is a question at play in his favorable construal of these new disciples. Is there receptivity because of their nobility or does their receptivity constitute their nobility? We are yet caught in the problem of the mixture of status perception with Luke. He is seemingly fixated on the status of those who come to believe, these powerful Gentile women and men. There is, however, a different way to think about nobility presented here. It is the nobility of welcoming and searching. The Beroeans are often read as unrelenting biblicists who tirelessly examined (v. 11) the Scriptures. The energy of examining the Scripture is, however, bound to the eagerness of welcoming the newness of the gospel. Indeed the examining is energized by the welcoming, and the welcoming is enfolded in the examining. Here is a new possibility of faithful life in diaspora where the risk of loss can be overwhelming. This new possibility is a form of discipleship that welcomes the reality of a new word from God and examines the Scripture as inseparable actions of faithfulness to the God of Israel. Paul and Silas are yet what they were in Thessalonica, world over-turners, revolutionaries in flesh bringing a disruptive word. Yet in Beroea a difference is being displayed that the church continues to struggle to see. This is a pattern of discernment born of a community attuned to the Spirit where a newness from God will be received by God's people as they practice a form of risk-filled hospitality and a freeing exegesis of Scripture. Such freeing exegesis follows the Spirit's working in the world to gather sight of the life-redeeming ways of God. The people of God in Beroea are in fact not that different from the people of God in Thessalonica.

We need . . . to approach the Bible as if it were a parable of Jesus. The whole thing is a gift, a challenge, and an invitation into a new world, seeing yourself afresh and more truthfully.

Rowan Williams, *Being Christian: Baptism, Bible, Eucharist, Prayer* (Grand Rapids: Eerdmans, 2014), 29.

Their difference pivots on a simple desire: they want to listen to what God is saying.

17:16–34

A Rhetoric of Desire

Who is this man who has come to Athens? This is the crucial matter at this point in Luke's story. The Paul rendered in this speech embodies a new spirit. Luke performs a new human in these words given to Paul. This disciple of Jesus has been captured by the Spirit, taken up in the Spirit's embrace, and now he offers a fresh word that will never grow stale. The word he speaks binds diaspora Jews and marketplace Gentiles in a gracious invitation. The idols are the backdrop of his words. They are not new. Every child of diaspora understands what it means to be surrounded by idols. They mark the boundary of difference, the wall of separation, and the point of divine hatred. Death follows idolatry. No one seriously devoted to the God of Israel would traffic in the common religious currencies of Athens. In Athens, Jerusalem is a shut door. Until now.

What is extraordinary in this story is Luke's Paul, not Athens. Too much of the history of interpretation of this text is dazzled by Hellenistic glamor. Like people spellbound by celebrities, Christians have too often read this text fixated on those famous names, Epicurean, Stoic, Areopagus, and Athenians. This has much to do with a longstanding proto-European/European obsession with idealized Greek culture. For centuries Christians have wanted to "get back to the Greeks" and capture the supposed cultural genius of the modern West's imagined intellectual ancestors and even progenitors of modern thought. So this text is often overdetermined. It is asked to say more than it can and speak to matters that are not its concern. It is asked to perform creation, even the created order, and even a natural theology. At the site of a European fetish, that is, idealized Greek culture, interpreters have fantasized a natural order found in a potent religious intuition embodied among the Athenians, the pinnacle of human thinkers where refined intellects are aimed in the right direction, but just not far enough.

Such ways of reading this text are profoundly supersessionist and anti-Jewish, because they have ignored the miracle Luke is performing with Paul's words. Here is a serious Jew touching the unclean thing, Gentiles. Luke's Paul at this point mirrors Luke's Peter (chap. 10), but where Peter needed the Spirit to press him to join Gentiles, Paul here extends himself into a Gentile world to offer a way into God's beautiful new world. Paul, formed in Torah sensibilities, is rightly greatly disturbed by the idolatry all around him, but now he will do something absolutely stunning and marvelously productive with his outrage. He will not turn away from the idolaters, but toward them. This is what the gospel demands—a reaching toward and a reaching out to the point of touching and holding. Paul is reaching out to those Gentiles who could not be more removed from his world of covenantal faithfulness. The man who agreed to the stoning of Stephen now stands surrounded by stones that evoke his righteous fury, yet he must yield to the Spirit who now calls him to a new word.

What do you say to those radically outside yourself, radically different from you? What do you say to those whose religions and rituals you have been trained to loathe? What Luke will have Paul say is controlled by an extravagant fantasy born of the Spirit. The fantasy is not in what Luke writes or what Paul says but in what the Spirit hopes. The Spirit wants the hearers of Paul's words to hear and receive the invitation from God to them. These words aim to draw these Gentiles into the body of Jesus and into one Spirit with Israel. So Paul's words will join the synagogue to the marketplace, encircling all the creatures that traffic these sites with the love of God. These words of Paul are no missionary ploy. They present a transformation enacted by the Spirit that turns the logic of idolatry in a different direction. God wants the Gentiles. God desires those who desire idols. This is the truth that shapes these words. Here we witness a rhetoric of desire. This speech is driven by the irrepressible longing of God to embrace wayward creatures by every means possible. What do you say to those radically outside yourself, outside your theological vision? When your speech meets divine desire, the Holy Spirit will tell you what to say in order to create the new in and through your words. That new is a relationship aiming at a marvelous joining.

Paul is caught up in the Spirit who is doing something new with Israel's ancient understanding of idol production. The idol is a collective self-deception, a point of facilitation where human fantasy and wish, circulating around material realities, generate distorted hope. The idol facilitates a hope of control of both my life and the life of the gods, that is, to draw the gods into common cause with me for sustaining my life. The production of the idol is the production of the human, because through its creation a self is also created and through its worship and devotion that same fabricated self is sustained. Idol production is the folly of the Gentiles who know not God or themselves. It is *complete* ignorance of the God of Israel, the creator, and the gracious reality of being creatures. Yet Paul will not turn Gentile ignorance toward God's condemnation, but toward God's condescension. Now an acceptable day has arrived, and with the arrival of such a day the religious activities of the Gentiles may be touched and handled and drawn toward light and life. The point is not the hidden truth of idolatrous practices. The point is that divine desire now enfolds idolaters in hopes that God's body will draw them away from the body of the idol.

Luke's logic here will be echoed in some measure in the groundbreaking counsel of Bartolomé de Las Casas, who performed a similar theological generosity in reflecting on the religious practices of Amerindians. Las Casas would not turn away from the indigenes even as his church used their "idolatry" as an alibi for colonialist terrorism. For Las Casas, the religious practices of the indigenous peoples, even human sacrifice, did not condemn them to damnation but only served to show them to be people loved and wanted by God.[4] Of course, Las Casas's example is separated from Luke by centuries of supersessionistic interpretations of Scripture, which lost the abiding implications of this moment of Gentile acceptance. It is also separated by a swirling ocean of colonialism and theological imperialism. Yet Las Casas did spy out a trajectory that draws its line from Luke, who shows us a God who by the Spirit will press into disciples the divine wanting, longing, and claiming of creatures.

---

4. Bartolomé de Las Casas, *In Defense of the Indians* (DeKalb: Northern Illinois University Press, 1992), 221–48. See Willie James Jennings, *The Christian Imagination: Theology and the Origins of Race* (New Haven, CT: Yale University Press, 2010), 100–102.

This is why God demands of all people the turning-toward that is repentance (*metanoein*, v. 30). To be sure, Luke never departs from the story of Israel. All this is within their vision, and as such it will seem to some that the entire speech presents pure ethnic and theological chauvinism. Yet this is the danger of diaspora living: you embody a claim that reaches to all those you encounter, even if they do not believe what you believe. And now once again, the difference of Israel from the other nations is being performed as a different Israel to other nations. Paul speaks to these Gentiles of the assertive love of God made known in Jesus whose body now stands between life and death. This new time of repentance is rooted in the resurrection, not death, gift and grace, not subjugation and imperialism. What awaits all people is a new judge, one who is filled with righteousness and set ablaze with justice. This way of repentance invites peoples and nations to see a future that is moving irrevocably toward this new human, the judge of the living and the dead. This, of course, is where this rhetoric of divine desire meets its greatest opposition. All religious speech, no matter how carefully stated, no matter how ecumenical and affirming, no matter how polite, shatters at the resurrected body of Jesus. Because to speak of the resurrection of Jesus is no longer religious speech, but speech that challenges reality, reorients how we see earth and sky, water and dirt, land and animals, and even our own bodies. This is speech that evokes a decision: either laugh at it or listen to it, either leave or draw near to this body. It is his body or your stones.

18:1–11

A Community in the Double Bind

To be within the prophetic is to be for a moment in synergy with God, sharing in the full measure of the temptation to lose patience with God's people, yet intoxicated with the divine longing for the creature.

A people is forming in Corinth. Some are Jewish refugees, having come there by escaping life threatening conditions in Rome under Emperor Claudius. Luke never allows us to forget the pains of diaspora. Jews had been driven from Rome because their religion was seen as an enemy religion of the state. Others of the Corinthian diaspora are there among the Gentiles, especially among those Gentiles who worship the God of Israel. This will be a community formed in the double bind. From one side they are a despised people under Roman rule and from the other side they are now caught in what appears to be an intractable theological debate, fueled by an organized opposition to the new message. Luke brings us deeply inside the intensity of that intramural struggle. Each Sabbath gives witness to the heightening of the tensions. Finally, the tensions overwhelm Paul, and his actions and words speak a truth that is not true. He shakes the dust from his clothes. He pronounces judgment on his Jewish opposition. He claims he has done all he can, and he announces his attention has shifted to the Gentiles (v. 6). He gives up. His energy collapses, and this is completely understandable and paradigmatic. Jesus himself drew near this collapse, echoing God's ancient frustration with a sojourning people created by God's own mighty hand and outstretched arm. Love will sometimes threaten to abandon, but it never does. Paul is caught in the threat of an action that God will not follow. God does not follow abandonment, because God has brought abandonment into the divine life. The abandoned now have a home in God if they want it.

Many Christians have lived in a distorted reading of this moment, imagining in Paul's frustration an aspect of a divine plan of substitution and this heated turning away to be God showing God's own backside to Israel. Nothing could be further from the truth. The truth here is the truth of frustration, reaching the full measure of the temptation to lose patience with God's people. This is a moment of prophetic synergy, when the co-laboring with God becomes fully human and fully divine (v. 10). Paul has joined God's own loving struggle with God's people. Now next door to the synagogue, God will continue to woo diaspora, calling them home. A motley band is being formed next to the synagogue, Gentiles and Jews of Corinth. This will be the church, always next to the synagogue, always born within a lover's quarrel with their beloved, and always positioned to be the witness God uses to call to Israel. Formed next door to the synagogue, the church must always give an account of itself to Israel

for Jesus' sake. However, this is not sentimental. This is deadly serious. Once again Jewish opposition will deploy the weapons of the
state against these disciples of Jesus. This again is tragic, not only
because they seek to unleash the violence of Rome against the followers of Jesus, but also because it shows a forgetfulness of the truth
of diaspora. They are insignificant in relation to the state.

An analysis of prophetic utterances shows that the fundamental experience of the
prophet is a fellowship with the feelings of God, *a sympathy with the divine pathos,*
a communion with the divine consciousness which comes about through the
prophet's reflection of, or participation in, the divine pathos. The typical prophetic
state of mind is one of being taken up into the heart of the divine pathos.
Sympathy is the prophet's answer to inspiration, the correlative to revelation.

Abraham J. Heschel, *The Prophets*, vol. 1 (New York: Harper Torchbooks, 1962), 26.

"A matter of questions about words and names" (18:15). Gallio's
words make the point that is as clear as the noonday sun. Why
should he or anyone else care about an intramural Jewish theological debate? Gallio lumps Paul and his would-be persecutors into the
same sack of contention. From his perspective there is no crime here
and no criminal worth noticing. Equally troubling, Gallio reminds
Israel of its difference from the Roman state, even if they did not
need reminding. What worries them does not worry Rome, what
concerns them does not concern Rome. Disapora people must
always make the case that their well-being is aligned with the well-
being of the state, and in this regard with these upstart disciples, they
have failed. But this is a potent temptation rooted in the *Realpolitik*
of life at the margins. This potent temptation will be inherited by
the church, and at many times and diverse occasions will become
an ecclesial and social quagmire. The problem is not that the church
should be oblivious to the well-being of the state but that churches
have felt and continue to feel compelled *to make the case to the state*
that what is important for our well-being should be important to the
state. We should never imagine such a hoped-for synergy of concern.
Nor should we ever equate our churchy struggles with the struggles
of the world, our tensions with the crushing tensions of people trying to find fresh (violence-free) air to breathe, water to drink, and

food to eat. If there is a case to be made to the state it is about the well-being of its citizens and of the creation itself. We press for the flourishing of the world and not for the flourishing of the church. God will see to the latter. This portion of the narrative ends with an inexplicable act of violence. It is not clear if this is violence done by Jewish opposition to the disciples or anti-Jewish Gentiles. The crucial point is that Gallio did nothing to stop it. There in front of all to see a human being was beaten, and not just an abstract human but a Jewish man was beaten, and the state paid no attention. This is the way of the state. It will see only the violence it wishes to see and respond only when its interests are at stake. Yet Luke puts eyes on this act of senseless violence just as he reminds us that Paul was spared, by the hand of God, from what would have been his lot had the state actually joined the opposition in seeing him as a threat. What is most important is that we call out the violence and the injustice, especially if the state refuses to do so, and even more so if the violence flows from the actions of the state.

18:12–28

A New Kind of Couple

Luke does not give us with Priscilla and Aquila a domestic order or a vision of gender complementarity, but disciples together. This is by far the best working definition of a Christian couple.

The couple returns. Priscilla and Aquila, a refugee couple, having left Rome under its threatening conditions, now join Paul on his journey. We learned at the beginning of this chapter that they shared with Paul a common artisanship, tent-making, and equally crucial, they shared in the ministry of Jesus and the itinerary of following where the Spirit leads (vv. 2–3). We see the couple now within the reality of service and ministry. This is not Ananias and Sapphira, though many of the same elements are present. Like Ananias and Sapphira, Priscilla and Aquila's lives are shaped in the quotidian realities of survival, and like the earlier couple they have been enfolded in the demands of discipleship. Yet unlike the idolatrous couple, they have joined Paul and the work of the Spirit as a couple. As a couple, they travel with him willing to face the cost of discipleship. Although the details of their life are slight in Luke's narrative, Priscilla and Aquila are a couple under ideal conditions: they are not consumed with self-preservation but with a shared life that yields to the Spirit. Indeed Luke does not give us a domestic order or even a vision of gender complementarity, but disciples together. This is by far the best working definition of a Christian couple.

Luke, at this point, confirms Paul's theological stability. He is a faithful child of Israel. He has not left the sensibilities of his people or left his people (vv. 18–19). He is also a faithful collaborator with the Jerusalem church (v. 22). What has fully emerged in this smaller narrative-apologetic for Paul is the seamless joining of worlds, Jew and Gentile, through his body. Paul is moving between worlds now, from Jerusalem to Antioch, from synagogue to the Jesus-cells in Gentile homes, from faithful Jews to God-fearing Gentiles and all those in between. There is an in-between, biracial character to Paul's life now that we must never forget to note. What does it mean for a disciple of Jesus to move between worlds, traveling back and forth along old lines of hostility and distrust? This is the calling of the Spirit for Paul and the couple, Priscilla and Aquila. There is always great risk when you travel between worlds. You always edge up against the accusation of weakened allegiances to and even betrayal of the one for the other. You also live with the burden of enacting what others are usually spared, cultural authenticity. This may be a burden unique to Christian faith at its founding, to gesture love in the bland gestures of the everyday. So Luke acknowledges Paul's heavy commitment in the lightness of normal actions, keeping his vows by getting his hair cut, visiting synagogue and church, speaking and listening. Equally important, the movement between the two is not the struggle, but the site of struggle. Christian life is, at its very heart, a freeing movement between worlds that weaves together that which others never imagine together. This is the Spirit's doing who always uses the in-between spaces to create the new, a space of redemption where we can together strain to touch the fullness of Jesus' body.

"For Priscilla and Aquila" (18:24–28). This chapter ends where it began, with the couple, Priscilla and Aquila. Commentators have made this chapter primarily about Paul and secondarily about that interesting figure, Apollos, the Alexandrian. Both are in fact

powerfully present in this chapter, but the couple has what Cynthia Ozick would call narrative power.[5] They had been left in Ephesus by Paul, but also seemingly by the Spirit as well. Apollos appears, learned and filled with eloquence and power. Luke provocatively presents this powerful Alexandrian intellectual who is already a follower of the Way but in need of further instruction. That instruction will come from this unlikely source, an itinerant couple, refugees from Rome and now in Ephesus. Here is more than the exercise of leadership from an unlikely place, this couple, though that should be seen and celebrated. Now we see the couple in better light, a new glory in which a pedagogy emerges between them, one powerful enough to teach the powerful, and bring clarity and precision to faith where there had been great zeal but fragmentary knowledge. Priscilla and Aquila helped Apollos. If in fact this is the Apollos who will make such an indelible mark on the life of the church, then this couple framed his work and angled his efforts toward excellence. Luke shows us what a couple can do joined to Jesus. They can speak truth to power and instruct the powerful. This is a reality of the couple that the church has never grasped in its fullness, that is, to be a micro-cell of insurgency, an intimate event of revolution that might draw others to a deeper understanding of the life of God in flesh.

19:1–20

By Water and Touch

Both the water and the touch become the stage on which the Spirit will fall on our bodies, covering us with creating and creative power and joining us to the life of the Son. Through the Spirit, the word comes to skin, and becomes skin, our skin in concert with the Spirit.

19:1–7

We have reached a clarifying moment in the ministry of the Spirit and the work of Paul. Luke rehearses events that are similar to what we have already experienced in the narrative, all of which announce

---

5. Cynthia Ozick, "Ruth," in *Reading Ruth: Contemporary Women Reclaim a Sacred Story*, ed. Judith A. Kates and Gail Twersky Riemer (New York: Random House, 1994), 215.

the reign of God performed through the overwhelming presence of the Spirit. Luke also brings forward his concern to signify both the importance of John the Baptist and the one for whom John was a forerunner, Jesus. John was preparation. The way of repentance he declared in Israel was the stage for the one who lived that life of repentance for his people. John was a person, but Jesus was a person and a place of living. John was an event that flashed across the landscape of Israel. Jesus was the bringer of a new time that extends to all space. The questions that Paul asks are diagnostic and all-encompassing. These questions are asked of those who heard the word of John and entered the way of repentance. These were not people who needed convincing. Their commitments to a new way were clear. Yet the questions are crucial. "Did you receive the Holy Spirit when you became believers?" (v. 2) "Into what then were you baptized?" (v. 3) These questions expose not simply gaps in their discipleship but lack of clarity of its *telos*, its end, goal, and fulfillment. Clearly John the Baptist presented a renewal movement in Israel, a calling home, a clarifying work establishing the divine claim on a beloved people with a purpose. That purpose was to trumpet a new day in Israel. Paul is of that new day, and soon these disciples of John will also be of that new day.

Baptism in Jesus' name signifies bodies that become the new day. There is a glorious repetition here that is absolutely necessary. Paul repeats the apostolic gesture and the Spirit comes again. Again they speak in tongues and again twelve disciples have entered the journey with Jesus and entered the flow of the Spirit. The saving work of God is always new, always starting up and again with faith. Some churches have gone so far as to see in this moment of baptism a baptismal formula that is superior to later Trinitarian developments. However, the point here is not canonization but contextuality. Paul invites these disciples to *baptize their discipleship in Jesus*, and thereby join their lives to his in such a way that they will lose their life in the waters only to find it again in the resurrected One. Here we see the Spirit's tendency and technique. The Spirit lovingly joins the caressing of our skin through the water and the laying on of hands. Both the water and the touch become the stage on which the Spirit will fall on our bodies, covering us with creating and creative power and joining us to the life of the Son. Through the Spirit, the word comes to skin, and becomes skin, our skin in concert with the Spirit.

19:8–20

Paul lives between Jew and Gentile, speaking to both. Luke again reminds us of the tension that resides in the in-between space. This space, constituted by the body of Jesus, is ground zero for Christian existence. This is what public space means for a Christian. It is the space between commitments, allegiances, and alliances where we give witness to God's sovereignty over flesh and blood, in space and time, and in the now. Public in this sense sutures inside/outside, native/alien, and Jew/Gentile through the bodies of disciples, like Paul. Luke again shows us Paul in the synagogue, but by now we have come to expect that he will not be exclusively there. Luke knows too much, just as Paul knows too much and just as we must remember what we know. In the duration of time, opposition will rise up as some people begin to see the implications of this Jesus-message, that a new day of God's reign has come that will bring together Jew and Gentile, diaspora concern and Gentile need, worshipers of the one true God and wayward worshipers of many other gods. We should never forget the element of duration that runs through Luke's narration. Paul was in the synagogue for three long months in incredible strength and clarity about a message that was redrawing the lines of community and communion. It is not surprising that some of the diaspora did not see in faith but only in fear and "spoke evil of the Way before the congregation" (v. 9). Nor is it surprising that Paul withdrew from them and set up shop in the lecture hall of Tyrannus.

Paul and these disciples are caught up in an expansive word that was never contained by the synagogue, but by the permeating reality of the Spirit, it captures both synagogue and lecture hall. Paul and these new disciples will give witness to the claiming power of God over the creation. This is what the miracles will signify. Luke has always been clear about miracles, as a sign of divine retaking and holy restoration of a wayward creation (Luke 4:38–41; 5:13; 6:19; Acts 5:15–16). This is a work manifest by bodily touch, presence, and relationship. Not all three must be present for miracles, but all three are certainly implied. This extraordinary element of this story has always been the skin. The skin of Paul by the Spirit is given salvific resonance such that objects that touch his skin also touch divine presence. The life of objects became one with the life of God. This suggests not a transformation of the objects but a connectivity that presses deep into the materiality of the divine embrace. Here deliverance is at the surface of objects, on the plane where skin and cloth carry a saving sensuality. We, Christians of a desensitized era, would do well to remember this reality of sensuality. Touch matters to God because we are God's creatures, created to be touched repeatedly by God. Touching is often intercepted by economic utility and isolating pleasure, yet here we see a glimpse of an eros in which touching marks a divine yearning for a pleasure that heals and sets free and that will reach into eternity.

"Seven sons of a Jewish high priest" (19:13–14). The sons of the high priest could not see what they should have been able to see. Much like the magician Simon (8:18–21), they discerned power instead of presence and did not sense the ecology of touch and relationship that moved in and through Paul and these disciples. So in their efforts they were wounded by the one oppressed by evil. It matters little who the evil spirit knew or did not know. What is far more important is that these would-be exorcists imagine their delivering work outside the bonds of relationship with Jesus or his servants. This is a perennial danger for those who wish to do serious intervention against the demonic forces of this world that oppress humanity and the creation. The danger is to press into technique imagining its tight execution as the key to loosening death's agents' stranglehold on life. Technique is crucial and vital, especially if it signals serious commitment and energy. These sons of Sceva did in fact challenge the demonic, and they did in fact seek to free someone from its deadly grip. Yet they had not placed themselves in the space of the Spirit and the life of Jesus where touch, presence, and relationship situate our actions in God's own life and turn us always toward that life. So they are wounded in their attempt to do the good, and if this mysterious house (v. 16) might have been the house where the Christ-community gathered, then their fleeing in injury and failure carries even more serious implications. It signals what is

always possible for those who wish to do the work of Jesus without constantly pressing into the life of Jesus. We too may be overcome by evil. Yet these sons of the high priest, although only mentioned briefly in Luke, also represent wayward spiritual practices obsessed with corralling divine power. These are practices not aligned with the giver of life, the Lord Jesus.

This text and others like it have not always been handled with care by Christian interpreters. Christians have imagined a clearinghouse at play in this story that collapses all non-Christian religious practices and ways of life, all indigenous homeopathic practices, and all native (non-Western) visions of life and earth, sky and water as constituting the site of magic and aligned with or subject to the demonic. Christianity's colonial legacy has rendered this text terrifying, instilling in the colonized minds of many readers a deep suspicion of any words, rituals, gestures that do not display an obvious Christian orthodoxy. But what does it mean to turn from magic to the living God? What does it mean to see in particular practices and rituals an end? First and foremost, this text shows us believers who see the limitation of such practices and choose to bring them to light, exposing them in confession and disclosure (*exomologoumenoi kai anangellontes*, v. 18). We are on the ground of renunciation here, where the intimate spaces of hope infested with practices and gesture that lean toward futility and false gods are opened and cleared out by the Spirit, and hope is placed on a true path, as echoed in the famous words from the hymn "My Hope Is Built on Nothing Less," by Edward Mote (1797–1874), "my hope is built on nothing less than Jesus' blood and righteousness." This limitation is one unearthed by believers, not imposed on them. It is *their* recognition that a particular practice or belief will not yield what they imagined and is not encircled by the ecology of divine touch, presence, and relationship. *They see* the limitation and have chosen the better way. This is the heart of what will grow into the formal and informal practices of renunciation by which those who become believers come to see, disclose, and renounce those practices, no matter how sacred, intimate, or exalted, that will not free them from the demonic and will not draw them closer to God, even if they are called Christian practices that claim the name of Jesus. Renunciation therefore must always come from within a community and never be imposed on a community. The imposition of renunciation in the history of Christianity has led to the inculcating of deep cultural self-hatred in many peoples and forms of Christian life that are obsessively policing. Such forms of faith deny and destroy much more than they affirm and build up, and thus they undermine the holy work of renunciation.

19:21–41
The City Is Shaken

Confronting those powers that oppose God often means confronting those seeking to protect their wealth. Paul had been in this kind of situation before, where his actions directly challenge the cultural economy and financial arrangements of a city. Paul faced the slavers/owners of Philippi (Acts 16), who had him tortured and imprisoned, and now an equally dangerous threat of direct action against him and his colleagues looms in Ephesus. Once again these disciples of Jesus are disrupting the smooth flow of production and consumption of goods and services. Demetrius, an artisan and a businessman, clearly sees the ramifications of the gospel Paul is preaching. It will not be good for business, in fact, if taken seriously it will destroy their source of livelihood. It is exactly how that destruction will occur that is so powerfully clear to this man.

The gospel not only exposes the fetish, that is, the object of veneration, but also its production. Both object and production come into view as anthropocentric endeavors, human-made but also concealed in the making. This of course is not new knowledge. It is a truth at the heart of the Jewish diaspora and a pillar of the faith of Israel, but now that truth has intensified through the Spirit and is being woven into the hearts of Gentiles. They are now being exposed to idol production and consumption as never before. The logic of idolatry, once a messianic secret, is now spread abroad in new hearts. We are the inheritors of this knowledge. We understand the logic of idolatry is not in the idol alone, but also in the economies of production and consumption that order lives toward futility and death. Sadly, Christians continue to underutilize this precious knowledge by not bringing into view and calling into question other realities of idolatry, from processed and disease-producing foods, to machines that destroy the environment, to practices of consumption that foster greed and disregard for life. Demetrius grasped the obvious: their financial world is threated and would be overturned by this gospel Paul was preaching.

Demetrius is also shrewd. He makes the connection for his listeners between their economic well-being and the prevailing religious ideology. This gospel threatens our trade and our temple (v. 27). Demetrius has evoked a powerful mix and a winning strategy for fostering hatred and mindless violence. If you want people to hate deeply, hate down to the bone, then suggest that someone or something threatens their financial stability *and* their theological beliefs. If you want people to be willing to kill without hesitation, suggest that these same enemies will weaken the social and political standing of a place and a people by their disrupting actions. Ephesus will diminish in glory as the temple of Artemis diminishes in glory as our businesses diminish in productivity and sales. Once this logic is unleashed on a people, no people has the power to resist its powerful impulse, because it conjures the spirit of fear, and failure, and reminds people of their vulnerability as creatures in this world.

The actions that follow Demetrius's speech indicate a truth of the creature witnessed by the response of the crowd. There is desperation inside the anger of their shout, "Great is Artemis of the Ephesians!" (v. 28). The crowd is always susceptible to the fear that now clothes the creature. The crowd is the creature exposed in its vulnerability. So nationalistic slogan, religious incantation, or enthusiastic cheering are used to conceal this vulnerability. The volume of a crowd is never an indication of the strength of their faith, but always their vulnerability and oftentimes their fear. The crowd needs faith. A crowd that gains faith shrinks in size and becomes a congregation. The crowd that becomes the congregation happens one-by-one, as those who have found the narrow way to life join together (Matt. 7:13–14). But this crowd is far from faith. Those of the diaspora know this. Luke reminds us of these realities, as the presence of Jews among this Gentile crowd only intensifies its fears. The mindlessness of this crowd, the confusion of their actions, easily finds a focus when Jewish bodies appear. There is no crime here, no imminent threat, only Jews, but that is enough to unleash violence. This story and the damnable logic displayed therein will mark the future of the church and of Israel and also marks our time. Luke is no futurist, no prophet in that sense, but he has shown us a dynamic that was and is still deployed against those who believe in the God of Israel. The tragic history that enfolds Christians is that we have forgotten the difference between the crowd and the congregation and have followed those crowds that have hated Israel. We have also succumbed to the seductions of idolatry embedded in the smoothly connected operations of production to consumption to profit and back to production again. What remains for Paul and the disciples is to stay away from the crowd and flee its fears and its temptations and look for the congregation.

20:1–16

The Journey of Jesus, Again

Paul has become like Jesus. Luke frames the journey of Paul inside the journey of Jesus. This one like that one has set his mind on Jerusalem. This one like that one looks to the day of Pentecost. Paul now gathers together those who knew his ministry and shared his life. They are signs of the Spirit's working in him, and they represent a geographic spread of diaspora, Jew and Gentile together. This is the sign of gospel in effect—a mixed group moving in the same direction. What place is ready for such a group? This is a form of nomadic existence in the Spirit that echoes the path of Israel, from the days of unleavened bread to Pentecost. These disciples of Jesus travel in the future and toward the future. Luke, however, brings us to an interesting story, somewhat understated. Paul is speaking and a young man, Eutychus, is falling asleep. This story is quite understandable given Luke's narrative and Paul's experience. How does one give an account of the miraculous penetrating the quotidian? How do you speak of an assertively speaking God who directs by the Spirit while allowing yourself to be guided by the Spirit in your speaking? There is too much to say, and it is filling the hours like buckets being filled with water, until there is no more time, but still more to say.

Eutychus is caught in the middle of ecclesial speech in the making. He is in the midst of what will soon become an often overwhelming discursive practice.

Paul and this youth Eutychus perform a kind of dark humor in Luke's story. It is a dark humor that continues in the church and continues to be instructive. There is something beautiful and spectacular in this moment of Paul as he opens the rivers of living water that have been flowing through him, but there is also something tragic at the window. There sits someone young in a very dangerous position who cannot take all this in and who cannot sustain the energy or attention to stay with Paul. So he falls asleep and falls out of the window. The text is ambiguous about whether he is actually dead (vv. 9–10). But the point is clear. Paul's overabundance of speech and inattentiveness had direct bearing on what happened to this youth. My point is not Luke's point. Luke is offering up a Jesus performance in Paul. Paul goes to this youth who has fallen and injured himself. He takes him in his arms and raises him up. Even without clearly indicating whether in fact Paul raised Eutychus from the dead, Luke again patterns Paul's actions after Jesus.

The youth is raised up! He is brought back from what looks like death to life. Yet we must not lose the irony of this event that echoes to our time. We who speak of the saving life of God are often not mindful of the bodies that listen and the dangerous positions they are in *as they listen*. Nor do we consider enough the danger we put them in as we place the weight of the word on young bodies. In an upper room filled with the Spirit and the sounds of salvation, a young person fell out of the window. Our task, like Paul's, must not only be to go and raise the child up, bringing them back to life and health, but also to be mindful of the effect of our words on the ears of the young.

20:17–38

Communion or Counterfeit

Luke paints with rich colors at this point in the story. He gives us Paul recounting his journey fully within the bonds of the Spirit. There is vulnerability and honesty in these words that mark them as the strange way a servant of Jesus speaks of their suffering and their willingness to suffer. These words, however, are not transferrable. They can only be participatory, only a sharing in the suffering of Jesus. Luke marks the journey of Jesus in the journey of Paul and places the life of Paul in the life of Jesus. This participation in Jesus' suffering is not on some ephemeral plain but involves death threats and assassination plans on the one hand, and arrest, incarceration, and torture on the other hand. Paul is following Jesus as a body at great risk of death. God knows intimately what it means to be a body at risk in this world, a body in imminent danger. Paul now knows this too. But imminent danger is the reality of so many people in the world. So what then is the difference? Paul is showing us that God has drawn that risk into the divine life so that the risk and dangers that may confront us in life will not define our life. Indeed Paul here articulates his life redefined by the pain and hope of Jesus. Luke is giving us the beginnings of a cruciform existence, where my life has been taken from me and given back to me, but not as my own but as God's own life. The value of my life has been transferred to God, and I no longer hold it in my hands or by my efforts. Paul's is a body in the Spirit, having released control of it to God and given himself, without remainder, to the ministry of Jesus Christ.

20:17–27

No one can force someone into this way of life. Paul's words depict a singular commitment and an individualized emptying. As Calvin noted of Paul in this passage, "God has become the governor of his course" and his "calling is the rule of a good life."[6] Calvin captures an intimacy exposed through which a disciple declares that the logic of sacrifice is now the logic of their life. Something has turned in Paul. His zeal has merged with love, and he speaks from the position of a compassion-filled co-laborer with Jesus, sharing in the divine ransom of the many by the one. These are the heady days when what it means to be a servant leader, an elder, a pastor, or a priest is being

---

6. John Calvin, *Commentary on the Acts of the Apostle*, vol. 1 (Grand Rapids: Christian Classics Ethereal Library, 2009), https://www.ccel.org/ccel/calvin/calcom36.i.html.

formed in the crucible of threat and danger. "Behold the lamb of God slain" echoes in these words of Paul.

There has always been great danger of confusion with these words of Paul. The first confusion would be to confuse the sacrifice. Paul is not Jesus, he is not the lamb slain. He has only partaken of the slain lamb, and now the sacrifice of Jesus is in him, filling him with purpose. The confusion, however, is understandable because Luke has given us all the familiar Jesus signposts. The difference is not one of appearance but of power. Paul can save no one, not even himself, but he is being used by the Spirit to announce the salvation that has penetrated time and space, existence and death, breaching every wall of resistance. Disciples in general and pastors in particular still fall victim to this confusion, mistaking the grace Paul lives in with the duty Paul is under. Paul's suffering is spectacular and his commitment compels us to look, but this should not distract us from the *eros* of communion. Paul is being embraced by God and he is yielding to the Spirit, and he invites his listeners to do the same. Yet this points to a second type of confusion that lurks as a danger with Paul's words, and that is to confuse the invitation with an injunction.

No one should be compelled to sacrifice in the way of Jesus. The church has been and continues to be guilty of the ideological use of sacrifice as a way to feed an addiction for control of bodies. It was and is this addiction that distorts the truth of the self-giving of Jesus, turning it into simply an example of the kind of sacrifice others must give, especially women, children, and those imagined as needing heavy domestication. This, however, is not Paul's aim. An intimate world of becoming one with their lover is being opened in this discourse in which this disciple has found his way to union with God, and he invites others to find their way here as well. So his admonition to the other disciples is to find their way so that they might see clearly. See what?

20:28–32

Counterfeits. Keep watch—the image of optic work is very powerful here, and it moves in two directions. The one direction involves self-discernment. We should imagine this as the deepest level of self-care that is inextricably bound to the ministry itself. The newness of the message is at stake in the powerful habits of old ways of thinking and being in the divided world of Jew and Gentile. Luke has already shown us would-be disciples who greatly misunderstand the gospel, and that strong drift toward the old tempts all disciples. The followers of Jesus must sense when the drifting back toward the old is taking place—the lust for power, the desire for control of others, or the fears of diaspora, fears of cultic loss, cultural death, or theological uncertainty—and press more deeply into the Spirit as their anchor. If not, they may become only shadows of the gospel. This is where self-care begins, in truth, the truth of the newness of the gospel that is outside us, drawing us to a new way of living with and for others.

The other direction is toward those who have been found in Jesus. Luke deploys the foundational image, ancient in Israel and deeply intelligible in agrarian societies, of shepherd and flocks of sheep. They are called overseers (*episkopous*, v. 28) made such by the Spirit. This designation appears here in its intense Trinitarian context, as if Luke is exposing the very womb of God to us. Here a people have been born out of the triune God's own suffering, pain, sacrifice, and blood. There is a stark vulnerability at play here that encircles the shepherds, making their lives deeply consequential for the lives of the people of God. Luke has brought forward that ominous dynamic witnessed in Israel of old in the jagged relation between prophets and people when the lives of many may be destroyed by the unfaithfulness of one. But something more serious than ancient prophetic unfaithfulness is at stake now as Paul speaks frantically about the counterfeits. He knows the risk of the gospel for both Jew and Gentile, who have entered a fragile liminal space between the old world and the new. The unprecedented is the order of the day as these converts are seeking to yield to the Spirit and follow divine instruction into an unfamiliar reality of life together.

This is the primal vulnerability that is church rooted in the new and uneasy social and political space created by the Spirit of God. This space requires disciples willing to live floating in baptismal water, their feet no longer held in place by the soft soil of kinship, empire, family, or even religion. These followers of the savior are held afloat by the Spirit working through love for one another. Paul's words capture the truth of the earliest church but also the truth of every church: those who launched out into and live in the deep waters of the Spirit where Jew and Gentile are joining are especially vulnerable to winds and currents and captains who wish to chart the way for us. The Jesus movement draws people who see its potential as a source of unprecedented power, and they bring enough personal charisma, theological knowledge, and social skill to exploit the gospel to its fullest possibilities. Such exploitation is not new news, yet it is still poignant news, and Paul understands that false words can easily slide under truthful speech, and false shepherds, hungry like the wolf, can easily gain power. The famous words of benediction (v. 32) offer the only response to the reality of primal vulnerability: live in the grace of God that is able to build us up (*oikodomēsai*). True stability is being grounded in the grace of God. That grace is the compass we need for living where past, present, and future revolve around the divine life and those who have come away with God. Churches continue to struggle with seeing the crucial difference between a stability rooted in the old ways (of family, nation, or religion) and one rooted in grace.

20:33–38

It does come back to money and possessions. Paul's testimony at this point: "I coveted no one's silver or gold or clothing" closes the circle of his admonition to these Ephesian elders and reveals an angle of discernment through which we can see the real and the counterfeit. Simply put, real overseers position themselves to give, and counterfeit overseers position themselves to take. We embody economic circuits as we also embody economic desire. Economic desire, the desire to support oneself and have enough resources to survive, is not the problem. The horror is found in the circuit, the system of exchange of goods and services that would flow unchecked through our bodies. Paul's words press against the economic circuit of his day, where slavery was a given and everything was shaped by the master/ slave relation. In such a world, one either moved toward being a master with slaves or one moved toward being a slave. Paul's words overturn that movement by resisting economic mastery and refusing the place of the master. Indeed he placed himself in the position of the

one who gives, that is, the slave, yet he is free. This is the freedom
Jesus enables and that we are called to embody, a freedom in the flow
of the economic circuit and a power to redirect its current toward
life. The church struggles mightily in this very matter. Often our failure is a failure of sight. We fail to see the circuit at work all around
us and in us and thereby reduce this revolutionary word of Paul to
a sentimental gesture of almsgiving or, worse, to an apologetic for
economic self-sufficiency. An economic system must be overturned
in us, and it begins with the overseers. Luke has always been clear
about this matter. Indeed his comments about money and possession echo the founding moment of the congregation of Spirit-filled
disciples who sold their possessions and gave the money for the sake
of the common. Their own needs did not disappear. Those needs
simply merged with the needs of the common, and together they
sought a shared flourishing life.

21:1–14

A Jerusalem State of Mind

*How can disciples follow the Spirit and yet follow segregationist
thinking? This is the dilemma of the church. This is our
ongoing struggle with the newness of the Spirit.*

Jerusalem is not only a place but a state of mind. Paul knows this now
as he journeys in Jesus' steps, putting his life on the line in the holy
city. The Spirit does not speak in this passage. The Spirit screams.
The prophetic voice flows through bodies like water flows down
river banks, and in every case those yielded to prophetic unction say
the same to Paul—incarceration and torture await you in Jerusalem.
And with this holy word, the saints draw a conclusion for Paul: don't
go! From start to finish in this passage, it is clear that the journey
is outside their control. Luke reminds us that travel in this ancient
world depended on the commerce patterns of ships. The disciples
get where they need to go by going wherever the ships need to go.
They are an order of hitchhikers: they go where they must by going
where they can. This is the constrained travel itinerary of the ancient

world but also of the Spirit. There is a tension in this text that echoes a blues refrain. Something beyond anyone's control is going on, and all must speak of it, worry about it, cry and plead together about it, but ultimately there is little anyone can do. That is the blues. Paul is coming full circle at this point in the narrative. We again meet Philip, and God has been good to him, for he has daughters, four who can ride the wings of the Spirit and prophesy (8:40). Agabus returns and with him comes prophetic word as well (11:27–28). The Spirit has informed other disciples as well. They all share the painful knowledge of what waits for Paul in Jerusalem.

Why are these tragic interactions revealed at all? Why do we need to see a life that appears to be trapped by fate? Jerusalem is the reason. It is the place where prophets suffer, which means it is the place that resists the Spirit. The Spirit is once again headed to Jerusalem, this time in and with Paul. This is the Spirit's journey, and we read this text poorly if we read it fatalistically as the story of a lone man destined for tribulation. Here we encounter the truth of the Spirit's own struggle and God's own lowliness and humiliation. The Spirit moves with us in the quotidian realities of life, marking our time as God's time and God's time as our time. This is not an example of a man looking to be a martyr, nor is it some sick kind of providence in which God foreordained Paul to suffer and die. This section of Luke's narrative requires that we keep the real history of God clearly in sight, so that we do not turn this into an abstract story about the mysterious hand of God that allows human suffering. This is about the Spirit's striving in Israel, among the people created by God's own hand. Paul has joined his body to the Spirit's burden. There is a profoundly Trinitarian character to this entire set of mournful exchanges, less because of the number of times this word of suffering and pain is announced (20:22–23; 21:4, 11–12), and much more because of its christological repetition. Just as with Jesus, the Spirit leads an obedient one who will do the will of God into Jerusalem. God journeys again into rejection and suffering, and Paul is the companion of God. The prophetic voice here is a disclosing voice, bringing us into an intimate space—the inner life and anguish of God. Again Jerusalem, again.

21:15–40

The Anguish of Diaspora

21:15–21

Diaspora is inescapable. Its concerns shape the contours of Luke's literary work, and now his narrative strains, to the point of possible collapse under the weight of those concerns. If Luke has tried valiantly
to weave a story of collaboration between the apostles and Paul and a
bridge that connects Jew and Gentile, then both are crumbling even as
Luke's account tries to hold it together. Yet this is not a tragedy. This is
the truth of Pentecost and the joining demanded by the Spirit. It was
a truth out beyond the full grasp of these earliest disciples, and it is a
truth yet beyond our full grasp. Who will believe our report? Paul is
again in the presence of James and the other elders, offering careful
testimony of the work of the Spirit. At this moment Paul is the Spirit's
advocate, giving specific evidence of the hand of God. He bears witness to a God fully at home among the goyim (Gentiles). The only
response to such unprecedented divine action is praise.

God is praised when lives are turned toward redemptive light.
Yet this praise, like so much praise, happens within the constrained
conditions of diaspora. God is praised rightly and truly, but there is
a concern that polices that praise, weakens its reach into the lives of
its hearers. James and the other elders speak as one voice of the very
familiar, Jew and Gentile. They say that there is Jew and there is Gentile, equal now before the face of God but separate in worship of that
same God. This is a difference that requires a different way of life that
must be acknowledged even inside the gospel that has come from
God. This is a form of segregationist theology, yet we must understand it as inside diaspora anxiety. Paul is deeply familiar with that
anxiety. Luke has repeatedly narrated it, and now it is overwhelming.
So much is at stake at this moment, because diaspora is about life
and death, hope and despair, and the struggle to maintain identity.

The good news is that the good news has been taken seriously.
Thousands believe the word about Jesus and the word of Jesus *and*
are also zealots for the law (*zēlōtai tou nomou,* v. 20); their lives
are marked not only by the observance of Torah but also by its
protection. They watch over the identity formed by Torah to uphold

it, sustain it, and keep its honor.[7] These two realities of gospel and Torah are not in competition. They are in fact one. Paul, however, has been presented as someone who tears asunder these realities and has done so where it matters most, in diaspora space ("Jews living among the Gentiles," v. 21). The accusation is not true, but even as a lie it has the power of a truth, because it touches the dangerous realities of life in diaspora where a people could be washed away, body, mind, and/or soul. This accusation carries the punch of a double fear, both the loss of direction for life, especially young lives, being adrift in a sea of Gentiles and the death of a people, drowned in that same *goyim* sea.

21:22–25

What, then, is to be done? Given diaspora anxiety, James and the elders offer a plan of conformity. This is the appearance of conformity for one whose Jewish identity and commitment to Torah was never in question. But Paul is now pressed by the disciples of Jesus into the bio-politics of authenticity. Prove to those who will see you that you are true to your identity—this is what their plan entails, so Paul will move through the rite of purification, paying for it for himself and others. Thereby he will show that he exists in a safe sameness with these others, observing and guarding the law. This performance of authenticity is meant to address diaspora anxiety, but diaspora fear cannot be overcome in this way. James and the elders, these followers of Jesus, have not followed the Spirit all the way into Gentile space. Indeed they rehearse the initial decision (noted in Acts 15) that Gentiles need not become Jews, but only follow the contours of a life sanctified to God. The Jerusalem leaders see parallel worlds, Jew and Gentile, but that is not the world created and now being recreated by the Spirit.

Paul is in the hands of diaspora anxiety, and that anxiety is in the disciples of Jesus. This is absolutely ironic, because the disciples of Jesus have spoken and yet speak in other tongues. They have experienced language (and thereby experienced life) in peoples other than their own. Although these other nations were represented by

---

7. Johnson, *Acts,* 374.

God-fearers and Jews from the diaspora, the gesture irrefutably pointed toward the Gentiles and the world. The Spirit has shown them that they can enter another people without fear of being lost in another people. How can the Spirit who joins and diaspora fear that separates exist in the same body? How can disciples follow the Spirit and yet follow segregationist thinking? This is the dilemma of the church. This is our ongoing struggle with the newness of the Spirit.

We are yet committed to separate but equal thinking, yet imbibing diaspora anxiety. We often long for homogeneity, which is the desire for a sameness that helps us cope with a diversity that we cannot anticipate or control. That longing leads to the futile performance of authenticity masquerading as commitment to God but in actuality only plays to a watching crowd. Church after church has not grown forward from Pentecost and like James and the elders creates plans of conformity destined to fail. The fundamental difference between the Jerusalem church and our churches is that they struggled to imagine an expansion of Torah-filled life into Gentile space that would alter Jewish space without loss of identity. We who live on the other side of Christian colonialism have watched the emergence of a soul-killing, people-destroying expansionism that forced peoples into a Christian sameness, an orthodoxy of body and dress, comportment and character that has numbed the minds of many and presented the faith as exquisite subjugation.

The struggle was and continues to be a struggle of sight and hope. Like James and the elders we must see the Spirit who enters lives without destroying lives and joins with us, becoming one with us, while remaining the Spirit of God. We must see a Spirit that joins Jew and Gentile and joins peoples without destroying peoples, and yet the Spirit expands into our lives and becomes new in us, new every morning. The Spirit would draw us into that newness where peoples do not lose themselves but find themselves through the addition of others.

21:26–40

Paul tried to follow the plan of conformity birthed in the minds of James and the elders, but it failed. It was destined to fail, because diaspora anxiety is never satisfied by conformity. Once it imagines difference concealed in sameness, nothing can be done to change that image. So diaspora Jews ("Jews from Asia," v. 27) saw Paul engaged in his performance of authenticity through purification, but Paul's performance could not hide what diaspora imagined they saw—the mark of a traitor. So Paul will face what all those who are imagined as traitors must face—the struggle to have his own voice heard in the midst of a loud and false narrative that he cannot hope to defeat. These diaspora Jews from Asia narrate Paul as demon. He teaches against our people, our law, this place, and he defiles us (v. 28). Paul has not spoken nor can he speak in such a moment because the crowd has been brought to life. Luke has shown us this crowd before (Luke 23). It is the personification of the human in pain, fear, and desperation, and the crowd turns on Paul's body, as they had turned on Jesus' body. Paul is beaten without mercy.

"They were trying to kill him" (v. 31). The gift was closed inside this horror. Paul, like Jesus, was offering himself to God and to them, but the crowd, easily gripped by fear, cannot receive the gift. It can only see threat. This is the way of the crowd, because this is the way of the human. Our weakness and vulnerability is on full display once we enter our mode of crowd. This is chaos, and the empire knows how to handle chaos: with the chaos of military force. The military arrives and seizes the body of Paul. We should speak of it this way because now Paul is simply an object of offense that must be removed from the crowd. From the perspective of the tribune, Paul is just another would-be revolutionary stirring up political ferment. His question, "Are you the Egyptian insurgent?" reminds us of the optic through which this Jesus movement will be seen by the empire—just another religio-political faction that needs to be managed. The concern of empire will be if this faction is an actual threat to the regime or just another religious barking dog with no bite. This is the reality of our theological conflict seen from the lens of a violence-infused world: these conflicts between Jews and these other theological upstarts are merely intramural squabbles that, if unchecked, may lead to real problems. Paul, the Jew, standing there next to tribune and soldiers, asked from the crowd what he could never have gotten on his own: silence. So he will speak in the worst possible condition for speech, in a space filled with soldiers, tension, and fury, with his body bruised and probably bloodied. The Spirit

has brought him full circle. He now stands like his savior, speaking to his people in their own tongue. Paul shares in so much at this moment with his savior and his people. He shares in Jesus' suffering and his people's pain. He shares in their subjugation to Roman rule and his savior's constant plea to his people. His words will hang in the air, suspended between anger and hope. A prophet speaks to diaspora in faith, but will they hear?

22:1–28:31

The Disciple-Citizen

22:1–29

Dangerous Speech

The disciple of Jesus is a desperate citizen because she knows that lives are at stake in the operations of the state, her own life, and others. Desperate citizenship does not take citizenship lightly but presses it to its absolute limits to perform the good for the sake of Jesus Christ.

22:1–22

Paul speaks inside of misperception. The crowd does not see him through the truth of his own words. They only see him through the lies born of diaspora fear. How does one speak in such a situation? This will be the dilemma for countless Christians who will follow Paul, and even for us now. How do we speak when surrounded by rumor and false words, by accusation and complaint? How do we speak dogged by a history of our own doing, of hateful speech and action? The only actual way forward for Christians and for Christianity is testimony. Paul will offer a witness that will also be the self-witness of Jesus. Such witness is never thoughtless. Luke weaves a beautiful word performed through the mouth of Paul, bringing together powerful rhetorical elements from Greek *apologia*. Paul claims diaspora in its full reality—a commitment to the way of Israel's God in and among the wayward (Gentile) places of this world. He is a Jew (*eimi anēr Ioudaios*; v. 3). Paul announces the familiar. This is indeed family speech.

His pedigree is without dispute and his earlier actions against those of the Way clearly align him with the protective strategies of diaspora and the kind of violence he himself received at the temple.

Must zealousness always be aligned with violence? It seems that diaspora fear makes this so. How can one stand against the forces that would kill and destroy a way of life if not by making use of the tool of death, violence? Paul testifies to the seductive power of violence (vv. 4–5) and in so doing exposes the entanglement of zeal with fear even for the people of God. Such entanglement can only be broken by the Son of God, who collapsed violence onto his own body. Paul experienced this collapse on the Damascus road, that site of diaspora life. Paul now exposes the intimate space of the revolution—Jesus speaks to him and he hears Jesus. This exposition of the intimate is what brings Christian testimony to life. It is living words about the living word. Paul's dramatic account would not have sounded utterly strange to his hearers because it outlines the way of the prophet and the operation of the prophetic. But its placement is absolutely unprecedented. Paul's testimony disrupts the connection of violence to zeal and reverses the flow of Jewish faith, no longer against Jesus but toward him, no longer over against his disciples but with them. Religious zeal has found its righteous home—in the body of Jesus and away from the power of violence.

Paul keeps all of this in the family of God. Ananias is of the people of God as Paul is. The story Paul proclaims reveals the shared sensibilities of those who know, live, and love Torah, except something different is being narrated here. A resurrected Jesus is directing and guiding, drawing a life faithful to Torah toward an embodied *telos*, an embodied purpose. The zeal for the way of God that was immersed in a brutal and bloody sanctification now gives way to a new orientation—toward the Gentiles. The pathos of Luke's narrative is overwhelming at this point. Paul's words have cut deeply into his hearers as they struggled to imagine his speech as an authentic word from the Lord. The *goyim* are the opposition, the ocean that would wash away Israel if not held back. So how can this Jesus to whom Paul testifies be anything other than the destroyer of Jewish life and identity? The crowd speaks its fear-formed truth again: kill this man before he destroys us. The crowd thinks in absolutes:

kill or be killed. Paul with these words is performing a future that is almost impossible for a crowd woven in diaspora fear to see. Paul's Jewish body is now the horizon on which God wants Israel to see freshly the Gentile body. How can one who is fully connected to and deeply embedded in their own people also be *at the same moment* the portal to another people and a site for joining? Only through the Holy Spirit. The new that Paul speaks can only be accepted in faith or rejected with violence.

22:23–29

The crowd's fury was now too much. Paul had gestured this join-ing—a Jew among the Gentiles by the will of God—and at that moment became absolute threat and absolutely expendable. Yet to the representatives of the Roman state this entire matter was beyond them, so their response was the state response—torture the pris-oner to get at the real issue. When the state is confused, they torture people to alleviate their confusion. The tribune and the soldiers have heard the words of Paul and the shouts of the crowd, but they have not yet heard anything to make intelligible this public passion. They have not heard a revolutionary who would challenge Roman rule. So what is the issue? Surely, there must be something beyond the theo-logical intricacies of his speech that drew out mob violence? Paul

---

In any nonviolent struggle, civil disobedience is a tactic that must be employed strategically. Dr. King learned from Gandhi and taught the civil rights movement the basic, four-stage process that leads to effective civil disobedience. First, a campaign against injustice must do its homework and gather the facts. Second, we attempt to negotiate with the ruling authorities. Only after they've refused us can we move to stage three: self-purification. Because civil disobedience is a decision to personally embrace the suffering we have sought to prevent, it is not simply a strategic opportunity. The opposition may open the door, but we must always be sure we have prepared ourselves before we step through it. Only then, after examining our own willingness to suffer until enemies become friends, can we move to stage four: direct action.

William Barber II, with Jonathan Wilson-Hartgrove, *The Third Reconstruction: Moral Mondays, Fusion Politics and the Raise of a New Justice Movement* (Boston: Beacon Press, 2016), 77.

understands the way of the state and deploys its logic against its rote actions—I am a Roman citizen! With these words, Paul performs desperate citizenship. This is in fact the only kind of citizenship for a disciple of Jesus. It is one that plays the game of the state, working with its identity politics to defeat its use of violence. Desperate citizenship does not take citizenship lightly, but presses it to its absolute limits to perform the good for the sake of Jesus Christ.

The disciple of Jesus is a desperate citizen because she knows lives are at stake in the operations of the state, her own life, and others. This kind of citizenship depends wholly on one's level of vulnerability in this world. The vulnerable enter citizenship with a purpose different from the elites, for whom citizenship is only an embroidery to their existence. It only adds to their strength and aids the accomplishing of their desires. Vulnerable people reach for citizenship to stave off death. Paul is a Roman citizen by birth, but at this moment he has joined the hope of the weak, to turn the law in their favor and draw down the power of the state to harm. The disciple-citizen bends the will of the state away from violence and toward the protection of bodies. Luke has passed a threshold in his narrative. We are now in the realm of the disciple-citizen with Paul, where he must negotiate the tight space between diaspora fear and state power while remaining focused on the work ahead—to announce the joining of Jew and Gentile in Jesus through the Holy Spirit. Paul's testimony now exposes a political density that we have in our day and time almost completely forgotten.

22:30–23:35

Between Rocks and Hard Places

Jesus encourages Paul. This is what Jesus does. He encourages us in the midst of struggle and especially at what seems like the beginning of an intensification of suffering.

22:30–23:5

We are back at the prison. Luke's narrative is woven through captivity, release, and more incarceration, and judges, tribunals, and the constant work of giving an account of oneself and one's actions. This is not incidental to his story. It is the ground of intelligibility for the discipleship he inscribes. The disciples of Jesus must face the technologies of incarceration because they are the fundamental tools used to resist the work of the Spirit. Luke's story from this point to its end is simple: Paul in prison, Paul chained, Paul facing the threat of death yet faithful to the resurrected Jesus. Every step he takes is labored and measured. They must be, because his options are gone. Now his actions are synchronized with Jesus' actions, and he will wear the tangled garment of the disciple-citizen. Standing in front of the council is terribly dangerous space. Paul is struck even as he begins to speak (23:2), which indicates that they are not there to actually hear what he has to say.

The action of the high priest is not surprising given his intoxication with violence. Something terribly tragic is being played out in this scene where theological disagreement has entered absolute brutality. This is where the integrity of theological discourse collapses. It does not collapse in the consistency or inconsistency, coherence or incoherence of its ideas, or at the warrants for its claims. It breaks apart precisely at the place where fear becomes focused on a person, and then hatred gives birth to the desire to silence and destroy. The church is yet to learn the sad lesson of the action of the high priest. This is the well-worn path of theological minds that must have their way, so utterly convinced of their clarity that they listen to their opponents only to find an opportunity to shut them up or unleash violence on them. Paul's response is the template against such theological violence. It is hypocrisy, and he names it as such by calling the high priest a whitewashed wall (*toiche kekoniamene*, 23:3) and cursing him. This leader is one whose appearance conceals the decay and death that is at work in him. Behind the wall are only the remains of drained life.

Paul's indignation is holy, and it finds perfect pitch in his exposition of this hypocritical posture of the high priest. This is how we must respond to the violence that infects all debate, especially theological debate—by strongly denouncing actions that undermine the witness of the people of God. Yet the cursing of the high priest is disturbing ("God will strike you!", 23:3) because it suggests vengeance and harkens back to ancient quid pro quo thinking in which violence is returned for violence. Paul's response, however, returns the violence back to its perpetrator as a judgment that will be rendered by God. Striking Paul invites divine vengeance. The use of violence always stands in the shadow of divine vengeance. Paul's words raise the question whether it is possible to curse the use of violence and those who use it without succumbing to the seductive power of violence even in hope of divine retribution. Might we hope less for vengeance and more for divine justice to be realized in space and time soon and very soon? The high priest contradicts the law of God in his embrace of violence in order to silence his enemy. Paul has little chance of being heard by someone whose theological orthodoxy has been compromised by the will to power. So another stratagem comes to mind for Paul. He must speak the truth in a space that is not ready for the truth.

23:6–11

"I am on trial concerning the hope of the resurrection of the dead" (v. 6). Paul's theological witness turns with his political witness, and he understand the power of his words in this hostile space. Luke fills in the details here so that we may sense the volatility of this situation, but Paul's words capture both Sadducees and Pharisees in something neither is ready to hear—that the hope of the resurrection has been realized in Jesus. Even the seemingly affirming words of the Pharisees that "a spirit or an angel [may have] . . . spoken to him" (v. 9) falls terribly short of the message that Paul embodies. Indeed the resistance of the Pharisees is all the more astounding given that Paul is speaking on the same theological terrain that they occupy. Of all people, they should hear him. Yet once again Luke shows us Pharisaic resistance to the Spirit of God. The word of resurrection that Paul speaks is a new starting point for the theological imagination of both Sadducees and Pharisees. There is, however, a chasm between this new starting point and the theological dissension that now encircles Paul in this setting. Sadducees and Pharisees have given into the violence that tempts theological discourse, and Paul's life is threatened at this moment. Violence has been chosen over hope, and death over resurrection. Throughout the history of the church when these horrible

choices have been made, the claims of our faith have been seriously compromised.

The irony of this event also often escapes our reading of this section of Luke's narrative. Paul is in the complexities of the disciple-citizen. The words of the Lord frame that complexity for us: "Keep up your courage! For just as you have testified for me in Jerusalem, so you must bear witness also in Rome" (v. 11). This is an extraordinary moment through which Luke narrates the intimacy of life with God for Paul. Jesus encourages Paul. This is what Jesus does. He encourages us in the midst of struggle and especially at what seems like the beginning of an intensification of suffering. The words of Jesus point to Paul's destiny, to bear witness. His life is in Paul's life, and Paul's life is in his life. God takes bodies and places with absolute seriousness. Paul's body in Jerusalem and then in Rome—this is the divine desire for us to be where witness must be given and for God to be with us in the giving of that witness in difficult places. This intimacy will be the engine that drives everything Paul will say and do now. Every moment is now a Jesus moment in which and through which Jesus will breathe every breath with Paul, hear every sound, and speak in Paul. Paul and Jesus will be like two musicians who have become one in song, each leaning in to hear the other and expressing a sound that speaks the one sound they want heard.

23:12–35

Paul, the disciple-citizen, will face the purest form of violence at the hands of some of his own people: assassination. Here the power of death to seduce us reaches its absolute strength. Children of the covenant make covenant with death. There had been plots against Paul before this (Acts 9:24; 20:3, 19), but this strikes at the heart of life, because those who would kill Paul make death their intimate partner, offering their own bodies to it if they fail to unleash its power on the body of Paul. Assassins marry death and thereby become its agent. They join in death's constant planning to take as much of life as possible, even the lives of its agents. The tragedy of assassins is that they do not realize that they are death's mark as well. Forty people bind "themselves by an oath neither to eat nor drink until they had killed Paul" (v. 12). They promise themselves slow and painful death to the extent they fail to bring the quick death of Paul. Indeed to engage in any planning to kill for nationalist, military, political, or economic reasons is to enter the slow and painful death of the killers. There is no nobility in planning the death of another, nor may we justify it for the expediency of saving a life or a way of life. Such planning is already death, already a gesture of obedience to death, announcing it our lord and master.

No pain comes close to the kind of pain in which one's own people seek your death. Who can bear the pain of being seen as a traitor? Who can walk the trail of betrayal? Luke brings us to this Jesus space found in the plight of Paul. Here we search for sight of love and understanding surrounded by the thick fog of hate and violence. But first Paul must be saved. Paul's young nephew hears of the plot and Luke gives us a short story worthy of an exciting novella. This is the story of the future saving the future. This young man will act for the sake of Paul and the gospel to thwart the agents of death. None of the events that Luke gives us in this short story are beyond belief. Indeed given the volatile nature of the religious and political landscape in Jerusalem, Roman officials acting in extraordinary ways to keep the peace makes complete sense. Paul's young nephew exposes the plot to the tribune, and now the state will deliver Paul. Soldiers, horses, weapons, and military protocols are all called on to do this work. These are strange times, and Paul is in a strange place. At this moment, the state will do for Paul what it would not do for Jesus, deliver him from the hand of death. The irony does not escape Luke as he narrates an impossible situation for Paul. Again this is desperate citizenship enacted at the site of diaspora fear transmuted into extreme violence.

Paul's desperate citizenship is performed at the in-between space, between those of Israel who desire his death and a state trying to stave off possible religious anarchy and political upheaval. What does it mean to be in the hands of the state for the sake of the gospel? Make no mistake—the state is no friend of Paul or the gospel. It holds no warmth for this disciple of Jesus, but at this moment it is needed for Paul's survival against the people of God. This is the sheer horror of this portion of Luke's narrative. Rome thwarts the designs of those who would kill Paul, and here it is absolutely crucial we see two different historical interpretive trajectories of these events. The first way to read this is to read the necessity of the state as protector. Such a reading has from time to time and place to place intoxicated the church. It finds the state as the default mechanism against the excesses of religious zeal and violence. Here the state protects its citizens from threats, especially religious threats, against their lives. This way of seeing the state is terribly shortsighted and fails to see the beginning, middle, or end of the matter. From the beginning the state was willing to incarcerate, torture, and kill anyone deemed problematic, including the disciples of Jesus. In the middle, Paul's life hangs in the balance, and the hand of the state that now protects him could easily be the hand that kills him. At the end, Paul will have to work to convince the state to spare his life. The state, in the final analysis, does not have the power to resist the seductive power of death, because it will kill again and again. Yet to read the state as protector is an all-too-common way of reading this moment. Such readings always deny the real histories of violence and fantasize a safe space against violence inside the military operations of the state.

Another interpretive trajectory presents itself precisely in the space of Paul surrounded by soldiers on horseback and on foot. He travels with them away from danger to danger, being led by the Spirit of God. This way of reading remembers that Paul is in God's hand, not the state's power. Paul is not in a state of emergency, but of emergence. The gospel has created the unprecedented, and the new that the Spirit has called forth demands a response by both the state and the people of God. Together they are caught up in the work of God, and the word will be spoken to both by one whose body has been made vulnerable in the presence of both. Paul gives witness to Israel and to Rome. We must remember the word of Jesus to Paul, "Keep up your courage!" The work of witness must go toward the state and toward Israel, toward Gentile and Jew. Paul is a site of joining, and joining always has deep political consequences. This way of reading this moment in Paul's journey refuses to climb inside the managerial interpretive lens of government officials because that lens is much too small to capture what is going on. As the tribune said, "I found that he was accused

concerning questions of their law, but was charged with nothing
deserving death or imprisonment" (v. 29). There is no depth perception here, only a reading of surfaces. Paul travels with a word
about him that cannot possibly do justice to who he is or the word
he brings with him. Caught between Israel and Rome, Paul is not
being delivered from the former to the latter. He is drawing both
to a destiny in God and a decision for or against the resurrected
Lord in a space and a time from which there will be no escape.
Even if we wish to imagine that the state can protect what it does
not understand, that is, the religious against the religious, it cannot even protect itself from that which it imagines it understands
so well, the seduction of violence and the power of death. This is
precisely the deliverance that the resurrected Jesus brings.

24:1–23

The Political Is the Theological

Paul is not safe either among his own people or in the hands of the
State. His safety is between both in the hands of the Spirit. Paul's
work of witness now exposes its political density in ways that we
should never take for granted. Paul must face a Jerusalem delegation
that comprises powerful people: the high priest Ananias, elders, and
a lawyer, that is, a professional orator and advocate skilled at knowing what to say to those in power to get what he wants. Tertullus, the
lawyer, is a hired intellectual gun, and the world is filled with such
people who use their considerable intellectual skill, verbal dexterity,
and eloquence not for the pursuit of justice or truth, but for money.
We do not know whether Tertullus is Jew or Gentile, but that is not
important for understanding his purpose in this story. What is crucial is that he is intellectual and legal power being marshalled against
an innocent man. Luke here marks judicial sin that speaks to a wider
sinful condition—intellectual prowess in league with death. How
many women, men, and children have been sentenced to prison,
torture, and death through this kind of demonic connection? How
many well-trained men and women have used their gifts to destroy
life? Here we see the discursive arts fully corrupted, and what makes

this even more horrible is that such corrupted discursive arts are being used by the people of God.

Tertullus's words frame a false story of a dangerous rebel in their midst. Paul the "pestilent fellow" (v. 5) was captured by the Jews themselves, he says, gesturing a bit of Jewish self-determination (against Roman occupation) while at the same time suggesting cooperation and collaboration with Rome in maintaining political and social stability through Roman rule. Brilliant, but evil. Tertullus's words become the platform for the others who had come with him to launch their testimony. "The Jews also joined in the charge by asserting that all this was true" (v. 9). They build on the discursive power of Tertullus. This is the way of the world, and it has historically been also the way of many churches in many places, operating alongside and inside the machinations of brilliant but evil orators, lawyers, advocates who become our hired guns. Yet what has been more damnable has been our failure, a Christian failure to educate against the misuse of intellectual skill, verbal dexterity, and eloquence. Too often we have been mystified by such gifts and have idealized them abstracted from the real history of the horror

> There are two different forms of intellectual life, one that functions as if Jesus' cross, resurrection, and the coming of the Spirit does not matter and the other fully captured by these world-shattering and life-creating realities.

they have created and the suffering they continue to inflict. We have been too quick to rush to their defense, announcing the inherent goodness of such gifts and the glory of those who exhibit them without counting the cost of their use. Tertullus has become a weapon of unrighteousness, and we must always ask ourselves, how might we prevent the creation of such weapons?

Paul matches the oratorical and intellectual skills of Tertullus. We could count him as a weapon of righteousness pressing against this unrighteous weapon for the sake of Jesus and his own life. Paul weaves a legal and theological defense inside an alternative narration of the events. The facts are simple and straightforward: he went to the temple to worship. He caused no disturbance, he followed Jewish law and custom. He did the right thing. His accusers are not present and those now accusing him are not eyewitnesses. This is hearsay. Thus the charges should be dropped. Yet Paul also weaves the gospel into this argument—I share a hope with my accusers in the resurrection from the dead, and that hope has been realized. This word of truth deeply upsets my kin-opponents, Paul is saying. That is why they speak against me. Paul claims the power of the storyteller who tells the story of Israel rightly, aimed toward life eternal. Yet Paul and Tertullus do not represent similar intellectual gifts used for good or evil, because to see them in this way only sees the utility of the gifts. Such a way of reading this pivots on circumstance and situation. So Tertullus, in this way of thinking, could easily be Paul's defender if the money is right. Tertullus and Paul represent intellectual life before cross, resurrection, and the coming of the Spirit and intellectual life after these world-shattering and life-creating realities. Paul now speaks inside the hope of resurrection and as one who yields to the Spirit. His words aim at faithfulness and gesture divine presence. He certainly wants to win, finding justice against false accusations, yet the arch of his discursive work bends toward the resurrected body of Jesus. He speaks in witness to the hope of resurrection.

What would it mean to educate people inside this hope? What would it mean to immerse, that is, to baptize intellectual ability, verbal dexterity, and eloquence inside the body of Jesus, inside his death and resurrection and his sending of the Spirit, so that our words, no matter of what we speak, arch toward hope and give witness to resurrection? Here we might tease out from Paul's rich defense the possibilities of such an intellectual baptism. Of course, we must note that none of this makes any difference to Felix, "his Excellency," who does not care about Paul or his opponents beyond how he might keep this political situation from hurting him and how he might make use of it for his own gain. Felix knows that there is no real case against Paul here, and the lightness of his concern is matched by the lightness of Paul's incarceration. He allows Paul to "have some liberty" and have his friends visit him and take care of him (v. 23). In showing Paul to be no threat to the Roman state, Luke does something else as well. He shows the low levels of interest or enthusiasm for the gospel in the halls of political power or in the sight of the empire. Luke is showing us the formation of an opinion about the gospel that always flows through empire: it is foolishness. Paul's witness to Rome formats a judgment against empire precisely in the formation of empire's judgment against the gospel. Paul sees hope, and the empire sees folly. This is the difference between sight and blindness.

24:24–27
The Assimilated Couple

This is not a natural break in the story but a continuation of the actions of Felix from verses 22 onward. It forms a nice segue to Paul's next audience with Roman officials. It also shows us the complex world Paul must navigate where he must confront an alternative mixture, an alternative joining of Jew and Gentile. This is cultural assimilation, where Jew and Gentile join within the social ecology of Rome. Felix and his wife, Drusilla, represent assimilated existence where the way of life within empire has become their way of life. Felix is not Jewish. Other historical sources tell us that Felix was once a slave who made his way out of slavery and up the political ladder.[1] His critics suggested that while he functioned as a Roman official he yet acted like a slave. This, no doubt, is a critique not only of his failed leadership but a word of insult about his pedigree. Class bias is often inescapable for those who find themselves in positions of power without sharing in the same social formation of the master classes, then and now. Felix was interpreted as a man in power with a slave's mentality, an uneasy fit. Luke, however, allows us to see an additional uneasy fit, Drusilla, his Jewish wife, living against diaspora life. Together they form another couple. Yet unlike Ananias and Sapphira or Priscilla and Aquila, this couple is of the empire and of Roman culture. They represent assimilated life.

24:24–25

Other historical sources fill in the story of Drusilla.[2] She married Felix after leaving her former husband in what seemed to have been a marriage of political and social convenience for her and him.

---

1. C. Kavin Rowe, *World Upside Down: Reading Acts in the Graeco-Roman Age* (New York: Oxford University Press, 2010), 71–72.
2. Josephus, *Antiquities of the Jews* 20:141–43, cited in Luke Timothy Johnson, *The Acts of the Apostles* (Collegeville, MN: The Liturgical Press, 1992), 418, 423.

Together Jew and Gentile, former slave and formerly unfaithful wife formed a union that fit the social ecology of Rome and the political economy of empire. This is the way assimilation works. It fits us to survive and thrive in a world not of our own choosing or making. And in return it would conceal and if possible destroy our people's histories by drowning them in a wider narrative of national or cultural existence. Roman culture was skilled at the technologies of assimilation. Both through force and seduction, it convinced multiple peoples that the peace it provided (*pax Romana*) included a superior way of life bound to its imperialist culture. Israel was accustomed to the horrors of assimilation. Diaspora life stood against that very power. But now Paul faced an example of that power in that Felix and Drusilla were Gentile and Jew fully inside Roman subjectivity. The good news is that they called for Paul. The calling itself is hopeful as they heard Paul "speak concerning faith in Christ Jesus" (v. 24).

Luke notes three nodes of Paul's discourse: justice, self-control, and the coming judgment. Commentators tend to focus in on the second node, self-control, as being the most problematic for the ears of this couple (or at least Felix) given their scandalous beginnings. Paul is most certainly engaged in something far more radical than moralistic sermonizing. These ideas of justice, self-control, and the coming judgment point to the wider narrative that he has already been telling repeatedly of a world made right through Christ Jesus. Indeed if we hold them together we find justice noted before self-control and held on the other side by judgment. Thus self-control is inside a trajectory that moves from justice to judgment. The justice that Messiah Jesus has inaugurated, a justice that will overturn the forces of violence and death and that sets captives free will culminate in his judging the living and dead. Too often the church has isolated self-control from this lovely trajectory from justice to judgment and even forgotten justice and simply gone from self-control to judgment in its proclamation. Yet Paul's words to this couple are about more than their relationship. They are about their life together within the life of Messiah Jesus. Thus Paul's words to Felix and Drusilla do an additional work: they challenge the power of assimilation by offering an alternative story within which to place their lives. Paul has brought forward all the power of diaspora life concentrated in this word of faith in Christ Jesus. It is a word that calls them out of Roman assimilation to new life. Maybe this is what frightens Felix. He hears, and maybe Drusilla hears, the shattering of Roman subjectivity in the message of the gospel. If the gospel is rightly proclaimed, then it will always challenge assimilation by reminding us that we live inside a Jewish story that cannot be assimilated but burns away all that would cover its truth: Christ Jesus is the giver of life, and your life is now inside his story.

Sadly the church has too often failed to challenge the power of assimilation and in fact has often been in league with empire-like assimilation. Christians have time and again preferred the strange mixture, the troubled joining of assimilation where indigenous peoples have been forced or seduced to take on alternative identities for the sake of survival and under threat of death. The faith has been presented to many peoples within a tragic calculus of loss and surrender where their own cultural practices and ways of life were rendered demonic, or deficient, or relegated to a past that can no longer be productive of life. Such a vision of assimilation has been hard at work in Christianity, especially since the modern colonial period when becoming Christian meant for so many becoming Spanish, Portuguese, English, Dutch, French, German, or American, and so forth. That long historical reach of assimilation in league with Christianity can only be effectively countered with an alternative vision rooted in the life of Jesus, his justice, his self-control, and his coming judgment that frees us to enter into a new possibility of life together and of joined difference. Yet Felix and Drusilla resist that possibility and remain locked in Roman sensibilities. Paul is asked to go away (v. 25).

24:26–27

Felix is of the old world, the world of empire politics. So he invites Paul into the dance of money and power. Paul will be repeatedly invited to audience with Felix for one sole purpose—to grant Paul the opportunity to gain his freedom by becoming captive to the way of empire politics. Paul could offer Felix money for his freedom.

Money often means freedom. That formula has been with us for a very long time and remains an effective medicine against incarceration. It is the rule unaffected by its few exceptions. Those with money in this world rarely go to jail or remain in prison for long. Those with money can buy their freedom and turn the judicial system into a barking dog with no real bite. We could do like many people do and live in the naivety that those with money and power engage in less criminal behavior, but Felix destroys that belief. He exposes the truth that those in power are often attuned to the processes of exchange that permeate the judicial system. Many working in the judicial system follow a financial quid pro quo that yields purchased freedom and creates another common formula—poverty often means incarceration. As we noted from the first moment that disciples of Jesus were placed in jail, we must question not only the narrative that all those in prison deserve to be there but also the morality of the prison itself, knowing that the prison has always existed inside economic and political desire and the flow of money and power. The prison has always been inside the market just as much as it is inside the state.

Luke brings us into the tension of Paul's imprisonment. For two long years, Felix invited Paul into the old world, and for two long years Paul refused entry. What does it mean to be offered repeatedly the opportunity to bribe your way to freedom? Surely Paul could have found ways to get the money and gain his release, but his work of witness closed off that option. We too quickly bypass this crucial aspect of Luke's narrative that will become even more important as we move to its conclusion. Paul must wrestle against the burden of prison time, that special kind of time that carries with it a deep sense of the absurdity of waste and the pain of slow loss especially for those who know their innocence. Paul is suffering witness, bound to his encourager, Jesus, and so too are those who suffer in prisons today who carry the knowledge of their innocence. Felix plays with Paul's life, just as the lives of so many women, men, and children are used to make a political point that reveals a tragic disregard for life. The question this portion of Luke's narrative asks us is, will we remember those in prison whose lives are stretched from the decisions of one judge or ruler or politician to the next and who are always in danger of being forgotten in the play of political favors and maneuvers? Paul is left in prison, and to know this and remember this is a witness of the gospel.

25:1–27

The Citizen-Disciple

How do you think, sleep, dream, eat, and live when your life hangs suspended in a legal process that moves painfully slow and is governed by a judicial system not concerned with the truth? This is the plight of so many, and it must become the deepest concern of the church.

25:1–12

The tight space of life for Paul, the disciple-citizen, has just gotten even tighter. His enemies are closing in on him, and he has only one option: press more intensely into the work of witness. A new political player has entered Luke's story: Festus replaces Felix, but the politics have not changed. Paul is yet pawn, and this is yet the ecology of empire. Diaspora anger has given way to diaspora obsession over Paul, and his enemies want only his death. Paul, in their eyes, is no longer a part of the people of God, a member of the covenant family, but a traitor who must not continue to draw the breath of life. It is astounding that those who want Paul dead are the chief priests and the leaders of the people (v. 2). Those who should be able to see faith in God being renewed only see faith being destroyed and have placed themselves in league with the demonic and the power of death. These wayward leaders of the people of God eagerly petition the new Roman official to aid them in the work of assassination. Earlier in Luke's narrative he showed us a demonic covenant mapped on top of the holy practice of fasting in which forty people vowed to neither eat or drink until they successfully carried out Paul's assassination (23:12–14). And at this point in the story, we can only marvel at the faithfulness of Paul's enemies to that covenant, because two years have passed and their bloodlust has not abated.

It was the same simple plan. Send Paul back to us, and we will kill him on the return journey. Festus, like Felix, was willing to do a favor for his Jewish subjects, and like Felix he would use judicial ritual to cover over a decision he had already made before such ritual could be enacted. It had to be acted out, so Festus took his tribunal seat, the official seat of judgment, and launched legal theater. The scene Luke paints in verses 6–12 is horrifying. Paul is surrounded by his hateful accusers shouting charges against him. As horrifying as this is, we must never lose sight of the humanity of his enemies because they believe they are doing a good and righteousness thing. They by any means necessary (by lying and bearing false witness) are seeking to bring about the death of a heretic, one who they believe is a direct threat to diaspora faith and life. Ironically, Paul's enemies represent a circle of faith, but it is faith that has gone bad. Faith can go bad, as the history of Christianity has shown us when God's people enter into a shared blindness that turns love of God and zeal for the divine into intense hatred and a willingness to kill.

Paul is surrounded by this circle of bad faith, and he stands in front of a corrupt Roman official who is willing to give him over to the assassins. The choice that is no choice is presented by Festus: "Do you wish to go up to Jerusalem . . . ?" (v. 9) And the truth that Festus wants to deny Paul makes visible: ". . . I have done no wrong to the Jews, as you very well know" (v. 10). The truth must be spoken into this tragic legal theater in order to break through the lies that often circulate in the formality of legal proceedings. The only choice for Paul is to choose witness. He appeals to Caesar. We now see that the appeal to Caesar was an act of a desperate man trying to survive. Paul has not now nor has he ever trusted the judicial process. His trust is in God. He is out maneuvering his enemies and living to fight another day. This is what disciple-citizens must do, recognizing always that they are caught in a deadly game. This appeal to the emperor places Paul more deeply within the social ecology of Rome and even more subject to its political winds. Although Luke is narrating not only Paul's innocence but also the innocence of the disciples of Jesus as political revolutionaries in the sense that Rome would understand it, he is also showing us what life is like for those who are subject to judicial processes and political machinations that have absolutely no regard for the well-being of defendants.

How do you think, sleep, dream, eat, and live when your life hangs suspended in a legal process that moves painfully slowly and is governed by a judicial system not concerned with the truth? Paul's plight echoes in the situations of so many women, men, and children today who are tempted to hopelessness and despair as they wait for a justice that they struggle to believe will ever come. Luke gives us a Paul in waiting, and while he waits the Spirit is present, strengthening him, holding him in the knowledge that his witness to the rulers is bound to the witness of the Messiah Jesus. Yet we must appreciate the fact that Luke looks into the incarceration of Paul, giving us the details of his struggle. How much more should the church today follow the trajectory of Acts and learn the stories in detail of those who suffer behind bars and move in painful and arduous sojourn through the world's judicial systems. We need to know them for the sake of Jesus, and we need to act on their behalf for the sake of the gospel.

25:13–27

Paul will again encounter another powerful couple, King Agrippa and his sister Bernice. If they are a couple it seems to be in the realm of a shadowy scandal. This Agrippa was the son of Herod Agrippa, whose demise we find in Acts 12. Like his father he ruled as a subject of the Roman empire, his power flowing out of its power. Bernice his sister lived with him after the death of her second or third husband.[3] Thus it may be a stretch to call them a couple and more accurate to call them two Jewish-Roman powerbrokers. Yet like Felix and Drusilla, they are fully assimilated Jews who perform Roman sensibilities. Clearly, they operate in both Jew and Gentile worlds and are at ease in Rome's political economy. Festus moved King Agrippa and Bernice to center stage in the judicial drama of Paul, and Paul now finds himself needing to give account of himself to those who have their lives established in empire. Agrippa and Bernice are asked

---

3. Justo L. González, *Acts: The Gospel of the Spirit* (Maryknoll, NY: Orbis Books, 2001), 265–66.

to examine this man, not to determine his guilt or innocence, not to advocate for his freedom or his continued captivity, but to aid Festus in what to say to the imperial majesty, i.e. the emperor. It could be that a supportive word from them might help Paul's cause but the likelihood of such a word was not high. If Felix and Drusilla represented full assimilation, Agrippa and Bernice represent full and greatly successful assimilation.

They were part of the Roman ruling class and presented a mixture of cultures fitted for empire, and as such they were the rich who would have to struggle to enter the kingdom of God (Luke 18:28). That struggle was precisely because they had already chosen a kingdom and an emperor. Their mixture of Jew and Gentile followed the way of the world where people merge at the site of conquest and oppression, violence and the desire for power. Paul represented an alternative vision of joining in which Jew and Gentile found each other at the resurrected body of Jesus. This is not assimilation but joining, and the church has always struggled to know this difference. The former means loss, but the latter means gain. The former destroys the voices and histories of people and imposes an alternative story that imparts to peoples a derogatory gaze of their own people and culture in light of the glory of the new conquering culture. The latter invites peoples to share in each other's ways of life and come to know each other through the Spirit, who imparts the desire to love and the desire to be together in the love of God made known in Jesus.

The former is Rome and the latter is Pentecost, and the church has too often chosen Roman-like assimilation instead of Pentecost-formed joining. So Agrippa and Bernice request to hear from Paul (v. 22), which is good news. But this good news will be put to the test as this royal power couple enters this space with all the majesty and gravitas due their station in life, and Paul stands there in chains. This is the difference that could only be overcome if Agrippa and Bernice realize that Paul is free but they are held captive. At this point in Luke's master narrative, we wait to see what Paul will say, but we already have a sense of that. The real question is whether King Agrippa and Bernice, given their success and power, are ready to hear what Paul will say. This is always the question for those who have been assimilated to empire.

FURTHER REFLECTIONS
Citizenship and Struggle

Disciples of Jesus should be desperate citizens. The desperate citizen will press their citizenship as far as possible for the sake of thwarting death and its agents. Paul, as he moves through the political ecology of Rome, illumines this kind of citizenship. It is a citizenship that takes seriously the position of those most disadvantaged by empire, those trapped in its prisons, found begging on its streets, those receiving the brunt of its unleashed violence, and those made slaves to its economic machinations. The church constantly forgets that it must see citizenship from this position, because this was the position of our savior, who felt the force of empire on his own body. Instead, we too often imagine citizenship from the privileged position of options. We have in many times and places imagined we have options—to become involved in politics or not, to concern ourselves with contentious issues or not, to advocate for people or not, to claim our citizenship or not, or to speak out or remain silent. To have this kind of option already displays a position of privilege built on the prevailing economic arrangements and social structures.

There is an option proper to desperate citizenship—press against your captivity or die a slow death. This is the option for those who are treated as pawns in the economic and political games of others, where life becomes sacrificial. Jesus experienced life as a pawn as his life was imagined by the rulers of Israel as expendable for the well-being of the nation (John 11:50). Turning people into pawns is fundamental to the ecology of empire, yet its operation affects people differently. Some enjoy the benefits of empire and happily live in its service, while others quietly accept the loss of land, livelihood, or even life as the cost of enjoying the freedoms afforded by empire, and still others rebel against having their lives turned into instruments for use and are then designated as problems or even enemies. Indeed to be made a pawn is to be placed on the path toward slavery. The desperate citizen discerns every operation that places creaturely life on this path and presses against it with all the means at her disposal as citizen.

Why, however, is citizenship a necessity? Could not the disciple be one who lives outside any political system, any national identity, or any economic structure of citizenry? Should not the disciple be poised for rebellion, revolution, and a new order? The disciple of Jesus is already of the new order, already embodied revolution, already geared to perform rebellion in the everyday acts of living, sharing, and supporting others. As such, disciples of Jesus find themselves in and/or are called to enter spaces of creaturely subjugation where worldly powers must be exposed and turned back upon themselves. Those very spaces, especially since the advent of modern colonialism, tend to be constructed inside nation, tribe-nation, and/or corporation, and all may be understood as empire. Whether or not life in nation, tribe-nation, or corporation is inescapable is irrelevant. The point is the overturning of creaturely subjugation. The purpose of citizenship for a disciple of Jesus is to use the emperor's gold to break the emperor's hold on lives and to use the systems that construct pawns to shatter the chains of servitude. But this can only be done with clear-eyed awareness of those life-draining and death-dealing processes of empire being played out on the bodies of its most abused people. Thus citizenship represents the constrained conditions within which disciples must work, knowing that the only political position we should take is one calibrated to the goal of announcing the redemption of creaturely life, and the overturning of all that which would destroy God's creation.

The disciple-citizen, however, moves forward always like Paul— subject to the political winds, negotiating the forces crisscrossing their bodies and the bodies of others, and from that vulnerable position learns to read the bodies and actions of those with power who may harm or kill them. Such reading is endemic to the survival politics practiced by so many poor and oppressed peoples of the world who must painstakingly attend to the ways of the elites whose slightest decisions could radically alter their lives. The disciples of Jesus often live these same realities or must enter in with those subject to this level of chaos. Politics is indeed a game, a deadly one, where paying attention to the operations of power is serious business and central to overturning its detrimental outcomes. Too many Christians have imagined gospel work as something existing beside or parallel to this overturning work, as though we move continuously from gospel work to overturning work, and back again. Such an image mistakes the nature of creaturely life and the architectures of creaturely captivity to death and its agents.

Gospel work enfolds political work, just as God enfolds the creature and the creation through the body of Jesus. Yet that enfolding not only draws us into the divine life but draws the life of God into the constrained situations of creaturely life. This means that the incarnate life of God was life lived inside our political spaces, and from within those spaces God announced the divine reign and the emergence of a new citizenship, the citizenship of heaven. The disciple-citizen lives then in this new citizenship that makes intelligible their actions in the worldly republics they inhabit. We are citizens of heaven first, born anew into a living hope that unites us with women and men spanning across space and time (Eph. 2:19). Our actions inside worldly republics must be calibrated by this citizenship that reaches far beyond the hopes of any nation-state, any tribal-nation, or corporation (Phil. 3:20–21).

The dream of each nation-state, each tribal-nation, and each corporation is eternality. All form their actions and their politics to enact their permanence. We know, however, that the eternity they seek is only possible in the body of Jesus. From within his body and through the Holy Spirit we live already within God's eternal reign and within the eternal life given to the children of the living God. There and only there may a people find what no political maneuvering can achieve—life everlasting. Unfortunately, the reality of our heavenly citizenship has sometimes been interpreted in ways that evacuate its most profound implication—that we have been freed to risk everything for the sake of the gospel, pressing the inner logics of every nation toward good ends for the sake of a suffering creation. Our heavenly citizenship translates in the here and now into desperate citizenship in the fleeting realities of worldly politics. So while some work for the welfare of the empire, we work in empires for the welfare of God's creation. Christians can easily get this confused by forgetting that the ends of an empire are not our ends, its dream not our dream, and its circle of concern always smaller than our concerns. Our citizenship should be characterized by an urgency not born of the needs of the nation, but the witness of God's redeeming love.

26:1–32

The King and I

In art and life, the invitation is everything.

26:1–8

Paul speaks again. This is repetition drenched in risk. Paul's speech is a study in elegance under pressure and Luke's narrative is a study in the power of story. "Paul stretched out his hand and began to defend himself" (v. 1). This is his final great speech. Like an artist who, having entered the depth of her art and having performed it in multiple places and situations, now launches into a performance that summarizes and soars, Paul will now press into the depth of his experience and the depth of the gospel. This is another template-setting moment that will echo through the centuries to our present reality. Christianity is ultimately about both an experience and God, both the movement of God on us and the movement of God through us. We should never pit experience against revelation, the soul against the Spirit. Only folly comes out of that fabricated conflict. God cannot be honored in our speech unless we honor our experience with God, and our experience cannot be honored unless we honor the truth that God actually exists, has become flesh, and has spoken and yet speaks. Christian theologians took a terrible turn when they decided that our way, the creaturely way of knowing ourselves and God, had to be defended and defined much more than it needed to be discerned and articulated.

Paul speaks inside his intimate knowledge of God. From the inside he extends an invitation to King Agrippa and Bernice (and all who would listen and see). Indeed his story is precisely a story of the inside, inside the faith, inside his anger, inside God's dealing with him. All this is intimate terrain, and the crucial interlocutor for Paul at this moment is in fact Agrippa. Masterfully Paul is trying to weave the story of Israel, his story, and the story of God around the body of King Agrippa. In art and life, the invitation is everything. There at the place of invitation a bridge is being offered to join lives together by surprising would-be hearers or readers with a common journey and a shared truth that also belongs to them. Paul's is a life in review—born of Israel, rooted in their space and place (in Jerusalem and among his people) and rooted in their hope of the fulfillment of a promise made by God. Paul knows that Agrippa knows this story. It is a story he shares. Agrippa is royalty, bound to this story if not also bound to the Roman Empire. He is a man caught between two stories, one of hope and the other of empire, and Paul's opening story invites this assimilated king to his freedom.

"*Why is it thought incredible by any of you that God raises the dead?*" (v. 8). Paul's question is jarring because it is both obvious and yet inconceivable. For those inside Israel's story of faith the question puts marvelous pressure on that very faith by asking those who are listening to Paul how seriously they take the God in whom they believe. But for those outside of Israel's faith and in service to other gods there is also pressure—if you believe, does your belief reach into death and through death to a God who overcomes it for your sake? And for those outside of all faith, all that is left is the inconceivability of Paul's words, which for them gesture toward madness. Yet Paul is bridge-building from the resurrection of Jesus to the hope of the promise, from faith aimed toward hope to hope born anew through faith in Jesus, from death to life, and his body is the bridge. Paul is a bridge to scandalous hope. He proposes to transition the hope of Israel from its unseen God and messianic expectation to its God found in the resurrected Messiah Jesus. This is no small matter, because if the first hope imagined a changed world, this new hope sees the world changing from the starting point of Jesus' body.

26:9–16

Paul, who was inside diaspora fear and the resistance to this transition of hope, shares his own horrifying story. He was a killer and torturer. We must never forget this. To forget this is to lose sight of the power of God to transform those thought irredeemable. Paul offers a theological confession with political consequences. This is a political confession of theology in league with death. While we may try to soften the truth of his story, we cannot hide from its clear implication. Paul deployed all the weapons of death—incarceration, violence, torture aimed at coercing out of people a false confession—all because he saw "the saints" (v. 10) as a threat to diaspora and hated the theological vision these followers were espousing. If Paul must confess this, so too must the church, because we have been on many occasions in our history like Paul before his conversion, Paul intoxicated with maddening anger and willing by any means necessary to silence voices we perceived as a threat to our faith. For Paul the end of his allegiance to death and of being its agent came in the moment he encountered the resurrected Jesus.

This is yet what needs to happen in this world. Every road that leads to violence must become a road to Damascus, where faith aimed in the wrong direction becomes faith focused on the One who raises the dead. How might we end violence? This is the question for all ages, the question that has not been answered in practice, on the ground, in the flesh. This question must be sharpened to get to the root of our problem: How might we end violence bound up in religious zeal? All violence is at heart born of religious zeal, especially by those who imagine their violence to be nonreligious in origin, but rather violence that is cool, calm, objective, justified by protocols and procedures that will ensure safety, stability, and justice. But such a neat separation is an illusion, because all violence is religious violence. All violence acts in the place of God, gesturing toward the prerogative of the life giver to withhold the fullness and goodness of life. All violence is rooted in the false belief that we can bring life out of death and create the good out of the destruction of what we deem bad. Violence has always been the tool of those who pretend to the throne of the creator. Yet violence's seductive power is quite overwhelming, and only the foolish refuse to see its awesome temptation.

Paul's confrontation points the way forward from violence's power. The Jesus he meets on this road is no solitary figure but one witnessed by sound and solidarity. He speaks and he speaks of his joined life to those whom Paul is killing and torturing. Maybe the way from violence to a faith that overcomes its power is to see Jesus bound to the suffering, tortured saints who honor his name and to realize that God glories in such binding to flesh. God joined to our plight in the body of Jesus means a God forever bound to bodies, feeling their pain and knowing their horrors. This knowledge of God willing to be incarcerated, beaten, tortured, and killed is bound to the reality of direct speech. God speaks to Paul. In the speaking is the calling. This is always the case with God. If God speaks, God calls. The calling is away from a life of confused purpose, trying to secure a future that is no real future. The purpose of God is what calls us out of violence and into its opposite—the offering of life and that eternal. Only a purpose bound to the giving of life is strong enough to weaken the temptation to take life.

26:17–18

Paul pulls back the curtain and reveals the foundations of a world being pulled by the strong current of death back into the nothingness out of which life emerged. He has been sent by God to open (v. 18) eyes. We cannot see the darkness because we are in it. Here we must remember the density of this darkness that exists far beyond any optic register. Unfortunately, with the emergence of the racial optic within the advent of colonial modernity, darkness has been aligned with peoples of color, and their bodies have been encased in a forced and false alignment of darkness, blackness, danger, sin, deficiency, and deformity. Such a vision of darkness is blind to the truth. The darkness of which Paul speaks cannot be seen but only known in the light of Jesus Christ. This is a darkness not *of* the creation but *against* the creation. This darkness conceals and is concealed amidst aimless existence that moves away from God. No creaturely body could ever be this darkness, but all of us have been subjected to it.

Paul is at the center of the turning, like a sign that points in a new direction—from darkness to light and from the power of Satan to God (*tes exousias tou satana epi ton theon*, v. 18). Luke is reminding his readers of the disclosure of the demonic that he noted in his earlier volume (Luke 4:6). We did not know of our blindness in darkness and of our captivity to the demonic until the revealing of light and deliverance in Jesus of Nazareth. We can now see what we were incapable of overcoming until the overcomer appeared, telling us to fear neither the darkness nor Satan, because God has claimed the beloved creature. Paul has been claimed and now gives witness to the claiming actions of God intended to bring the creature as close as possible to the divine life. The forgiveness of sins in this regard must be read against the centuries of forensic incrustations that have caused Christians to read this stunning word of Paul superficially as though God has merely rendered a judgment of forgiveness for trespasses. This forgiveness, articulated by Paul, is life together with the Son, sharing in his life and faith through the Spirit. This is the new place of life from which to live life in communion with God and the other saints. This is the great gift, the great truth that now must be spoken with great urgency: God with us and we with God.

26:19–32

"King Agrippa, I was not disobedient to the heavenly vision" (v. 19). Paul has turned his performance toward an audience of one, King Agrippa. It is as if a great artist, like Aretha Franklin, has pressed her face and voice toward one single listener, and now, with all the power of her complex life squeezed into her sound, she sings in full voice toward the one. Paul is in full voice now declaring his life wholly intoxicated by the vision of God's victory. His journey has not been about sedition against the empire but the redemption of the world. He outlines again the path of divine desire toward the Jews first and then also to the Gentiles: God's hunger knows no bounds. God wants them all. Paul's repetition is the essence of artistic performance and of life. "The Messiah must suffer . . . and . . . by being the first to rise from the dead, he would proclaim light both to our people and to the Gentiles" (v. 23). These words are the rhythm and bassline, the tempo and the beat, and they must sound strongly into the air to set the stage for hearing the voice of God. This is a breathtaking word about a God who shatters fantasies about God in light of the revealed God—the crucified, dead, buried, and risen Jewish Messiah, Jesus. Paul has said this before and he will say it again, and it will define his sound and ours. To be Christian is to be defined by this shattering sound that brings joy and ridicule.

Festus interrupts Paul's flow. The performance is too much for him. "You are out of your mind, Paul! Too much learning is driving you insane!" (v. 24) Festus is in a different world than Paul at this very moment. Paul, in rhetorical flight and faithful witness, has entered the real world, and Festus remains in the false one. From that false world, Paul's words are understandable, but they make no sense. Festus, from his position, seeks to shatter an illusion that is no illusion. The only way he could end this illusion is to allow himself to be shattered through the words of Paul. But that would be difficult now. His power and his position as judge over Paul have increased his distance from the good news Paul is sharing, but Paul's response to Festus is meant as a quick retort that refocuses attention on his true audience, King Agrippa.

This is a moment for this wayward king. Luke has drawn a tight circle around Paul and Agrippa. The king knows and Paul knows. They share the story of Israel, and Paul invites this king living under Caesar's rule to remember his own throne bound up with the throne of other Jewish kings and the prophets who spoke to them. Paul calls Agrippa to act on the knowledge they share. But here we see the difference between the disciple and the assimilated king. As we noted earlier with Felix and Drusilla (25:13–27), assimilation turns the familiar into the strange and renders the story of a people null and void under the pressure of imperial domination.

Agrippa knows but he has learned not to know. Paul utters the truth born of cultural intimacy and diaspora hope: "King Agrippa, do you believe the prophets? I know that you believe" (v. 27). How does Paul know that Agrippa believes? Does he have insider knowledge of this King's beliefs? Is he guessing? Paul claims the knowledge that is common currency for diaspora people and that must be with this king as well. But he is also doing more—this is the question for the king of Israel.

Prophets have spoken to kings in Israel, and Paul placed Agrippa in the exact same situation as all the kings of Israel, under the word, subject to the word that has come and will yet come again. By asking this king about his belief in the prophets, he is asking him, do you believe that God has spoken and yet speaks? Once again a king during a time of occupation and forced assimilation is being asked the perennial question: Is there a word from the Lord? And once again the answer will not be given because this king cannot face the question. His response to Paul was cunning in that he understood what Paul was doing—drawing him so deeply into the story of Israel that he would be compelled to encounter the true storyteller of Israel, Jesus. "Are you so quickly persuading me to become a Christian?" (v. 28) The King James translation rendered these words so magisterially: "Almost thou persuadest me to be a Christian." We know they were spoken in jest and ridicule by this king, because he would not allow Paul's words to capture him. Instead he sought to turn the focus back on Paul, reminding him and all present of the true order of things: namely, that he is the judge and Paul the judged.

Agrippa will not be captured by this holy word, even or especially as a king firmly established in the empire. Paul is indeed the focus, and his final words to the king and his retinue clarify what is at stake for them all. "I pray to God that not only you [King Agrippa] but also all who are listening to me today might become such as I am— except for these chains" (v. 29). This is an astounding desire that he utters, one that imagines a life shared and mapped across other lives. Paul may imagine this because it has happened to him. Jesus has placed his life inside Paul, and what now unfolds for Paul is his life within the life of Christ Jesus. Paul offers a radical becoming, one that speaks a future that King Agrippa cannot see trapped as he is within the mechanisms of Roman assimilation. He cannot and will not imagine a new identity (worth having) witnessed by Paul, and so the only response is the common response that reaches through time to our present. They all rose to their feet and left. There is nothing here they want.

Their endeavors to maintain their identities as stable and reliant members of the empire worthy to command respect and wield imperial power were far more compelling than becoming like Paul. Indeed Paul was the opposite of what they wanted to be. King Agrippa and Bernice, along with the honored cohort, present to us that which obstructs the gospel—the desire to enter the form of the powerful man, a form not specific to gender or tribe, nor time or place, but one that suggests freedom, independence, and control of one's own life, and others' lives. King Agrippa and Bernice rose to follow that form and thusly indicated the direction one takes to move away from redemption and life. The opposite direction, which is in fact the direction toward freedom, is precisely toward Paul and his chains. This gospel preached by Paul interrupts the journey toward that self-sufficient powerful man and turns those who would listen toward the crucified God, who speaks to us from the other side of death, saying, "be like me."

Luke's powerful turn at the end of this episode again joins the body of Jesus to the body of Paul and declares them both innocent. Any concern that Paul is a terrorist bent on overthrowing the Roman government is now clearly false, verified in the words of Agrippa to Festus. Yet the melancholy in the final words of this chapter suggest not simply a tragic end to Paul but a continued yielding to the Spirit. Paul goes forward in chains to the emperor and to Rome. Even with all his shrewd political maneuvering, his skilled oratory, his finely sharpened survival skills, he is being led where he had not planned on going because in, with, through, and despite the shifts in his situation, the Spirit is working to sustain him in the good work. Yet we must not make of his captivity a matter of divine providence, but of divine presence. God is with Paul, guiding the witness bound up as it was in God's own desire to be known in the redemptive embrace of Jesus. While the complexities of our lives are never planned, one thing is sure: God desires to be known and embraced by us and through us to embrace a world held in captivity.

27:1–44

A Common Journey and a Singular Faith

The journey of faith, if it is one that follows the Spirit, will be one that draws us toward people who out of economic necessity live close to danger and on the edge of physical harm.

27:1–3

Paul is not in control of his life now. He is a prisoner being transferred to a different prison. In this regard, Paul is nothing more than cargo. Watching prisoners being moved is like watching the walking dead. They are alive, but they are not treated as living, breathing human beings with feelings and needs, hopes and desires. They are a task that must be accomplished. They are a movable feast of incarceration. Paul is not the only prisoner in this transfer. We read this story poorly if we forget the crucial fact that Paul is among the prisoners destined for relocation. What distinguishes this ordinary horror of being a prisoner-in-route is Julius, the centurion charged with getting this task done. What we learn of the centurion Julius that is of high importance is that he treats Paul humanely (*philanthrōpōs*, v. 3). Luke notes the rarity of behavior that should be the norm, but is not. Maybe Julius understood that Paul was no threat and that the charges against him did not merit intense surveillance of his every action, but regardless of his reasoning, Julius's actions speak of a kindness greatly needed in prison systems today. Paul is allowed to reconnect with his friends, and they are allowed to care for him. Paul is spared the isolation that torments minds and damages souls.

The actions of the centurion move in the opposite direction of our modern mechanisms of incarceration that glory in isolation and are addicted to practices of solitary confinement. Surely, Paul is no dangerous prisoner and therefore would not deserve what goes as standard operating procedure in so many prisons in this world, some would argue, but isolation and solitary confinement have never been about danger. They are about control and punishment woven in vengeance. We must resist the structures of vengeance that lay at the heart of our prisons that already enact the death penalty by starving women and men of human contact and slowly strangle their life force. Strangely, a centurion situated in the bloody and cruel regime of Rome could suggest to us a better way to treat the prisoner. Of course, the truth is that Paul should not be a prisoner in the first place. Freedom should be his normal state, as it should be for so many who are numbered among those in lockdown.

27:4–26

"*The winds were against us*" (v. 4). Some commentators have wondered about the purpose of this fantastic story in Luke's grand narrative. It is a beautiful rendering of a fairly common ancient literary convention, an exciting sea adventure. Unfortunately, too many modern commentators have fixated on the historicity of this event and on the possibility that this story exposes Luke's entire narrative to be more fiction than history. As Luke Timothy Johnson suggests, it would be a mistake to read Luke's work as if he functions with our categories of history and fiction or as if we gain anything in trying to parse out the one from the other.[4] History does matter in this story, not in the ways most commentators have imagined it, but in the way it has been captured by the divine life. Paul, the prisoner, numbered among the prisoners, is at risk. And now the risk and danger that had characterized Paul's life as a disciple join the risk of those working at sea and in service to the empire.

The journey illumines life on the ground and at sea where people out of economic necessity must live close to the edge of physical harm. This is the journey of the centurion, the ship owner, captain and crew, each focused on carrying out orders and/or making a profit. Paul's life is now inside their risky business and danger-filled lives. This is the history of so many in this world who are caught up in the dialectic of work and survival, pressing to make a living in the places where death hunts for them. The sea and life on the sea was never a preferred destination for the children of Israel. Death and chaos were imagined as bound up with the sea.[5] Yet those shaped in maritime cultures understand the dual reality of the water. It both gives life and takes it. It is both friend and enemy and must be respected at all times. Once you have committed yourself to the business of the sea and business with the currency of its chaos, then the cost of a wavering focus could be your life.

Luke gives us Paul at sea, which mirrors Jesus at sea among those who make their living on the water. Once again God is on the water, but this is a different reality of incarnation. Paul serves the God made flesh, and here in a place and time where the Holy is normally not imagined as present, speaking, and guiding, we find the Spirit working. This journey from the very beginning was difficult and risk-filled, because it took place at an inopportune time of the year when

---

4. Johnson, *Acts*, 450–52. Also see Beverly Roberts Gaventa, *Acts* (Nashville, TN: Abingdon Press, 2003), 349–56.
5. Johnson, *Acts*, 450.

the elements were against sea travel. The centurion, the owner of the ship, and the pilot together are trying to discern the best course of action, and Paul interjects. *"Sirs, I can see that the voyage will be with danger and much heavy loss, not only of the cargo and the ship, but also of our lives"* (v. 10). Paul speaks into a space where he is not invited. This is their business, not his. But he has made it his business, not only because his life is at risk with theirs but also because the prophetic voice is his, and he listens to the Spirit who has always been the Lord of travel and an eager companion on the road. The Spirit knows where to go and how to lead us. So Paul speaks from his expertise as one who follows the Spirit.[6] The centurion leans more heavily on the advice of the owner and the pilot, as would be expected. This is their world, not Paul's.

The centurion is not to be blamed for doing what anyone would do in his situation, that is, listen to those familiar with the risk of traversing the seas and accustomed to its negotiation. Yet Paul represents the One who is far more deeply familiar with risk, risk rooted in the love of the Creator for a fragile creation. They do not know it, but their risk at sea has now been taken up inside this wider risk, and their lives are now in the hands of a God who has overcome death. Should they have listened to Paul? Yes. But their response to Paul is a typical response to prophetic word that interrupts profit management and strategic planning aimed at survival. The word of God is rarely able to penetrate those lost in these calculations. Luke narrates an aspect of Israel's ancient resistance to prophetic word at the site of Gentile resistance where again we see the concerns of mammon override God's counsel. Luke continues to cast Paul in the body of Jesus, following the form of the Son. Like Jesus, Paul is on a boat at sea beyond the purview of those struggling to ride out a storm (Luke 8:22–24). But there is one significant difference. Where Jesus was called on and then calmed the sea, Paul at sea is ignored and subjected to the chaotic winds and the futile efforts of those in charge.

"All hope of our being saved was at last abandoned" (v. 20). We have to admire the efforts of pilot and crew charged with the safety and success of the voyage. They did everything they could to survive and

---

6. Justo L. González, *Acts: The Gospel of the Spirit*, 271–72.

yet finally winds and waves proved too strong to be escaped and the fear of death soon drained them of hope. It was at that moment that again the prophetic word came through Paul. The prophetic word always comes at the times when hope is drained, because God will not allow hope to die in this world. Luke captures the pattern of God's hope-restoring work in Israel and replays it on this desperate ship—the divine word came and was ignored, the people fall into hopeless despair, the divine word returns again and promises deliverance and a future in God. This (Gentile) ship is the site of the repetition of Israel's drama with its loving God. Paul speaks and announces the divine theft of this moment. They thought it was their journey and their history caught inside the repetition of work and risk, but Paul is turning their world right side up. They are in God's history and the Spirit's journey with Paul. Paul is their prisoner, but they are captive inside his mission. *"For last night there stood by me an angel of the God to whom I belong and whom I worship, and he said, 'Do not be afraid, Paul; you must stand before the emperor; and indeed, God has granted safety to all those who are sailing with you'"* (vv. 23–25). There is a proper hubris in this story that the church should remember. It is the hubris of a mission filled with hope and guided by faith that announces our life within the life of God. It is a hubris that dares to speak at the site of despair and chaos, saying God lives and so too will we live. Paul is the witness who will not give into fear, and he invites these wayward sea workers to take hold of his faith.

27:27–38

No one's feet are on solid ground now. Not Paul, the centurion, the owner, pilot, or crew. The only place of stability is Paul's faith in God. Paul will perform his faith in front of a crew suspended between exhaustion and desperation. They have not eaten in many days, which is a sure sign that their lives are under threat of death. So again bread will signify more than food. The pattern Luke knows so well he inscribes in this story: *"After he had said this, he took bread; and giving thanks to God in the presence of all, he broke it and began to eat"* (v. 35). (See Luke 22:18–19; 24:30–31.) What did Paul say?

"*None of you will lose a hair from your heads*" (v. 34b). An astounding claim made at the height of crisis, but it logically follows the words stated by his savior before he broke bread with his disciples: "*I will not drink of the fruit of the vine until the kingdom of God comes*" (Luke 22:18). The reign of God has begun on this ship being tossed by the wind and sea at the breaking of this bread. Paul again gestures a joining absolute and redemptive (he with the God he serves) in a public space crowded with crisis and troubled minds. Such a simple act has no power in and of itself, but placed at the site of chaos where death desires to reign and announced inside a word of praise for the God who delivers, it becomes the source of hope and the sign of divine love. The result: they were encouraged and took the bread. Even in our time no one's feet are on solid ground. This is not an allegory but reality. We are always on this ship, and the question for the church is not whether we will eat but when and where we will offer food and under what conditions will we invite those fear laden and troubled to eat.

27:39–44

It was time to leave the ship and cut their losses. The end of this fantastic sea voyage is not the end of risk for Paul. We must remember that Paul is yet a prisoner joined to other prisoners. His exercise of faith in the public space that is the ship does not negate his status as one held captive and therefore as cargo. Yet as the ship begins to disintegrate around them, his status as viable cargo also disintegrates. The soldiers plan to kill the prisoners (v. 42). Why? Because if they cannot be maintained as prisoners then they must be made corpses, which require no maintenance. Corpses cannot speak of their abuse or murder by their handlers. Nor will they be threats to the empire and its commerce. The temptation to turn prisoners into corpses is an ancient temptation. This part of Luke's narrative echoes hauntingly through history to the tragic case of the slave ship *Zong*. At the close of the year 1781, a slave ship traveling from Africa to Black River in Jamaica was lost at sea and running low on water. The crew of that ship, hoping to survive by cutting *their* losses, threw overboard

132 Africans, who were soon to be slaves.[7] The horror of this story is not only the massacre of these Africans but also an English judicial system that found the only crime to be in the fraudulent attempt to collect on the insurance. Paul the prisoner's death sentence reaches toward those Africans whose death sentence was carried out. Once again, a soldier stands between Paul and those who would kill him (23:23–35). The difference between Paul and the Africans thrown overboard was a simple command: No, you will not kill him or the others. The centurion acts humanely again toward Paul and fulfills divine prophesy and, in so doing, enacts a different world where lives are not balanced against profit or security. This is the world Paul brought onto the wooden world of the ship, and it is a world that yet needs to be brought fully into our world.

28:1–15

The Gift of Hospitality

There is a loneliness born of trial that attaches itself to body and mind, pressing us to turn toward despair. Only a word of life can silence that loneliness, a word found in other believers who understand the power of grace-filled invitation and hospitality.

28:1–13

What do you need after you have survived trauma? What if your life was saved by holding on to a slender thread of hope in the face of two kinds of threats, the threat of storm and wave, and the threat of men with weapons desiring to kill you? Some would call these different threats natural and human made, respectively, but the effect of surviving it is still the same. You are marked by it. For untold generations of peoples who survived harrowing travel by sea and physical torment before, during, and after being on board those ships, they emerged *boat* people with an intimate knowledge

---

7. James Walvin, *The Zong: A Massacre, the Law, and the End of Slavery* (New Haven, CT: Yale University Press, 2011).

of how precious life is and what it is like to come ashore disoriented and in need. The crew and human cargo of this ship arrive to the island of Malta, exhausted and shaken from what they endured. Standing there in cold rain, they were in need of help, and the Maltese helped them.

Luke draws his stunning narrative to a close in this penultimate episode with astounding Gentile hospitality. The natives showed no ordinary kindness (v. 2). Again we see the word we encountered with the treatment of the centurion toward Paul (*philanthrōpia*). The natives are designated here by the term barbarian (*ho barbaros*), which in the New Testament simply means foreigner, one alien to the world of empire. It lacks the racially inflected pejorative character it will come to take on later in our history. These natives acted in ways supremely human and stunningly gracious by making a fire and inviting these shipwrecked souls to join its heat. It is important for us to see the vulnerability of this ship-less crew, because such vulnerability fits the gospel. The gospel did not arrive in power but in weakness and humility. Paul experiences the hospitality of the Maltese precisely at the point of his urgent need. A template is forming here not simply for missions but for the living of the life of faith, where we recognize our vulnerability and our shared need for one another as the beginning point of sharing the gospel. The Maltese's action toward the shipwrecked was a surprise of grace and kindness that would be repeated in so many other contexts and with so many other peoples in the centuries that followed, and the church has never learned to see such kindnesses as what they actually are—signs of the Spirit's presence with peoples as precursor to a holy joining being orchestrated by God.

Paul's humanity is beautifully on display in this scene as he does the ordinary work of gathering brushwood for the fire. The disciple and prophet of God, the man dramatically fighting for his life through a problematic legal system, innocent of the charges being brought against him, the one who has already testified to the high and mighty and will do so again in Rome—that Paul gathers wood for the fire. Paul is, after all, simply a servant. But he is a servant among strangers, and their cultural logic, which Luke weaves together with ancient literary themes, shows itself in how they interpret Paul's actions. A snake's bite becomes the occasion for articulating a godless providence. They imagined that the bite had to be confirmation that Paul was a killer who even now would not escape lady justice. They were right. Paul was a killer, but he was inside a different providence. They watched Paul to see justice take its course, and they were again right. Justice was taking its course, but Paul was inside a different justice. Within the logic of the Maltese, the fact that Paul did not die meant that he must be a god. Here they were wrong. He was not a god, he only served the one true God.

Luke again maps the journey of Jesus on top of the body of Paul, but now drenched in Gentile hospitality. Publius appears in the story as a man of means and power on the island who "entertained [them] hospitably (*philophronōs*) for three days" (v. 7). Three days of Gentile hospitality was followed by Paul mirroring the actions of his risen savior and healing Publius's father of fever and dysentery (v. 8; see Luke 4:38–39). Luke is painting a resurrection scene here both inside the Gentile hospitality and in what follows, with all the infirmed of the island coming to Paul and being healed. Salvation has come to Malta. Of course, Luke gives us no account of a word preached and received by the Maltese, and it might seem like a stretch to see conversion in this story. We might instead settle on communion and shared life with these indigenes, and if that is the case, then salvation has come to Malta in the way it should come to every people in the sharing of food and hospitality, service and healing in the name of Jesus. It would be difficult, however, to believe that Paul would not have explained in detail in whose name he healed and by what power such healing was made possible. Paul's gestures if not his words announce a new community in which the events of his time with the Maltese expose a desired pattern, help given, hospitality offered and received, and God present to heal. The Maltese offered them community and blessed them on their departure, as anyone would with the departure of family and friends. This too gestures the joining with God that Paul preached.

28:14–15

Paul is in need of such community. There is a tenderness exposed in these verses that shows us Paul's humanity and our own. Faith is always in need of company and support. Even Paul, especially Paul, is in need of such support. Luke has brought us a long way with Paul, and we have seen the weight of his suffering. Even Paul, especially Paul, filled with the Spirit, shaped in prophetic utterance, now feels the great weight of his trials. We know this because we cannot help but know it. Who would not feel such weight after accusations from his own people, multiple attempted assassinations, prison, chains, storm and shipwreck, and a Roman trial yet waiting? There is a loneliness born of trial that attaches itself to body and mind and presses us to turn toward despair. That loneliness pretends to be a friend who will speak the truth to us of our situation and our suffering. Only a word of life can silence that loneliness, a word found in other believers who understand the power of grace-filled invitation and hospitality. It is not a coincidence that Luke takes Paul from hospitality to hospitality, from a foreign space to a familiar one, from Gentiles who show kindness to believers who do the same. Such a gift does not make one a disciple of Jesus, but one cannot be a disciple without it. In Puteoli, Paul encounters believers where he had not expected to see them. As he approached his destination, he encountered more of the unexpected but appreciated believers. "*On seeing them, Paul thanked God and took courage*" (v. 15b). For Paul, his faith needed sight, and often times our faith needs the same. In the place where his future would be decided, Paul discovered a truth we all must remember: God is everywhere waiting for us to arrive.

28:16–31

The Calling of Hospitality

Luke's narrative was not about Paul. We make a terrible mistake if we make this singularly Paul's story. Even at its close, with Paul on center stage, this is not first his story, but the story of another. It is the story of an urgently longing God who has bound the divine life to the frailty of flesh. Once again we see what is in fact inexplicable—God who is everywhere comes to Rome with a fresh word. How can the God who is present be said to arrive at a place and a time? In truth, it is only because God has shown Godself to be present in the precise and specific urgency of the moment that we can then begin to see a Holy presence without measure and without limitation. God came to Rome. Paul came to Rome. These are two completely different sentences joined together simply by the Holy Spirit. Paul is being led by the Spirit and will also live in the gentle incarceration of Rome. We must hold these two realities together, the Spirit and incarceration. From the very beginning of Luke's narrative, the disciples of Jesus were destined for a constant encounter and negotiation with the prison system and with being designated criminals. So now, at the end of his story, the disciple of Jesus is under house arrest. This should not be imagined as though Paul was living in the suburbs, enjoying the peace and quiet of sequestered living. He is in prison with a soldier guarding him. Yet the Spirit is with him, present to guide and instruct. Luke has shown us that to be a disciple is to be bound to the Spirit and to be bound to the prison. Paul, like Peter and John and the many other disciples who found themselves in prison, learned that their lives were inextricably bound up with those placed behind bars and in chains. The trajectory remains: we remember those in prison as though we are there with them, because our faith grew in such places (Heb. 13:3).

Paul seeks after Israel, even now, after all that has happened. He could not do otherwise, led as he is by the Spirit of God. This God will never cease speaking to Israel, calling with a fresh word for the living of life within Torah faithfulness. So again Paul sits with the leaders of his people, this time in Rome, and gives witness. And again Paul sits in the midst of diaspora faith and diaspora fear with the stakes as high as ever. Rome is the home of the empire, where Israel's ancient faith could be swept away in the strong tides of Roman culture and military power. Luke has already shown us assimilated citizens of Rome whose Jewish faith has been rendered inconsequential to their lives (Acts 26:28–32). Paul has already spoken to those more concerned with their Roman status and identity than with hearing word of a new way of life born of the resurrected Jesus.

So now Paul speaks to those in Rome who have held the line, refused assimilation, and remained faithful and waiting. If we keep in mind the hard realities of diaspora life then we will read this text with sympathy. We should have sympathy for Paul, whose journey placed him in constant struggle with exhaustion of body and mind and whose patience at this point must be running thin. We should also have sympathy for these Jewish leaders in Rome who know the stakes of being associated with any sect that hints of sedition or heresy in the space of Roman ultimate power. In Rome, there is no room for political errors or theological experimentation. So Paul speaks in a constrained space and under constrained conditions.

Paul will have the chance to speak without the hostile rebuttals that have dogged him since his escape from Jerusalem. The space and the time will both be packed with people and with words. Paul speaks all day, "testifying to the kingdom of God and trying to convince them about Jesus both from the law of Moses and from the prophets" (v. 23). This is loving labor, like an artist singing her song yet again to the crowd she most wants to hear her, hear her heart and her hope. Paul has come to the great point of clarification—everything pivots on Jesus of Nazareth. Paul is trying to turn the reading practices of his own people in a new direction in, toward and through the life of Jesus. This has been the outrageous move from the first words of Luke's story to the last. It is an astounding act that can only be understood and accepted in faith and through the power of the Holy Spirit. How could the life of this crucified Jewish person be at the center of their story? Only God can hold such a position, and Luke has made it clear that such a conclusion is inevitable.

"*Some were convinced by what he said, while others refused to believe*" (v. 24). This is the situation that faith must face. The response to the gospel will always have this abiding mixture of acceptance and refusal. Yet this is much more than the struggle of the witness. It has its home in God's own life with Israel and the Creator's life with the wayward creature. God has spoken and given us life, and some were convinced and others refused to believe. God has delivered Israel with a mighty hand and an outstretched arm, and some were convinced and others refused to believe. The beloved child of God has come and redeemed the world, and some were convinced and others refused to believe. Acceptance and refusal, this twin inheritance of the disciples of Jesus must be endured for the sake of God's love. Paul has become one who shares in the passion of God for Israel. Here God the lover joins Paul, and Paul speaks like an ancient prophet. Paul's final statement to his own is not one of hatred but of a lover's anguish. Quoting Isaiah,

> "Go to this people and say,
> You will indeed listen, but never understand,
>   and you will indeed look, but never perceive.
> For this people's heart has grown dull,
>   and their ears are hard of hearing,
>   and they have shut their eyes;
>   so that they might not look with their eyes,
>   and listen with their ears,
> and understand with their heart and turn—
>   and I would heal them."
>
>   (28:26–27; citing Isa. 6:9–10)

Paul draws the line of love from ancient divine word and old frustration to this new word and more frustration. Yet frustration is not rejection. Far from it. Divine desire makes intelligible God's faithfulness, and God's faithfulness witnesses God's relentless love. Paul's final words to Israel have been read poorly in many churches over the centuries as a final breakup, and the beginning of an alternative relationship with Gentiles. Nothing could be further from the truth. The love of God for Israel reaches also to the Gentiles, binding them to Israel as a sign of God's faithfulness. This is what we have failed repeatedly to grasp. We are a sign of God's love for Israel and a site for joining where the two become one in and with Jesus through the Spirit. Yet we live on the other side of a history of horror where Christians have hated and killed Jewish people and turned our witness into a sign of segregation for the sake of survival. We have proven that the diaspora suspicion of the sect displayed in Rome has been justified through the centuries. The question remains whether faith can overcome both diaspora fear and the ambitions of empire. We have learned over the long centuries that diaspora fear and the ambitions of empire flow through both Jew and Gentile alike, and none can escape their pull without an alternative space and an alternative desire. The final words of Luke's story give us a glimpse of that space and that desire: "He lived there two whole years at his own expense and welcomed all who came to him, proclaiming the kingdom of God and teaching about the Lord Jesus Christ with all boldness and without hindrance" (28:30–31).

Paul is yet under the condition of incarceration, but even here we see the possibilities of an alternative space where economic flows have been rerouted toward a stunning new reality of hospitality. Paul welcomed all (v. 30). This action suggests not only an openness to the stranger, but also a reversal of diaspora fear. This faith that must be shared demands a sharing of life in the beautifully mundane realities of eating together and sharing common space. The fear of assimilation and loss has always been real for Israel and for other peoples, but here Paul's actions of welcoming the stranger suggest a joining without loss at the site of witness to a loving God. This God's reign has begun, which means the end of empire, not through sedition but through resurrection. The end of empire is the end of the *desire* for empire. No one can end empire. Only an alternative desire ends it. That desire has come from God who has invited us to life with the risen Messiah Jesus, God's only child. Faith in the resurrected Jesus draws us toward communion with the triune God through the Spirit, and only here can an imagination be formed that desires the multitude as God desires them, to be joined to the divine life forever.

> Come, thou Fount of every blessing,
> tune my heart to sing thy grace;
> streams of mercy, never ceasing,
> call for songs of loudest praise.
> Teach me some melodious sonnet,
> sung by flaming tongues above.
> Praise the mount! I'm fixed upon it,
> mount of thy redeeming love.
>
> Robert Robinson, "Come, Thou Fount of Every Blessing"

Paul welcomed all—Jew and Gentile alike, rich and poor—into his living space for the sake of the gospel. And again we see the boldness born of the Holy Spirit (Acts 4:31) displayed in preaching and teaching. Paul waits for his day in the court of the emperor, but while he waits, he serves. His prison will not keep him from being a disciple of Jesus and creating the site for the joining of peoples. Luke ends on a note of great hope not only for Paul, but also for the work of the gospel. He ends in possibility, our possibility of Christian life that picks up at the site of Paul in a house located in the heart of empire and marked by the incarcerated and a place that will not yield to diaspora fear or the lust for empire. This new space welcomes all to a faith that desires and joins. It is a temporary space for Paul, and temporary for us as well as we wait for a more permanent site that is being prepared.

FURTHER REFLECTIONS
Alternative Space, Alternative Desire

How might we live together in a life that shares all things, hopes all things, and overcomes the hatred that permeates this world? This question points to the constant search for a beloved community, an alternative communal living space that pushes against economic and social configurations destructive of life. Such a community has been and continues to be the dream of many people. What exactly constitutes an alternative space is always a matter of debate, but the desire to live together in some form of sustained and significant mutuality constitutes a hope that joins radically diverse visions of alternative common life. The dream of a communal life pushes against the grain of societies deeply committed to an individualism that must be performed in as many contexts of life as possible, geographically, emotionally, financially, intellectually—in the ways we love and imagine love, in the ways we build our futures, and even in the ways we face death.

Many peoples have enjoyed glimpses of a communal life where some aspects of tribal, village, or community life showed the possibilities of being profoundly life-giving and healing. Yet the possibility of sustaining even the glimpses of a communal life strain against the modes of fragmentation that have come upon us since the birth of the modern colonial period. The colonial period began the process of transforming the new world into private property and people into races. It disconnected people from land and turned animals into objects of utility and consumption. It tore into pieces the communal fabrics of many peoples, driving them toward community-killing forms of individuation. Nations and corporations continue to slice up the planet into ever smaller commodities, turning the world into nothing more than forms of property. We continue to live inside fragmented ways of seeing ourselves and our world. So the desire to have a life that integrates and weaves us together drives the dream of communal life.

The communal dream has often flowed in two complimentary directions: toward a community that imagines itself either as a space in the world for the world or a space in the world that seeks to overtake the world. Such spaces have been either religious or nonreligious in orientation. The former space is a space of witness against and even a means of escape from patterns of living that damage us and destroy the creation. The latter space is a space of insurgency that foments revolution by generating cells of resistance in as many places as possible, each marking a new way of living against despair, violence, or the status quo. But to create a community in either direction has always required the extension of a life into a place, a concrete space where people spread their bodies into the everyday realities of forming and living life. A body given—this is what makes a community. It is indeed a kind of sacrifice.

The church is formed precisely inside such giving. The body of Jesus constitutes the church, but we have yet to reckon with the communal density of his self-giving life. As the book of Acts closes, Paul finds himself inside a communal gesture—an openness to all who would come to him, sharing in a meal and learning of faith in Messiah Jesus. This gesture of openness echoes the desire of God to draw all who would come and experience reconciling love (2 Cor. 5:18–20). This gesture and the divine openness it signifies, however, require a concrete place and the possibilities of sustaining life. Geography matters for hospitality, and geography matters to God. We who follow Jesus are caught up in God's own desire to make his self-giving tangible, palpable, lodged in geographic space and concrete place. The Spirit who brought Paul to this place and time seeks to mark this space with divine presence.

The church has often failed to see the geographic dimensions of discipleship. We have failed because we have followed colonialist paradigms of fragmentation and commodification that have taught us to see the earth and the land, animals, and landscape, in pieces. We, like so many others in this world, see the creation and creatures as always potentially someone's property or possession and therefore as always capable of being sequestered and boundaried. We have followed patterns of conquest that naturalized division through ownership and literally mapped our sightlines of concern around, primarily, our property and, secondarily, our slightly wider areas of immediately interests. The space of the church for us is exactly the space the church owns, and no more, except in a highly spiritualized sense of space. And the places churches inhabit have become, for too many, inconsequential to the living of a shared life. Yet the point here is not the need for churches to expand their holdings, own more property, and expand their reach into more land and more communities. The point is to follow our incarnate God into places, extending ourselves into the space and joining with the peoples, the surroundings, the animals, and the ground itself.

The Spirit joins us to place *and* people, people *and* place, and from the site of joining presses us into an alternative life, a shared life. What constitutes the alternative? This has been the crucial question within the dream of a beloved community. What makes such a community an authentic alternative to the damaging realities of its society, and what sustains that community as an alternative? For Christians the only answer begins with the body of Jesus made present by the Holy Spirit. Just as Jesus drew his disciples into his love for God, his (Abba) Father, through the Spirit, marking the alternative in Israel through this intimacy, so too the alternative for us begins precisely inside this triune love and divine intimacy (John 17:20–24). This alternative connects and binds us to God and begins God's relentless pressing of us to deep and abiding connections with all that surrounds us, not only people but also the land, not only the land but also the animals, not only the animals but also the rhythms of particular, local life.

The struggle that attends life with Jesus is to yield to the Spirit and enter God's own desire to join us together. This has been the perennial problem the church has faced from the first moment desperate crowds pressed together not out of any desire for each other but only in want of help from Jesus. To get to Jesus they had to touch one another. The Spirit has instigated such complicated spaces where people are drawn, sometimes in surprise and sometimes in protest, toward each other in a divine hope that they will touch God's love for them by loving one another. That perennial problem has been enfolded in the contemporary challenges of the allocation and bifurcation of spaces that constantly render specific places inconsequential except as sites of commerce. This means that churches have simply followed the economic determinations of space that build patterns of interaction for us, shaping who we see and do not see, who we will know and who will remain absent from our consciousness and our life.

The mapping of space and the constructing of living places through city planning, land development, real estate operations, architectural reflection, zoning, and policy formation determine our communities and, to a large measure, dictate the vision of what life together might mean for us. This planned geography determines the reach of our discipleship and the material enactment of God's love in our communities. Thus disciples of Jesus must engage in two struggles. First we must begin to analyze, understand, and, if necessary, resist the geographic formations of life in cities, villages, towns, hamlets, and neighborhoods from urban to rural settings and everything in between. We must ask if we are being positioned against community or for community, positioned to know people different from us economically, politically, socially, culturally, and racially, or are we being herded into various kinds of homogeneities? Disciples of Jesus must pay attention to places because our presence carries a call to love our neighbors and our neighborhoods. Second, we must yield to the Spirit's leading us to join, recognizing that the Spirit of God may be calling us to break with a geographic pattern or help create a new one. In all this the Spirit is always leading us toward the communal, toward a sharing of life with those different from us.

We are the inheritors of God's own communal dream, one that would bind us together in the body of Jesus and overcome a world captive to a false vision of possession and fragmentation. Yet God's communal dream is not guided by the logistics of possession and sharing but by the desire for love to be made real among those born anew of the Spirit. It is love for one another that guides the giving and sharing and in this way presents the most radical option for communal life that we might envision—what if we lived as though the well-being of those around us, including our surroundings, was as important to us as our own lives? What if for the first time I felt the absolute depths of God's love and concern not only for the one who God has drawn into my life and me into theirs but also for the place I inhabit, the streets I traverse, the animals I see, and the plants I touch with all my senses every day? For those disciples so willing to be led by the Spirit into radical love, God will create a communal reality that answers back the groaning of the creation with a word of great hope: the children of God are now visible.

Postscript: A Place to Be Free

The image that ends the book of Acts, of Paul in a "prison house" receiving any who come to him, haunts me. That image imprints itself onto our present moment, weaving together the realities of incarceration, economic sustainability, and life within empire. Throughout the church's history, Acts has been called a contemporary text. In every time it speaks to the current realities of the church in the world. No more accurate assessment of this book could be made: It spoke to me of the now and the not yet in profound ways. As I wrote this commentary several things surprised me.

First, I did not expect to have been as sympathetic to diaspora as I found myself being. The diaspora of Acts is real, human diaspora, and in some ways it is like the diaspora I have lived with and in all my life. Diaspora communities in this world past and present live with a politics of survival that demands a clear-eyed and diligent suspicion of any who announce that they want to change us for the good or according to the will of the state or of a corporation or of God. For diaspora, hope for the future is built on sustaining memory of the past, of land, of people, of ritual, and, most importantly, of story. Cultural practice has always been fundamentally about how a people remembers place and how they envision their future in new places. Diaspora determines friend or enemy by how they support or undermine that crucial work of sustaining a sense of place, both past and present. Sometimes being seen as a friend or enemy of a people depends on whether you listen to their story and then live your life as though their story matters to you.

The tragedy that often attends diaspora people is that not enough people appreciate their story or find ways to lovingly enter their hopes. That lack of support often presses diaspora peoples to believe that they must go it alone, maintaining their history and its truth against all the corrosive effects of time and life in strange and sometimes hostile places. Such work makes diaspora life always susceptible to the forces of isolation and alienation that invite people to make peace with their segregation. Additionally, for diaspora, violence is a constant, unwelcomed interlocutor that always seeks to infect us with hate. The diaspora condition is one of constant temptation to take up the sword in our fantasies or in reality. When diaspora peoples watch their children killed in civil war, or by invading armies, or by ruling political parties and their cronies, or by the very policing forces sworn to protect them, they face the seductive power of death in its full force that says sweetly to them, "arm yourself, protect yourself and your people, and for the sake of your life, kill those who would destroy you." Acts is a plea to Jewish diaspora and every diaspora saying that there is a better way forward, a way to sustain your people not with violence, segregation, gated or walled communities, or fear but through faith in the resurrected Jesus and the life-giving Spirit. I experienced the book of Acts as an intensely political text in the sense that it illumined the cultural politic that shapes every people. And unlike other biblical texts, it suggests the sustaining of a people not by protectionism but through expanding a sense of belonging in the Spirit-filled action of joining.

This brings me to the second thing I noticed in this powerful book. Almost no one is doing what they want to do. The Spirit of God is pressing every disciple to do precisely what God wants done and not what they might envision. I was surprised by the assertiveness of the Spirit. In Acts, the Spirit of God truly directs, speaks, guides. If in the Gospel of Luke, God reveals the divine life in the Son, then in Acts the Spirit of God is making perfectly clear divine desire. Luke–Acts places us in the desire of God revealed in the Son's own yielding to the Spirit. His life of yielding becomes our life of yielding. God desires the interweaving of peoples, Jews and Gentiles, slave and free, male and female, into one through the Son and in the Spirit. From the Pentecost event, to constantly binding disciples together in prisons, to road journeys near and far, from Jerusalem to Antioch, from Troas to Rome, the God of Israel will wait no longer to join us to the divine life and to one another. There is an intentionality to the work of the Spirit that the church has ignored, to its shame. The Spirit presses us to join with people we do not want to join with or imagine intimate life with.

This imagining of a form of intimate life that transgresses boundaries and borders showed me yet another incredible work the Spirit performs throughout the book of Acts. The Spirit directly assaults the forces of assimilation bound up in empire. Assimilation is the great conveyor of social death and the way empire spreads its influence. We saw it so powerfully with Rome and those assimilated to its pseudo-cosmopolitan ways, where the worship of gods is acceptable as long as the emperor reigns supreme and the Roman state determines everyone's future. The joining that the Spirit presses forward overturns the assimilation process of empire by inviting disciples into a new common life. So Jews will eat with Gentiles, sharing in table and life with them and thereby taking on some of their cultural ways. Gentiles will enter the story of Israel through the worship of the one true God found in the resurrected Christ Jesus and thereby turn from the gods of their ancestors. We could call this a different kind of assimilation, one where, out of love and desire, disciples take on the ways of others. Disciples allow themselves to be assimilated for the sake of love; they do not demand or request others to assimilate to them. This is a message that Christians have rarely heard or understood but desperately need to live into today. Of course, there is confrontation and negotiation where some cultural ways and practices and some theological beliefs are troubled, transformed, or even set aside for the sake of life together. Yet it is life together in the Spirit of God as the goal that guides that thorny joining of peoples who never imagined themselves together. God surprises, and we have forgotten the surprise that is discipleship and the surprise we should be to the world as disciples.

The disciple of Jesus Christ is a surprise to the world, especially cultural and economic worlds where peoples live in balkanized conditions, segregated spaces, and sequestered living places, each working to sustain their cultural enclave. Disciples connect peoples at the sites of segregation, inviting a mutual enfolding of story within story: the stories of people enfolded in the story of God's love found in the resurrected Jesus and the stories of peoples enfolded in one another. This is precisely how a people's story may be carried into a flourishing future—by love for them found in others, and by others sharing with them in story, hope, and life. Indeed this work of the Spirit gifts us to one another as life partners, sharing in a common hope in the resurrection through Jesus Christ. Every empire resists this work of the Spirit because it undermines the dream of empire to control every peoples' stories inside its master narrative for how peace, order, and redemption can be achieved in this world.

Too often the church has confused its work of joining with the joining operation performed by empire. The Spirit is leading us to release ourselves into the lives of others for the sake of divine desire as God places desire for others in us through the Spirit. In this regard, we are an echo of the incarnation where nothing is lost and everything is gained. We bring who we are into this calling of the Spirit and find in the joining something new, a new creation born of the invitation to a shared life. The struggle I saw in the book of Acts and yet see here and now is the struggle of faith to stop resisting the calling of the Spirit toward those specific people we would choose to avoid. In contrast, the empire demands that people release themselves into its desire and wash away all that would hinder the smooth echo of its articulated economic and cultural goals and hopes. The Spirit joins for the sake of love. Empire joins for the sake of power. Empire seeks to manage difference, boiling it down to usable parts, which might be fitted together like cogs in a great machine. The Spirit breaks the machine by calling us toward one another into new forms of life together that witness a God who cherishes life in the multitude. Empire seeks parallel life in segregated space for the sake of order and the smooth operations of wealth accumulation. The Spirit seeks shared life in shared space for the sake of worship.

After having the experience of living intensely with this narrative for a while now, I see with much greater urgency the need for imagining and enacting forms of life together that transgress the boundaries we all know so well—racial, ethnic, economic, social, gendered, and nationalist. Acts clarifies for me the depth of change necessary for enacting the life of the common in the Spirit. The book of Acts presses questions on me that I am not yet able to answer regarding the shape and scope of the common life that ought to characterize disciples of Jesus. If Acts announces a new beginning with God, then I am convinced that we have not fully entered into that newness. That newness requires a new space in which to take hold of our freedom in the Spirit. Maybe our goal should be to form common life along the lines of Paul waiting for his day before the emperor—in a house where the struggle for justice meets radical hospitality and where people from every walk of life wander into a space filled with hope, surprise, and very good news.

For Further Reading

Anzaldúa, Gloria. *Borderlands, LaFrontera: The New Mestiza*. San Francisco: Aunt Lute Books, 1987.

Basil. *On Social Justice*. Crestwood, NY: St. Vladimir's Seminary Press, 2009.

Calvin, John. *Commentary on the Acts of the Apostle*, 2 vols. Grand Rapids: Christian Classics Ethereal Library, https://www.ccel.org/ccel/calvin/calcom36.i.html.

Campbell, Douglas A. *Framing Paul: An Epistolary Biography*. Grand Rapids: Eerdmans, 2014.

Crouch, Stanley. *Considering Genius*. New York: Basic Books, 2006.

Fischlin, Daniel, et al. *The Fierce Urgency of Now: Improvisation, Rights, and the Ethics of Co-creation*. Durham, NC: Duke University Press, 2013.

Gaventa, Beverly Roberts. *Acts*. Nashville: Abingdon Press, 2003.

González, Justo L. *Acts: The Gospel of the Spirit*. Maryknoll, NY: Orbis Books, 2001.

Holland, Sharon Patricia. *Raising the Dead: Readings of Death and (Black) Subjectivity*. Durham, NC: Duke University Press, 2000.

Jackson, George. *Soledad Brother: The Prison Letters of George Jackson*. New York: Bantam Books, 1970.

Johnson, Elizabeth A. *Friends of God and Prophets: A Feminist Theological Reading of the Communion of Saints*. New York: Continuum, 2003.

Johnson, Luke Timothy. *The Acts of the Apostles*. Collegeville, MN: The Liturgical Press, 1992.

Keating, AnaLouise, ed. *The Gloria Anzaldúa Reader*. Durham, NC: Duke University Press, 2009.

Keener, Craig S. *Acts: An Exegetical Commentary,* 4 vols. Grand Rapids: Baker Academic, 2012.

Knapp, Robert. *Invisible Romans*. Cambridge, MA: Harvard University Press, 2011.

Logan, James Samuel. *Good Punishment? Christian Moral Practice and U.S. Imprisonment*. Grand Rapids: Eerdmans, 2008.

Martin, Clarice J. "The Acts of the Apostles." In *Searching the Scriptures. A Feminist Commentary,* 763–99. Edited by Elisabeth Schüssler Fiorenza. New York: Crossroad, 1994.

_____. *Tongues of Fire: Power for the Church Today: Studies in the Acts of the Apostles*. Horizons Bible Study, 1990–1991. Presbyterian Church (U.S.A.), April 1990.

Mayer, Emanuel. *The Ancient Middle Classes: Urban Life and Aesthetics in the Roman Empire 100 BCE–250 CE*. Cambridge, MA: Harvard University Press, 2012.

Pelikan, Jaroslav. *Acts*. Grand Rapids: Brazos Press, 2005.

Rankine, Claudia. *Citizen: An American Lyric*. Minneapolis: Graywolf Press, 2014.

_____. *Don't Let Me Be Lonely: An American Lyric*. Minneapolis: Graywolf Press, 2004.

Rowe, C. Kavin. *World Upside Down: Reading Acts in the Graeco-Roman Age*. Oxford: Oxford University Press, 2009.

Sanders, Cheryl J. *Ministry at the Margins: The Prophetic Mission of Women, Youth, and the Poor*. Downers Grove, IL: InterVarsity Press, 1997.

Taylor, Mark Lewis. *The Executed God: The Way of the Cross in Lockdown America*. Minneapolis: Augsburg Fortress, 2001.

Tilling, Chris. *Paul's Divine Christology*. Grand Rapids: Eerdmans, 2012.

Witherington III, Ben. *The Acts of the Apostles: A Socio-Rhetorical Commentary*. Grand Rapids: Eerdmans, 1998.

Index of Scripture

Index of Subjects

CPSIA information can be obtained
at www.ICGtesting.com
Printed in the USA
JSHW041202270421
14032JS00001B/6